Virtues and Rights

Virtues and Rights

The Moral Philosophy of Thomas Hobbes

R. E. Ewin

Westview Press

BOULDER • SAN FRANCISCO • OXFORD

nwst
|ADK2773

Copyright © 1991 by Westview Press, Inc.

Published in 1991 in the United States of America by Westview Press, Inc., 5500 Central Avenue, Boulder, Colorado 80301, and in the United Kingdom by Westview Press, 36 Lonsdale Road, Summertown, Oxford OX2 7EW

Library of Congress Cataloging-in-Publication Data
Ewin, R. E.
  Virtues and rights : the moral philosophy of Thomas Hobbes / R. E. Ewin.
    p. cm.
  Includes bibliographical references and index.
  ISBN 0-8133-1239-6.—ISBN 0-8133-1238-8 (pbk.).
    1. Hobbes, Thomas, 1588–1679—Ethics. 2. Ethics, Modern—17th century. 3. Natural law—History—17th century. 4. Virtues—History—17th century. 5. Reason—History—17th century.
  I. Title.
B1348.E7W95 1991
171'.2—dc20   91-13883
                                                                          CIP

Printed and bound in the United States of America

        The paper used in this publication meets the requirements
 (∞)   of the American National Standard for Permanence of Paper
        for Printed Library Materials Z39.48-1984.

10   9   8   7   6   5   4   3   2   1

Contents

Acknowledgments

I have discussed Hobbes with many people over the years, and I owe a debt to all of them. I should especially like to thank Deborah Baumgold, Stephen Davies, Maurice Goldsmith, Michael Levine, Brian Stoffell, Alan Tapper, Brian Trainor, and Ted Watt. Each read all or part of at least one draft of this book and made helpful comments. Nevertheless, I take responsibility for what is said in the pages that follow.

R. E. Ewin

Works by Hobbes
Referred to in the Text

There are many editions of Hobbes's works. The editions that I have used are the following:

Leviathan, ed. C. B. MacPherson (Harmondsworth: Penguin Books, 1968), cited in the notes by chapter number and page number.

The Elements of Law, ed. F. Tonnies, second edition (London: Frank Cass and Company, 1969), cited in the notes by book number, chapter number, section number, and page number.

A Dialogue Between a Philosopher and a Student of the Common Laws of England, ed. Joseph Cropsey (Chicago: University of Chicago Press, 1974), referred to as *A Dialogue* and cited in the notes by page number.

De Cive and *De Homine* from *Man and Citizen*, ed. Bernard Gert (Brighton: Harvester Press, 1978). *De Cive* is cited in the notes by chapter number, section number, and page number; *De Homine* is cited by page number.

All other references to Hobbes are to *The English Works of Thomas Hobbes*, ed. Sir William Molesworth (London: John Bohn, 1839), referred to as *E. W.* and cited in the notes by volume number and page number. Reference is also made in the text to *De Corpore*, which is the first volume of *E. W.*

Introduction

Any reasonable interpretation of a philosopher's argument needs to pay attention to any statements that philosopher has made about how a good argument works. The usual example given when discussing Thomas Hobbes's method of argument is his discussion of the watch in *De Cive*. This is unfortunate because the example is misleading if one does not put due emphasis on Hobbes's remark that his concern is with putting things together, with "how men must be agreed amongst themselves that intend to grow up into a well-grounded state."[1] For Hobbes, taking a watch apart is an example of the resolutive or the analytical method, and actually taking a particular watch apart is not even an example of that: The sorts of parts in question for the resolutive method are not such parts of a man as his head and shoulders but such parts as his figure, quantity, and motion.[2] The sort of resolution in question is a conceptual dismantling, not a mechanical dismantling.

Hobbes used both the resolutive or the analytical method and the compositive or the synthetical method, and he thought that they served different purposes. The whole method of demonstration is compositive, he says,[3] and one is to teach others by use of the compositive method.[4] When Hobbes is attempting to produce demonstrations, as he says he is in his civil philosophy,[5] and when he is trying to teach others about civil philosophy, we should expect him to use the compositive method. Civil and moral philosophy are available to the less philosophically adept, who have not mastered geometry, by the analytical or resolutive method,[6] but Hobbes did have geometry to aid him and was conscious of the fact. If we are concerned about Hobbes's method, or his model of explanation, in his civil philosophy, therefore, a better example to take than his discussion of the watch is his discussion of the circle[7] because that is an example of the compositive method in action. And that is the example that I shall discuss.

The method involved, as I explain in chapter 1, is not that of seeking the actual causes of particular events. It is a matter of finding a procedure that would guarantee the production of this sort of thing *even if the procedure is not the one that was used to produce this particular thing.*[8] When Hobbes claims to have set out the cause of something in this way, he is not claiming that the cause actually existed or really produced the particular thing in question; he is giving a model for it. Hence the contract, as a model for the state, need not be an actual contract, and the natural condition of mankind need not have been actual in order to play a part in Hobbes's story of the generation of the state. Hobbes is quite clear that not all states began with a contract[9] and, as would be expected in that case, is not wedded to the idea that the state must have emerged from an actual natural condition.[10]

If we know the actual method by which something was generated, then we can infer the properties of what was produced from the method. If we do not know the actual method of generation but want to infer an appropriate method — a method that would guarantee the production of such a thing — then we must be able to establish the properties of whatever is in question without depending at all on inferences from the method of generation. Given the model of explanation set out in Hobbes's account of the circle, we should therefore expect him not to derive consequences from the making of a contract but to produce arguments independent of any contract to show that social life must have certain features the presence of which would be guaranteed if a contract *had* been the method of generation. The contract can then be a model for the state. Games-theoretic interpretations of Hobbes get his argument the wrong way around, dealing with the maneuvers that people might go through to emerge from an actual condition of mere nature. The relevant features of the state must be shown to be necessary quite apart from any detail that might go into the contracting; the model can be shown to be an appropriate one only *after* those features have been shown to be necessary to the state.

And Hobbes does argue in the way that his method makes appropriate. As I show in chapter 2, his argument about right reason in chapter 5 of *Leviathan* is just such an argument about sovereignty. It is an argument that an artificial right reason in the form of the sovereign must be set up if people are to be able to live peacefully together. Private judgment must be subordinate to the public judgment provided by the sovereign. The only alternative, on Hobbes's account, is that we live in our natural condition. And living in our natural condition would not be merely unpleasant.

Before ending chapter 2 I investigate further some of the implications of Hobbes's right reason argument. In particular, I investigate its implications for the liberty of the citizen and the idea of natural rights. Natural rights were held up by those Hobbes opposed as placing limitations on political authority and as limiting the sovereign. They could be used in that way only because the idea of natural rights goes with private judgment. If the sovereign determined for me what my natural rights were, then they would be positive rights and I could not appeal to them when objecting to limitations that the sovereign placed upon me. Hobbes, then, who believed the lauding of private judgment to be a great evil,[11] was bound to argue against the idea of natural right.

But Hobbes could not rid his theory of all natural rights. Despite all his arguments to show that social life requires that public judgment be given precedence over private judgment, Hobbes did not manage to remove private judgment from his theory. In its most obvious form, it remains as the inalienable right to self-preservation, which requires that I exercise my private judgment if it is to be effective. After having spent the first two chapters setting up Hobbes's argument, I begin whittling away at that argument in chapter 3 and going further into his moral theory by seeking responses that he might have made to the whittling away. In that chapter, I examine various ways in which Hobbes might try to explain this inalienable right and still maintain his thesis about public and private judgment. His failure to do so leaves him with a problem: The only right we have in our natural condition is the right to do whatever in our judgment is necessary for our preservation[12] (and dependence on private judgment turns that right, substantively, into a right to all things), but we retain that right in civil society. We must retain that right in civil society, on Hobbes's account, because the point of social life is to give security of life to each of us. If we retain in civil society all the rights that we had in our natural condition, how can we have left our natural condition?

In chapter 4 I examine the Hobbesian natural condition of mankind. This is not, as I shall show, a matter of explaining a particular state in which people might or might not be. The natural condition is a sort of relationship (a relationship in which *X* and *Y* have no common power over them and each is therefore his own judge), and different terms can stand in that relationship. Two particular people might stand in that relationship to each other; two families might stand in that relationship to each other; two sovereign states might stand in that relationship to each other. I might be in my natural condition with respect to one person but not with respect to another; there need be no simple yes or no answer to a question about whether I am in my natural condition.

How we left our natural condition is not a proper question. Hobbes did not believe that mankind had ever been in its natural condition all over the world, and his model of explanation does not require that he postulate any such time. But I am after a different point: There is a sense in which, at least until there is a common power over the whole world, we still have not left our natural condition completely. If there is somebody else in the world who is not subject to a power to which I am also subject, then I shall be in my natural condition with respect to that person. Security is something that we gain, not simply by leaving our natural condition as with one magical leap, but by having groups of larger and larger sizes so that they are less and less vulnerable to attack.

But there is a theoretically special form of the natural condition, and that is the form in which each person is in his natural condition with respect to every other person. This is what I shall call the radical form of our natural condition. And this form, I shall try to show, Hobbes believed to be impossible. In it, life would be solitary, poor, nasty, brutish, and short. It is not a possible continuing life for people. And it is populated, I shall try to show, not by complete people, but by creatures lacking the laws of nature. They lack the qualities disposing man to peace.[13] Those qualities are an important part of Hobbes's complete account of human nature. It is because of those qualities that it is natural for real people not to live in the radical form of the natural condition of mankind.

Not all of morality is a matter of convention, but Hobbes believed that even those parts of morality that were not conventional required a background of convention and, in an important way, depended on public judgment's being given precedence over private judgment. At the start of chapter 5, I discuss the conditions that Hobbes believed necessary for contracts to be binding and examine the role of the sovereign, who is the form taken by convention in his argument, in making them binding. Hobbes's account of obligation is not one that is dependent on self-interest, and it does not require the sovereign to coerce or threaten the person who is obligated. I am obligated if the other person has performed his part or if the sovereign is there to ensure performance on the part of the other. The function of the sovereign is to provide a guarantee of reciprocity. One issue that I shall want to take up later is whether the sovereign is the only way of providing the necessary guarantee, even given Hobbes's starting points.

In chapter 5 I also begin an investigation of Hobbes's laws of nature. My particular concern here is with the conditions Hobbes argues to be necessary if the laws of nature are to be effective, and thus with what he means by the claim that, in our natural condition, the laws of nature bind *in foro interno* but not *in foro externo*. This helps to explain the way in which even those aspects of morality that are not directly conventional require a background of convention if they are to be effective.

And then in chapter 6 I consider the way in which the sovereign is supposed to interpret the laws of nature and how they are to be understood. Given Hobbes's model of explanation, we should not expect him to be telling a sort of history, and we should not take literally the tale of people calculating and then agreeing on the laws of nature in order to leave their terrible natural condition. That will be an explanatory model, as is reference to the movement of a point in explaining what a circle is. The question to be answered is: What is it a model *for?*

The answer is that it is a model for the virtues. The claim that Hobbes was a virtues theorist might seem to be surprising, but there is plenty of textual support for it, especially after one has recognized that his tale of agreement on the laws of nature is merely a model. It is a complex virtues theory, too, because part of Hobbes's argument about the need to give primacy to public judgment is an argument to show that this virtues theory needs a rights theory to complete it, and part of his argument about the role of the laws of nature in setting up the sovereign to provide public judgment is that rights theories must be grounded in virtues theories. Rights theories and virtues theories have been treated recently as though they were exclusive of each other, but Hobbes shows that they are not.

But Hobbes's explanatory model has misled him in the case of the virtues. What he sets out as a model is not, in fact, a way that would guarantee the production of the virtues. It not only would not guarantee their production, it would also not produce them. But that model led him to give calculation and reasoning the wrong place in virtues. Understanding that, and getting the account of virtues away from the misleading aspects of the model, is the job that I undertake in chapter 7. And once we get that job done, we can see that the people for whom Hobbes believes government to be possible, those with the laws of nature, are also people who do not need the absolute sovereignty that he prescribes. Those with the virtues have, in possession of the virtues, their own motivation to behave in the appropriate ways, even though the effectiveness of the motivation will be limited by the fact that people do not possess the virtues to perfection, can be tempted, and sometimes differ about what would be the right thing to do. They will not *always* need the threat of a sovereign to make them get along peacefully.

There is in Hobbes, then, worthwhile contribution to current debate in moral theory. There is also worthwhile contribution to political debate. During recent years a simple opposition between conscience and the law has been fashionable, suggesting that if one disapproves of the content of a law one is morally bound to ignore the law. That position is certainly brought under severe attack by Hobbes, and he has presented good reasons for trying to shift the debate from issues simply about the content of the law to issues about the procedure by which the law was made and whether that procedure was just. That Hobbes was wrong in the more extreme claims in his theory of sovereignty does not mean that he was wrong about the need for public judgment and the need for citizens to be prepared to submit to a public judgment that is a fair procedure.

Notes

1. *De Cive*, "The Author's Preface to the Reader," p. 99.
2. *E. W.*, vol. 1, p. 67.
3. *E. W.*, vol. 1, p. 81.
4. *E. W.*, vol. 1, p. 80.
5. He says in "The Author's Preface to the Reader" in *De Cive*, for example, that the claim that monarchy is the most commodious form of government is the only claim in the book that he has not demonstrated.
6. *E. W.*, vol. 1, pp. 73-74.
7. *E. W.*, vol. 1, p. 6.
8. *E. W.*, vol. 1, p. 6.
9. Cf., for example, *A Dialogue*, p. 161.
10. Cf., for example, *Leviathan*, chapter 13, p. 187.
11. *Leviathan*, chapter 29, p. 365.
12. *Leviathan*, chapter 14, p. 189.
13. *Leviathan*, chapter 26, p. 314.

1

Hobbes's Method

Hobbes described a method of argument, or a model of explanation, that he thought would serve to achieve scientific knowledge. That method has frequently been misconstrued because of Hobbes's use of the term "cause." In a different way, to which we shall come later, Hobbes's method of argument crucially misled him in the conclusions he drew from his account of the laws of nature when he was dealing with sovereignty.

There were severe limitations on the conclusions that Hobbes thought could be reached by the use of this model, which reflects the fact that he thought that there were similar limitations on the sorts of things that could constitute scientific knowledge. What he thought of as science did not bear an especially close resemblance to what is popularly thought of as science nowadays, which is no great surprise: Hobbes wrote in the midst of a great debate about the proper scientific method, and his side did not win the debate.[1] One needs to be very careful, therefore, to avoid reading modern popular ideas of science back into what Hobbes wrote. As part of that, one needs to read carefully what he wrote when figuring out what sort of thing he was talking about when he used the word "cause."

Science, as far as Hobbes was concerned, could be knowledge only of conditional statements of the connections of names. That is to say, in modern terms, it was concerned only with conceptual connections and not with merely empirical connections. It could not be a matter of connections in an uninterpreted calculus: Hobbes had little time for algebra[2] but took geometry as his model and conceived of geometry as being the science of magnitudes and figures — he took geometry to be not an axiomatic deductive system but a series of constructive generations. His model was one in which the terms were interpreted empirically, but the connections he sought in that science, and saw it as the job of science to discover, were conceptual connections. Scientific knowledge, on Hobbes's account, is knowledge of conditional statements, and "whensoever a *hypothetical* proposition is true, the *categorical* answering it, is not only true, but also necessary."[3] Science, as far as Hobbes was concerned, was

> attayned by Industry; first in apt imposing of Names; and secondly by getting a good and orderly Method in proceeding from the Elements, which are Names, to Assertions made by Connexion of one of them to another; and so to Syllogismes, which are the Connexions of one Assertion to another, till we come to a knowledge of all the Consequences of names appertaining to the subject in hand; and that is it, men call SCIENCE.[4]

If the names (a term, of course, that does not mean the same thing as "proper names") have been aptly imposed, then, of course; in knowing the name we have significant knowledge of anything that properly bears that name. Geometry, as well as appearing to many seventeenth-century thinkers to be infallible or capable of producing definitive demonstrations, was very useful: It was an interpreted calculus that could be used in measuring matter and motion; in moving ponderous bodies; in architecture, navigation, and geography; in making instruments for all uses; in calculating celestial motions, the aspects of the stars, and the parts of time; and so on.[5] The combination of those two properties — geometry's use in producing demonstrations and its use in other applications — was largely what kept geometry at the forefront of Hobbes's mind. Nevertheless, in order to provide that possibility of definitive demonstration, Hobbes believed that geometry was concerned only with what we would now call conceptual[6] or logical connections: The connections are looked for at the level of the *names* and are not sought by empirical investigation of the things named.[7] The conclusion reached for practical purposes of building and moving large quantities is that *if* this thing has these properties, and thus properly bears this name, *then* certain other things follow. And they are intended to follow logically. Hobbes even provides a test commonly employed until recent times as a test of logical possibility: "When we make a generall assertion, unlesse it be a true one, the possibility of it is unconceiveable."[8]

That sort of conditional conclusion, Hobbes believed, could be known with certainty. The properties of particular things are sought by means of different methods and are not known with the same certainty, though clearly we can properly have greater or less confidence in different claims of this sort. Hence, even though we can know with certainty that *if* this thing is X *then* it is Y, we cannot know with certainty on that basis that it is Y: That unconditional conclusion can be known with no more certainty than the claim that the thing in question is X. Genuine science will not produce that sort of conclusion for us. To the extent that Hobbes was trying to produce a genuine science, we should not be looking for that sort of conclusion in his work. What he sought as a result of the scientific endeavor were apodictic or necessary statements — statements the falsity of which was inconceivable. He wanted logical truths. The causes that Hobbes sought were parts of the definitions of the things to be explained, and not everything had a cause:

> The reason why I say that the cause and generation of such things, as have any cause or generation, ought to enter into their definitions, is this. The end of science is the demonstration of the causes and generations of things; which if they be not in the definitions, they cannot be found in the conclusion of the first syllogism, that is made from those definitions; and if they be not in the first conclusion, they will not be found in any further conclusion deduced from that; and, therefore, by proceeding in this manner, we shall never come to science; which is against the scope and intention of demonstration.[9]

It is easy enough to miss this point and, as a result, to be mistaken about what Hobbes is arguing for and thus to misinterpret the argument that he presents. I shall give one example. In the last paragraph of chapter 20 of *Leviathan*, Hobbes, having presented an argument for legally unlimited sovereign power, deals with the objection of those who ask when and where such a power has been acknowledged by subjects. The objection he is dealing with is that he cannot have presented a logical truth if what he has presented is empirically false, and it is an objection that needs to be dealt with in the context.[10] His reply is that if those who raise the objection will look back at the evidence, they will see that the only commonwealths that have survived for long without sedition or civil war are those in which the powers of the sovereign have not been disputed. The empirical objection to what he has put forward as a logical truth, therefore, does not succeed.

Gregory Kavka[11] reads the argument differently. He says that Hobbes has put forward "empirical historical claims that, if true, would support the desirability of absolute sovereignty" and objects that Hobbes does not go on to back the claims with evidence. The cogency of this objection depends on the assumption that Hobbes is not trying to establish an apodictic truth about sovereignty but is arguing about which form of government is *preferable* to which other. But the latter conclusion is *not* the sort that Hobbes said he was concerned about establishing. Hobbes was, indeed, in favor of absolute monarchy; the arguments in support of that view were, he thought, mainly historical ones, and those appear in *Behemoth* and his edition of Thucydides. He takes up the issue in *De Cive*: "Though I have endeavoured, by arguments in my tenth chapter, to gain a belief in men, that monarchy is the most commodious government; which one thing alone I confess in this whole book not to be demonstrated, but only probably stated; yet every where I expressly say, that in all kind of government whatsoever there ought to be a supreme and equal power."[12] The passage makes clear that Hobbes thinks it worthy of comment when he argues for a conclusion of a different sort from that required by his method, and it also makes clear that his argument about sovereign power is not such a case. Kavka is mistaken about Hobbes's conclusion, that is to say, about the point of Hobbes's argument. In interpreting Hobbes here, we need to look for a different sort of conclusion, and preferably for one that does fit with his espoused method. Getting the point of the argument right helps in interpreting the argument.

The same considerations throw doubt on David Gauthier's claim[13] that experience replaces derivation from fundamental principles in Hobbes's political writings: Were this part of Hobbes's method of argument, he would hardly have felt it necessary to comment that he had not attempted to provide a demonstration in the particular case of argument about the superiority of monarchy as a form of government. Gauthier's example from *De Corpore*[14] shows only that Hobbes recognized that the resolutive or analytical method had its uses, a point about which Hobbes was quite explicit in the discussion immediately preceding that passage. It does not show that Hobbes resiled from the position set out in that discussion — that the compositive or synthetical method was the only method for demonstration.

Hobbes insisted that a calculus that was to constitute a science be interpreted; he had no dream of attaining genuine scientific knowledge by the use of pure reason divorced from experience and did not play down the role of experience.

> There be *two kinds* of knowledge, whereof the *one* is nothing else but *sense*, or knowledge *original*, . . . and *remembrance* of the same; the *other* is called *science* or knowledge of the *truth of propositions*, and how things are called, and is derived from *understanding*. Both of these sorts are but *experience*; the former being the experience of the effects of things that work upon us from *without*; and the latter experience men have from

the proper use of *names* in language: and all experience being, as I have said, but remembrance, all knowledge is remembrance: and of the *former*, the register we keep in books is called *history;* but the registers of the latter are called the *sciences.*[15]

Experience, prudence, or just plain common sense would lead somebody to leave his house as it burned to the ground in the Great Fire of London; he could have all empirical certainty that he would be reduced to ashes if he did not leave. But that is not an apodictic statement; it is not a statement the falsity of which is inconceivable and can be shown to be so by consideration of the names of the things involved. It is not science, and science is what Hobbes sought quite explicitly in his philosophical writings. Prudence is necessary to life, but it cannot teach us the universal truths we need, including, at least in Hobbes's view, the universal truths set out in his moral theory.

Why should Hobbes have bothered about science if experience also produced knowledge? Not simply out of a love of knowledge for its own sake: "For the inward glory and triumph of mind that a man may have for the mastering of some difficult and doubtful matter, or for the discovery of some hidden truth, is not worth so much pains as the study of Philosophy requires. . . . The end of knowledge is power."[16] Hobbes saw human life as being held back by reliance on piecemeal, unorganized knowledge. The lack of method outside geometry held back the development of knowledge in other fields. To deal with this problem, Hobbes tried to employ the methods of geometry and produce tight deductive arguments: "For all men by nature reason alike, and well, when they have good principles. For who is so stupid, as both to mistake in Geometry, and also to persist in it, when another detects his error to him?"[17] But he did not expect the job to be an easy one in the field of social life, even with the aid of tight deductive arguments:"For I doubt not, but if it had been a thing contrary to any mans right of dominion, or to the interest of men that have dominion, *That the three Angles of a Triangle should be equall to two Angles of a Square;* that doctrine should have been, if not disputed, yet by the burning of all books of Geometry, suppressed, as farre as he whom it concerned was able."[18]

Hobbes believed that the lack of development of the relevant science held back knowledge in the field of government or, more generally, civil affairs. This was the driving force behind the development of his moral and political theory. Here the need for science is, perhaps, not so obvious because the advantages to be gained from science in civil affairs are simply the avoidance of certain calamities. For those who take Hobbes to be a supreme individualist for whom people are naturally asocial, it is worth noting that he includes solitude among the calamities:

The utility of moral and civil philosophy is to be estimated, not so much by the commodities we have by knowing these sciences, as by the calamities we receive from not knowing them. Now, all such calamities as may be avoided by human industry, arise from war, but chiefly from civil war; for from this proceed slaughter, solitude, and the want of all things. But the cause of war is not that men are willing to have it; for the will has nothing for object but good, at least that which seemeth good. Nor is it from this, that men know not that the effects of war are evil; for who is there that thinks not poverty and loss of life to be great evils? The cause, therefore, of civil war, is that men know not the causes neither of war nor peace, there being but few in the world that have learned those duties which unite and keep men in peace, that is to say, that have learned the rules of civil life sufficiently. Now the knowledge of those rules is moral philosophy.[19]

Bear in mind still that Hobbes does not mean by "cause" what we would usually mean by it when we look for the cause of a broken vase or the causes of World War II. Nevertheless, he makes clear what he thinks the advantages of science are and where he thinks he is moving ahead of his contemporaries. And it should be clear, too, that he does think that he is moving ahead of his contemporaries. We should, of course, try to avoid proleptic interpretations of Hobbes[20] that read later developments into him, especially as games-theoretic accounts of his civil philosophy make it obvious that such interpretations are easy to fall into. But we should also bear in mind that he thought that he was breaking new ground, so we should not assume that he was trying to do only what his contemporaries were trying to do or that he was trying to answer only the questions that they were trying to answer. He was, as he makes quite clear, trying to go further than they went, and in ways that he thought very important. By reading his writings *too* much in the context of the debates of his time, one can miss his originality.

Of course Hobbes should be read in context, and there could be no understanding of him without that, but close attention to the Hobbesian texts is equally important and reveals the way in which he took over terms from others and changed their significance. He was not, for example, a believer in an actual contract as the foundation of the state, and one thing that he was concerned about showing was that contract theory, properly understood, led to absolute political authority rather than to limited sovereignty. He made similar changes with the idea of a state of nature and, I think, with the ideas of natural rights and natural law. He would have been foolish to use those terms had his use of them been completely unrelated to the uses they had for other writers of the time, but we need to be aware of the changes that Hobbes is making as he introduces his science of politics.

Hobbes thought that what was missing in what his contemporaries wrote on the subject was "a true and certain rule of our actions, by which we might know whether that we undertake be just or unjust."[21] He believed that whether something is just or unjust cannot be known by experience[22] but requires science. He held that earlier writers on civil matters had not established the science that they needed to carry out successfully the job that they had taken on. Hence he compares those who write in civil matters very unfavorably with the geometers: "What, then, can be imagined to be the cause that the writings of those men have increased science, and the writings of these have increased nothing but words, saving that the former were written by men that knew, and the latter by such as knew not, the doctrine they taught only for ostentation of their wit and eloquence?"[23] The great leap forward for Hobbes, and what distinguished him in his own mind from his contemporaries, was his use of a specific method in order to create a science of civil matters as he understood a science to be. In order to avoid the mistake of reading Hobbes too much in the light of the debate of his time and assuming that he could not be going beyond his contemporaries, we need to pay attention to his method and to read what he wrote in the light of that method. Perhaps he did stray from it, but, given the emphasis he placed on that method in his whole endeavor, we should give precedence to a reading that fits with that method over one that does not.[24] We should look for any connections in his writings that his method would give us, and we should look for interpretations that will fit his overall argument into that method. In detail he might well move away from it, but we should expect the structure of the large-scale arguments to fit the map that he had drawn for himself before setting out.

The statement about Hobbes's method usually considered by commentators is the example of the watch, given by Hobbes in the preface to *De Cive:*

> Concerning my method, I thought it not sufficient to use a plain and evident style in what I have to deliver, except I took my beginning from the very matter of civil government, and thence proceeded to its generation and form, and the first beginning of justice. For everything is best understood by its constitutive causes. For as in a watch, or some such small engine, the matter, figure, and motion of the wheels cannot well be known, except it be taken insunder and viewed in parts; so to make a more curious search into the rights of states and duties of subjects, it is necessary, I say, not to take them insunder, but yet that they be so considered as if they were dissolved.[25]

This is an example of Hobbes's resoluto-compositive method,[26] also known to him as the analytical-synthetical method. There are really two methods, the analytical method and the synthetical method.[27] They should not be run together and treated as one method, as they often are,[28] but should be sharply distinguished because they have different purposes: The synthetical method is the sole provider of demonstration and is the proper method for teaching,[29] although the analytical method can be used by people who are less philosophically adept but seek the truth.[30] The example of the watch is misleading unless it is read with Hobbes's statements about his method clearly in mind. As Hobbes tells us,[31] we cannot discover what is just or unjust by experience. Dismantling a particular state (whatever that would amount to) and looking at its component parts, the people, does not reveal to us the rights and duties that are part of a state as such. If it revealed anything like this, it would reveal to us only the rights and duties that were part of that particular state and would thus provide no universal statement of the sort that Hobbes required for a science. In fact, it reveals nothing of the kind; when we looked, we should see no rights and duties at all, because they are not the sorts of things that can be observed in that way. A different type of procedure is required to discover the sorts of things that Hobbes wanted to discover about rights and duties; opening up the machine and looking inside is not sufficient.

It is not entirely insignificant that one usually opens up a watch not to see how it works but to see why it isn't working. Even if one did open up a watch to see how it worked, one would not necessarily, on putting it back together again, put back everything that had come out: Any dust, for example, could be left out even if it had previously been affecting how the internal parts of the watch moved. In applying the name "watch" to the thing, we are making clear that some of the material matters and some, such as the dust, does not. We are also assigning to the thing a purpose, and in terms of that purpose we can sort out which bits of the material have significance and which do not.[32] Applying the name brings in a conceptual overlay, and it needs to be remembered that, on Hobbes's account, science deals with *names,* not with the things named. Looking at what Hobbes says in that passage about the watch, we might otherwise think of the watch as a particular mechanical item, each movement within it causally explicable as we now use the term "cause," and take it that this is what Hobbes was talking about when he said that philosophy consists of the search for the causes of things.

The point comes out clearly in another example that Hobbes uses in explaining his method:

How the knowledge of any effect may be gotten from the knowledge of the generation thereof, may easily be understood by the example of a circle: for if there be set before us a plain figure, having, as near as may be, the figure of a circle, we cannot possibly perceive by sense whether it be a true circle or no; than which, nevertheless, nothing is more easy to be known to him that knows first the generation of the propounded figure. For let it be known that the figure was made by the circumduction of a body whereof one end remained unmoved, and we may reason thus; a body carried about, retaining always the same length, applies itself first to one *radius,* then to another, to a third, a fourth, and successively to all; and, therefore, the same length, from the same point, toucheth the circumference in every part thereof, which is as much as to say, as all the *radii* are equal. We know, therefore, that from such generation proceeds a figure, from whose one middle point all the extreme points are reached unto by equal *radii.* And in like manner, by knowing first what figure is set before us, we may come by ratiocination to some generation of the same, though perhaps not that by which it was made, yet that by which it might have been made; for he that knows that a circle has the property above declared, will easily know whether a body carried about, as is said, will generate a circle or no.[33]

It is clear that Hobbes did not mean by "cause" what we would usually mean by that word today. He is not concerned about what might be called the accidental or matter-of-fact cause of some particular circle, as he makes clear at the end of the paragraph: The method of generation that we infer from the properties of the figure might not be the method by which this particular circle was made — it might, perhaps, have been stamped out in one action, not drawn by the movement of a point — but it is a method by which it might have been made. The meeting of that condition is not enough for the way we use the word "cause" today. The burning down of my house might have been caused by arson, but once we have established that there was no arson then we know that that was not the cause. Discovering that the circle was stamped out by a die rather than drawn by the movement of a point does not change Hobbes's claim about the cause of a circle in his sense of "cause."

Again, we need to remember that a Hobbesian science dealt with names and not with the things named. His method was not intended to explain to us the causes of particular things, such as the burning down of my house or the appearance on the page of a particular circle. It deals with universal statements. Hence, the cause he gives us for the circle, which he says might not be the method by which the circle was produced but is a method by which it might have been produced, is not just any old method by which it might have been produced: That particular circle might have been produced by somebody doodling with a pencil, but the method of generating it suggested by Hobbes is one that guarantees that the figure will have the defining properties of a circle. Understanding causes, as far as Hobbes is concerned, is understanding that sort of thing. The science he is concerned with deals with names, or concepts, and is an activity more closely allied to the analysis of concepts than to the scientific search after the cause of an outbreak of diphtheria as we would understand that causal search nowadays. Hobbes is not concerned with what, in fact, produced this particular circle or this particular society. The term "philosophy" covered a much broader field in the seventeenth century than it does among professionals today, but what Hobbes was trying to set up as a science is very closely related to the modern professional conception of philosophy.[34]

The idea that there could be an explanation the falsity of which is no objection to it sounds odd, but we need to keep in mind this that is not what Hobbes is setting out. He is not giving a false (but somehow satisfactory) causal account of how this particular circle came to be; he is giving a true account of what a circle is. What we learn from the apparently false explanation when we know that it could have been true is something about the properties present in what has been explained. And that can be an illuminating sort of explanation.[35]

The point is made clearer when Hobbes goes on to explain that only definitions are primary and universal propositions:

> Now, such principles are nothing but definitions, whereof there are two sorts; one of names, that signify such things as have some conceivable cause, and another of such names as signify things of which we can conceive no cause at all. Names of the former kind are, *body*, or *matter*, *quantity* or *extension, motion*, and whatever is common to all matter. Of the second kind, are *such a body, such and so great motion, so great magnitude, such figure*, and whatsoever we can distinguish one body from another by.[36]

The sense in which he uses the term "cause" in his discussion of the circle is further from our common use of the term these days than it is from the use Hobbes describes when he discusses the sense in which one proposition is the cause of another, as when "two antecedent propositions are commonly called the causes of the inferred proposition, or conclusion."[37] The relationship in question is a logical relationship that holds between names, not an empirical relationship that holds between things. And what is being explained is not particular things, but their *natures*: "by parts, I do not here mean parts of the thing itself, but parts of its nature; as, by the parts of man, I do not understand his head, his shoulders, his arms, &c. but his figure, quantity, motion, sense, reason, and the like."[38] The parts that Hobbes is referring to are the parts into which we resolve something when we set about explaining it, so what is to be explained is natures.

The method of generation that is to be sought, therefore, is not the matter-of-fact cause of a particular case. Knowing the generation of a universal is knowing such things as that "*a line is made by the motion of a point, superficies by the motion of a line, . . . &c.* It remains, that we enquire what motion begets such and such effects; as, what motion makes a straight line, and what a circular."[39] So even when he writes about motion and the reduction of everything to motion for the purposes of science, Hobbes is not talking about physics as we understand it now; he is still concerned with logical connections. The end of science is the demonstration of the causes and generations of things.[40] The whole method of demonstration is compositive,[41] which is to say that others are to be taught by the compositive method[42] even if the method of attaining to universal knowledge of things is analytical.[43] So we should expect Hobbes to work in terms of the compositive method when he is setting about teaching others; that is, we should expect his written works, and especially his more polemical works, to take the passage about the circle as the model for his argument.[44]

Civil and moral philosophy, Hobbes says, are available by the synthetical or compositive method, but they are also available to the less philosophically adept who have not mastered the first part of philosophy — namely, geometry and physics — by the analytical method.[45] But the method appropriate to demonstration and to the doing of science is the compositive method, the method exemplified in the passage about the circle.

Jean Hampton is clearly mistaken about Hobbes's methodology and his idea of the nature of philosophy because she is mistaken about the sort of thing he means by "cause." After quoting Hobbes's definition of philosophy from *De Corpore* ("Philosophy is such knowledge of effects or appearances, as we acquire by true ratiocination from the knowledge we have first of their causes or generations"[46]), she goes on to say: "In other words, science seeks to know about a world that is experienced by us as filled with change — objects move, they degenerate or generate, and they affect one another in many ways."[47] She refers to Hobbes as writing about "the causal connection of objects" despite his explicit statements that science deals with names and not with the objects named, and she generally continues in a way that makes clear that she takes Hobbes to be using the word "cause" as it would commonly be used today and to mean by "science" what we would mean by that word today. Hampton has misconstrued the role played by the model of geometry in Hobbes's idea of methodology in science or philosophy. She is referring to actual causes of particular changes in the world, whereas Hobbes's concern, as the passage about the circle makes clear, was not with matter-of-fact causes of particular things, but with a method that guarantees the result and which, therefore, "though perhaps not that by which it was made, [is] yet that by which it might have been made."[48] He was not investigating the actual method by which that particular circle had been produced. Science, on Hobbes's account, applies to particulars only as an interpretation of the calculus.

A similar confusion appears in Gregory Kavka's account of Hobbes's methodology. He accuses Hobbes of failing to distinguish properly between the logical and the empirical in that "Hobbes defines causation — the subject matter of science — as logical necessitation of the effect by its causes and correspondingly indicates that the test of whether a given set of accidents (properties) causes an effect is 'whether the propounded effect *may be conceived* to exist, without the existence of any of those accidents.'"[49] Clearly, Kavka is working on the assumption that Hobbes is using both "science" and "cause" in modern senses and that what concern Hobbes are the causes of particular things. Hobbes has made perfectly clear that science deals in universal statements and that it operates at the level of names. The test of conceivability is quite useless if the issue is who broke the vase or any other particular causal question of that sort. Nevertheless, despite the existence of well-known objections to conceivability as a test for logical necessity, it is at least in the ballpark as a test for the sort of conceptual issue that Hobbes said he was dealing with: an issue at the level of what consequences can be drawn from a name. In that same passage, because Kavka mistakes Hobbes's use of the terms "cause" and "science," he reads Hobbes's paragraph about the circle as a simple confusion of the logical and the empirical.

Those confusions must be avoided. We should keep in mind what Hobbes meant by science, and the level at which science operated for him, when we read his accounts of what philosophy is: "By Philosophy, is understood *the knowledge acquired by Reasoning, from the Manner of Generation of any thing, to the Properties; or from the Properties, to some possible Way of Generation of the same; to the end to bee able to produce, as far as matter, and humane force permit, such Effects, as humane life requireth.*"[50] He proceeds immediately to make some remarks about geometry, and then he recurs to the definition:

By which Definition it is evident, that we are not to account as any part thereof, that originall knowledge called Experience, in which consisteth Prudence: Because it is not attained by Reasoning, but found as well in Brute Beasts, as in Man; and is but a Memory of successions.of events in time past, wherein the omission of every little circumstance altering the effect, frustrateth the expectation of the most Prudent: whereas nothing is produced by Reasoning aright, but generall, eternall, and immutable Truth.[51]

From those comments, and especially from his reference to "some possible Way of Generation" without insisting on discovery of the actual way of generation, we can see that Hobbes is not concerned about giving a historical account of the rise of the government under which he lived, and he is not concerned about giving prudential, probabilistic arguments about which form of government is better than which others, even if he did clearly have his own views about such matters. He is concerned about necessary truths, and when he writes about government he is concerned with necessary truths about government, which will hold for any form of government. That sort of science will still be useful, as geometry is useful: It can be applied to the world, as an interpreted calculus, to explain or predict events.

Considering what Hobbes wrote about his method and by reading what he wrote elsewhere in the light of that, we can see that the story of the contract is not intended as a story about how states actually came into existence. Other writers of the time who were concerned with contract theories, people such as John Selden, thought in terms of an actual contract that set up the state and also guaranteed various rights to the citizens. The application of Hobbes's method gives the contract so different a role that it might even be misleading to describe him as a contract theorist. Hobbes thought that different states might come into existence in different ways: some by conquest, others by alliances formed among families, and so on. He said that "there is scarce a Commonwealth in the world, whose beginnings can in conscience be justified."[52]

His story about authorization is not to be taken literally as a story about how states were set up; it is an application of the method of the circle to the idea that the sovereign can do no injustice, a point for which Hobbes argues in a way that does not depend on any actual authorization: The real reason behind the idea of authorization is that, as an artificial right reason or second-order decision-procedure between contending views of justice, the sovereign determines what is just for us to do and, therefore, can do no wrong. If you and I disagree about what justice requires or allows and, faced by a need for common action, agree to settle the matter by tossing a coin, then, no matter what the rights and wrongs in our initial debate, I shall act unjustly if I refuse to comply when the coin comes down favoring you. Authorization might not be the method by which that situation was created any more than the method Hobbes describes must be the method by which a particular circle was created, but it is a method that *might* have been used and one that guarantees the outcome: If the figure was made that way then it must be a circle, and if the sovereign was set up that way then it is impossible that he should do wrong.

David Johnston suggests[53] that the doctrine of authorization in *Leviathan* reflects Hobbes's "increased sensitivity to the importance of public opinion as an element in sovereign power" and involves the subjects more fully in the sovereign's acts than earlier versions of Hobbes's argument had done. Public opinion is a matter of what people believe. Their attitudes and beliefs might be affected by a requirement of actual authorization to institute a sovereign, but Hobbes does not require an actual contract. The doctrine of authorization is better understood as an explanation of why the sovereign can do no injustice;[54] it reflects the fact that, in Hobbes's theory, the function of the sovereign is to *establish* what is just in the face of disagreement about such matters,[55] and peaceful coexistence requires that we be prepared to submit to such an arbitration procedure.[56] Given that the sovereign has the function of a coin tossed to resolve a dispute, it is substantively unjust not to do what the sovereign requires. The doctrine of authorization captures the idea that my being committed to the procedure means that I am committed to the outcome.

This is the sense in which the sovereign's word defines justice, and it explains away the contradiction that Jean Hampton claims to have found in Hobbes on this subject.[57] It is clear that the sovereign does not analytically determine justice because injustice is possible without a sovereign: If a covenant were to be made in the natural condition, according to Hobbes, then performance by the first party means that the second party is bound to perform because the conditions that invalidate a covenant of mutual trust do not then apply.[58] That is to say, injustice will be done if the second party does not perform when the first party's prior performance has given him security of reciprocity. But within civil society, the sovereign's edict substantively determines justice.

The story of the contract, similarly, is like Hobbes's story of the method of generating a circle. The contract is, then, merely a model in Hobbes's argument. If the plane figure was, in fact, produced by the method that Hobbes described, and if we know that it was, then we can read off its properties from that fact. If it was not produced in that manner, or if we do not know that it was, then we cannot read off the properties in the same way but must establish independently that the plane figure has those properties before we can say that the method is its cause or is a possible cause that would guarantee the outcome. In the absence of an actual contract we cannot read off obligations from the contract. And if there was never a time when men all over the world lived in their natural condition,[59] then it cannot be that all societies were formed by a contract that enabled people to emerge from that natural condition. In order to be able to derive the method of generation from the plane figure, we must be able to show, independently of that method of generation, that the figure has the relevant properties — that it actually is a circle. In the same way, to derive contracting as the method of generation of societies, Hobbes would have to be able to show, independently of any contracts, that societies must have the relevant features; he cannot read off those features from a nonexistent contract. We should expect his arguments to be directed toward showing the necessity of the relevant features in any society.

The contract as a method of generation for societies, then, will be a model called for at the end of Hobbes's argument, in effect summarizing his conclusion; it cannot be the logical starting point of his argument. He will have to show by independent argument that human social life necessarily involves the rights and duties that might lead us to say that even if no actual contract produced this particular society, it could have been a contract that produced it; that is, that the contract is a way of producing this sort of relationship. And that is how Hobbes does argue: He sets about showing that life for a community of people necessarily involves rights and duties the content of which is not determined simply by the judgment of the person whose rights and duties they are. To put the point in anachronistic terms, Hobbes argues that right and duty are a priori concepts ("I seem . . . to have demonstrated by a most evident connexion, in this little work of mine, . . . the absolute necessity of leagues and contracts"[60]), and he argues that those concepts can be operated only in a context of public judgment.

And this argument leads us toward an answer to a question about what significance the contract could have for the issue of political obligation if there really was no contract. If there really was a contract that I signed, then we have at least the rudiments of an argument to show that I have an obligation. If we can show that it would have been rational or prudent for me to sign a contract, then we have the rudiments of an argument to show that I have an obligation only if we can also show that I behaved rationally or prudently and signed the contract, or so it seems. But these questions do not arise when dealing with Hobbes's theory. We should look for the conditions of obligation in the story for which the contract is a model, and we find it in the laws of nature and in the necessity for conventional decision-procedures. Later, I shall take up the issue of how Hobbes's moral theory fares when it is read in the light of this model.

The model of the circle, I think, gives the structure of Hobbes's large-scale arguments. Most of the conclusions that he wants can be drawn from those arguments without going to the lesser ones. He does, at times, make empirical assumptions, most notably about the frequency with which people disagree and their willingness to press their points. They are at least very plausible assumptions, and we shall deal with them as we need to. We should note, though, the falsity of Kavka's claim that, on Hobbes's account, "the psychological principles that ground political philosophy are known by introspection and can be demonstrated no other way".[61] He cites the final paragraph of the Introduction to *Leviathan*. But in the previous paragraph of that work, having said that the similitude of thoughts and passions is such that he can know what the thoughts and passions of another are by introspecting on his own, Hobbes goes on to say:

> I say the similitude of *Passions*, which are the same in all men, *desire, feare, hope*, &c; not the similitude of *the objects* of the Passions, which are the things *desired, feared, hoped*, &c: for these the constitution individuall, and particular education do so vary, and they are so easie to be kept from our knowledge, that the characters of mans heart, blotted and confounded as they are, with dissembling, lying, counterfeiting, and erroneous doctrines, are legible onely to him that searcheth hearts.[62]

It is not the *principles* of psychology that we learn in this way by introspecting, but simply what hope and fear are. This, on Hobbes's account, is simply how we come to learn the meanings of these words. And Hobbes says that no proposition other than a definition ought to be considered a principle.[63]

Notes

1. Part of the story of the debate can be found throughout Brian Easlea, *Witch-Hunting Magic and the New Philosophy* (Brighton: Harvester Press, 1980).
2. *E. W.*, vol. 1, pp. 316-317.
3. *E. W.*, vol. 1, p. 39.
4. *Leviathan*, chapter 5, p. 115.
5. See *E. W.*, vol. 1, p. 7.
6. The *Oxford English Dictionary* has one usage of "concept" from William Harvey in 1663, then no other until the 1820s.
7. Cf. Sheldon S. Wolin, *Politics and Vision: Continuity and Innovation in Western Political Thought* (Boston: Little, Brown & Company, 1960), pp. 246-247. After the feigned annihilation of the world, what man re-creates is meanings. But Wolin's claim that "while philosophy was confined to an imaginative act of 'privation,' that act of annihilation with which political philosophy began had, in an age of civil war and revolution, an implicit foundation in reality" is misleading. The turmoil of the time no doubt provoked Hobbes to think about politics, but a physical dismantling of the state was not part of his method. To dismantle the world into the right sorts of parts would not be possible physically (*E. W.*, vol. 1, p. 67).
8. *Leviathan*, p. 113.
9. *E. W.* vol. 1, pp. 82-83.
10. H.L.A. Hart, in his *The Concept of Law* (London: Oxford University Press, 1961), chapter 4, section 3, and part of chapter 6, raises this sort of objection as one of a battery directed against the claim that every state must have a legally unlimited sovereign. He takes John Austin as his target, but the arguments could be directed against Hobbes.
11. Gregory S. Kavka, *Hobbesian Moral and Political Theory* (Princeton: Princeton University Press, 1986), p. 9.
12. *De Cive*, "The Author's Preface to the Reader," p. 105.
13. David Gauthier, *The Logic of Leviathan* (Oxford: Oxford University Press, 1969), p. 3.
14. *E. W.*, vol. 1, p. 74.
15. *The Elements of Law* 1.6.1, pp. 24-25.
16. *E. W.*, vol. 1, p. 7.
17. *Leviathan*, chapter 5, p. 115.
18. *Leviathan*, chapter 11, p. 166.
19. *E. W.*, vol. 1, p. 8.
20. Cf. the warning in the Introduction to Deborah Baumgold, *Hobbes's Political Theory* (Cambridge: Cambridge University Press, 1988).
21. *E. W.*, vol. 1, p. 9.
22. *The Elements of Law* 1.4.11, pp. 16-17.
23. *E. W.*, vol. 1, p. 9.

24. Pace Kavka, *Hobbesian Theory*, p. 10: "It may be concluded that in interpreting Hobbes's method we are well advised to look more at what he does than at what he says." My point is that what he does is something that needs to be worked out in light of his statements about what he was doing.

25. *De Cive*, "The Author's Preface to the Reader," pp. 98-99.

26. E. W., vol. I, p. 66.

27. E. W., vol. 1, pp. 68ff.

28. But not always: As one example of a commentator drawing the distinction, see J.W.N. Watkins, *Hobbes's System of Ideas: A Study in the Political Significance of Philosophical Theories* (London: Hutchinson University Library, 1965), especially pp. 66-68. Gauthier (*The Logic of Leviathan*, pp. 2-3), as an example of the opposite tendency, runs the two together and fails to recognize their different functions.

29. E. W., vol. 1, p. 80.

30. E. W., vol. 1, p. 74.

31. *The Elements of Law* 1.4.11, p. 16.

32. Gauthier, *The Logic of Leviathan*, p. 4, recognizes the importance for Hobbes's method of claims about the function of the commonwealth. I take up that issue in chapter 6.

33. E. W., vol. 1, p. 6. See also pp. 69-71.

34. Cf. Wolin, *Politics and Vision*, p. 250: "Hobbes gives us a strikingly modern conception of philosophy."

35. Cf. Robert Nozick, *Anarchy, State, and Utopia* (Oxford: Basil Blackwell, 1974), pp. 6-9.

36. E. W., vol. 1, p. 81.

37. E. W., vol. 1, p. 43.

38. E. W., vol. 1, p. 67.

39. E. W., vol. 1, pp. 70-71.

40. E. W., vol. 1, p. 82.

41. E. W., vol. 1, p. 81.

42. E. W., vol. 1, p. 80.

43. E. W., vol. 1, p. 69. Note, though, the passage that follows in the text: "But the causes of universal things (of those, at least, that have any cause) are manifest of themselves, or (as they say commonly) known to nature; so that they need no method at all; for they have all but one universal cause, which is motion." This plays down the significance of the analytical or resolutive method in the philosophical endeavor.

44. Michael Oakeshott, *Hobbes on Civil Association* (Oxford: Basil Blackwell, 1975), p. 28, recognizes that Hobbes always uses the compositive method in his civil philosophy: "Hobbes tells us that his early thinking on the subject took the form of an argument from effect (civil association) to cause (human nature), from art to nature; but it is to be remarked that, not only in *Leviathan*, but also in all other accounts he gives of his civil philosophy, the form of argument is from cause to effect, from nature to art." But Oakeshott suggests that it does not matter which method was used.

45. E. W., vol. 1, pp. 73-74.

46. *E. W.*, vol. 1, p. 3.

47. Jean Hampton, *Hobbes and the Social Contract Tradition* (London: Cambridge University Press, 1986), p. 45.

48. *E. W.*, vol. 1, p. 6.

49. Kavka, *Hobbesian Theory*, p. 8. The quotation from Hobbes comes from *De Corpore*, chapter 6, section 10, and the emphasis is Kavka's. Gauthier (*The Logic of Leviathan*, p. 3) says that Hobbes takes consequential relationships indifferently as causal or logical entailments.

50. *Leviathan*, chapter 46, p. 682. Cf. *E. W.*, vol. 1, p. 81, where Hobbes says that we can conceive no cause at all of particular things.

51. *Leviathan*, chapter 46, p. 682.

52. *Leviathan*, "A Review and a Conclusion," p. 722.

53. David Johnston, *The Rhetoric of Leviathan* (Princeton: Princeton University Press, 1986), p. 82.

54. Cf. also Baumgold, *Hobbes's Political Theory*, pp. 24 and 48-55.

55. I take up this point in the next chapter.

56. *Leviathan*, chapter 15, p. 213.

57. Hampton, *Contract Tradition*, p. 243.

58. *Leviathan*, chapter 14, p. 196.

59. *Leviathan*, p. 187, and *E. W.*, vol. 5, p. 183.

60. *De Cive*, "Epistle Dedicatory," p. 93.

61. Kavka, *Hobbesian Theory*, p. 9.

62. *Leviathan*, pp. 82-83.

63. *E. W.*, vol. 1, p. 82.

2

The Denial of Right Reason

Hobbes has a much-overlooked argument in favor of his doctrine of sovereignty.[1] That he thought the argument important is suggested by the fact that it was the first argument he produced in favor of that doctrine in *Leviathan*. It is the argument about right reason. Almost everything that Hobbes wants in his doctrine of sovereignty can be derived from this argument, with reference to the passions necessary only to give part of the explanation of why the sovereign must have enforcement powers. Reference to *particular* passions suffered by particular people would not fit his explanatory model, which requires universals. Certainly he needs no premise about all people being completely self-interested or extremely nasty, and he makes no claim that all people are like that, though such claims are often attributed to him.[2]

We begin with a rough outline of the argument. The fundamental problem of human life in a community, according to Hobbes, is that people have different ideas and plans that come into conflict. The central idea involved here is that of *disagreement*. People have different ideas about what is valuable or what is reasonable,[3] and, therefore, different ideas about what natural law requires or allows. Hobbes is quite clear about this: "If every man were allowed this liberty of following his conscience, in such differences of consciences, they would not live together in peace an hour."[4] If people really agreed all the time, we should have no government and no need for government:

> Being distracted in opinions concerning the best use and application of their strength, they do not help, but hinder one another; . . . For if we could suppose a great Multitude of men to consent in the observation

of Justice, and other Lawes of Nature, without a common Power to
keep them all in awe; we might as well suppose all Man-kind to do the
same; and then there neither would be, nor need to be any Civill
Government, or Common-wealth at all; because there would be Peace
without subjection.[5]

So disagreements of this sort, and not merely conflict of interests or
clashing passions, cause the problems that civil society is required to
overcome. And again, people's use of private judgment, and the
disagreement consequent thereto, is one of the central differences
between bees and people enabling bees to live in natural agreement and
precluding people's entering that happy state:

These creatures, having not (as man) the use of reason, do not see, nor
think they see any fault, in the administration of their common
businesse: whereas amongst men, there are very many, that thinke
themselves wiser, and abler to govern the Publique, better than the rest;
and these strive to reforme and innovate, one this way, another that
way; and thereby bring it into Distraction and Civill warre.[6]

And Hobbes sums it all up with his claim that what enables us to escape
the terrors of our natural condition is the "laws of nature, the sum
whereof consisteth in forbidding us to be our own judges."[7]

Community requires common or corporate action, so the problem is
how to have common action — even common action that amounts to no
more than a common policy of not interfering in certain aspects of each
other's behavior or that amounts to no more than community decisions
about permissions and requirements, despite the differing ideas and
plans of the citizens. Sir Robert Filmer failed to understand this part of
the argument: "To reduce all the wills of an assembly by plurality of
voices to one will, is not a proper speech, for it is not a plurality but a
totality of voices which makes an assembly be of one will."[8] Hobbes's
claim is that common policies must be followed even in some cases
where such agreement cannot be reached,[9] and that is the point of his
distinction between a multitude and a people or person civil;[10] where
we have no natural unanimity of wills and a common policy is needed,
we must have an artificial will. This, he says, is the will of the artificial
person that is the state.

Filmer did not follow the point, and it is one that is easily
misunderstood. We often think of common action simply as people all
doing the same thing, or all doing the same thing in a coordinated way:
Perhaps I cut the grass and you rake up the leaves and clippings, but we
are acting together to tidy the lawn. A certain unanimity is presupposed

in cases of that sort. But there are other cases where we must have common action because we are part of a corporate body and corporate action is needed. Perhaps there must be a decision, even if there is disagreement about the matter, on such issues as which side of the road we shall drive on or whether we are at war with a neighboring country. What declares and goes to war is a *country*, not merely the army or the politicians or random citizens, and the decision involves everybody in the country even if there is disagreement. I might oppose the war, but, as a national of the country that has declared war, I might find, if I am in the wrong place when the declaration is made, that I am locked up as an enemy alien, and the bombing of my house has a different significance from the bombing of the house of a citizen in a neutral country. I might disapprove of the decision to go to war, but I am caught up in it in important ways: A corporate body of which I am a member has made a decision in the face of my disagreement, and I am bound up in that just as much as a member of a business corporation is bound up in the decision of the corporation to make investments that he, personally, would not have made. In my personal capacity I am not at war, but as a national, whether I like it or not, I am. A corporate body such as a state needs a procedure for reaching a decision despite lack of unanimity, and that is the focus of Hobbes's concern.

People who are completely self-interested or otherwise nasty (the position attributed to Hobbes by John Eachard, who puts into the mouth of Philautus the words "I have taught thee to be true; . . . that the world is wholly disposed of, and guided by *self-interest*"[11]) will, no doubt, come into conflict, but honest and intelligent people can disagree, too, and decent people will sometimes be prepared to fight for what they believe to be right. In fact, decent people will sometimes be prepared to fight harder for what they believe to be right than nasty people will be to get what they want. At a certain stage, the price that a nasty person is having to pay will become too high, so the package of aim and price will cease to be what he wants; a decent person fighting for what he believes to be right, on the other hand, rather than merely trying to get what he wants, will be less likely to be put off by the fact that pursuing the plan is making life uncomfortable. The point of the plan was not simply to make that person's life comfortable. This might be exemplified by some of the states at war in the 1940s.

Some people are simply nasty, and most people, no doubt, are nasty some of the time. Hobbes was clearly aware of that and regarded it as a serious practical problem for those responsible for running the life of the community. Nevertheless, it is not necessary to the underpinning of his first argument for sovereignty, and, though he suggested that thoroughly decent people were few, he did not say that everybody was completely self-interested. There are, he said, two helps to the force of words in keeping men to their covenants, one being fear of the consequences of breaking them and the other glory or pride, which implies that there are some who will act from better motivations than fear even though "this later is a Generosity too rarely found to be presumed on."[12]   But there are empirical assumptions in Hobbes's theory, and the empirical assumptions about how frequently and deeply people will disagree, how insistent they will be on having their own way when they differ, and so on, explain some of the excesses of Hobbes's conclusions. In particular, they help to explain the enormous powers that he attributes to the sovereign.

The argument about right reason is fairly straightforward. It is set out in chapter 5 of *Leviathan:*

> And as in Arithmetique, unpractised men must, and Professors themselves may often erre, and cast up false; so also in any other subject of Reasoning, the ablest, most attentive, and most practised men, may deceive themselves, and inferre false Conclusions; Not but that Reason itselfe is always Right Reason, as well as Arithmetique is a certain and infallible Art: But no one mans Reason, nor the Reason of any one number of men, makes the certaintie; no more than an account is therefore well cast up, because a great many men have unanimously approved it.   And therefore, as when there is a controversy in an account, the parties must by their own accord, set up for right Reason, the Reason of some Arbitrator, or Judge, to whose sentence they will both stand, or their controversie must either come to blowes, or be undecided, for want of a right Reason constituted by Nature; so is it also in debates of what kind soever: And when men that think themselves wiser than all others, clamor and demand right Reason for judge; yet seek no more, but that things should be determined, by no other mens reason but their own, it is as intolerable in the society of men, as it is in play after trump is turned, to use for trump on every occasion, that suite whereof they have most in their hand.   For they do nothing els, that will have every of their passions, as it comes to bear sway in them, to be taken for right Reason, and that in their own controversies: bewraying their want of right Reason, by the claym they lay to it.[13]

Appeal to right reason or to truth, Hobbes is saying, will not resolve disputes if the disputes are about what right reason reveals or about what the truth is.   We might agree that we should accept the true answer to whatever question exercises us (we might agree that the economic policies we should adopt are those that will save the country, for example), but we differ about what the true answer is.[14] On first discovering disagreement where common action is necessary, we should, no doubt, discuss the matter in a reasonable way, each presenting the case for his own opinion and assessing the case the other person presents, each being concerned with the truth and not with personalities or attempts to establish who is boss. We should, to take over Hobbes's example, at least check our sums again rather than proceed immediately to dispute if we are the sort of people who will seek peace where it can be found. Concern for truth, or for right reason, should be the governing principle at this stage.

Hobbes does not bother to make that point, but it is worth interpolating; that he does not make the point is one possible reason why he has been misread. Hobbes assumes such discussion in the right reason argument just quoted: We are to settle things in the normal way if we *can* reach agreement, because preparedness to discuss things is part of the preparedness to accommodate oneself to others required by Hobbes's fifth law of nature.[15] The natural law foundations of civil law in Hobbes's theory therefore build in such discussion. This role for discussion in seeking agreement, and then the role of arbitration, was common ground to Hobbes and other sorts of natural law theorists, but Hobbes's historical setting explains why he was more concerned in his arguments with those natural law theorists who insisted on their own version of the truth and were, in the name of that version of the truth, prepared to plunge the country into civil war and kill a king.[16]

Truth and right reason do not wear lapel badges to identify themselves; even with concern for them as the guiding principle of debate, agreement at the end cannot be guaranteed. Even academics and people in public life, devoted as they are to truth and the public good rather than to personalities and preferment, manage to differ. If we still differ after all the reasons in favor of each position have been given, then we differ when there are, apparently, no more reasons to be given. If there must be common action anyway, then somebody must give way. That is unavoidable. This is not, as Gauthier suggests,[17] a shift on Hobbes's part to a theory of truth as depending on an agreed, conventional standard. Hobbes is moving right away from questions about truth toward questions about what must be done if we are to live peacefully together; he argues that the question "What is the case?" is less important than the question "What are we bound to do?"[18] The introduction of an artificial right reason does not determine what is true, but it does make possible the determination of what is to be done in the face of continuing disagreement about what is true. It introduces a public level of judgment that takes precedence over merely private judgments and thus avoids the problems caused by conflict between the private judgments.[19]

Hobbes makes clear that what matters is that the procedure or arbitrator be agreed to or be fair. There can be no requirement that it get things right or produce the correct answer: "Nor doth he covenant so much, as that his sentence shall be just; for that were to make the parties judges of the sentence, whereby the controversy would remain still undecided."[20] Whatever resolution the arbitrator comes up with, at least one of the parties to the dispute will think that the arbitrator has made a mistake. That an arbitrator makes mistakes in this way, therefore, cannot be an objection; it is a necessary part of the arbitrator's serving the function that he has.

So much is clear in the right reason argument as Hobbes has set it out. "No one mans Reason, nor the Reason of any one number of men, makes the certaintie," so the sovereign, being but a man, does not give us that sort of certainty. Any sovereign can make a mistake in a judgment of equity, as can any judge, but the judgment stands nevertheless, "not because it is his private Sentence; but because he giveth it by Authority of the Soveraign, . . . which is Law."[21] His edict does not guarantee us that we have the truth. The artificial right reason does not play that role. What it does is to bind people to a course of action that might run contrary to their own private judgment; that it is a matter of *binding* them is made clear by Hobbes when he compares refusal to accept the artificial right reason with a cheating insistence that trumps in every hand should be the suit of which one holds most. This, he says, is intolerable in the society of men, and we can take that fairly literally:[22] No doubt we can get by while a few people are like that, mainly by using our superior numbers to force them to fit in, but if too many people were like that then we should "either come to blowes, or be undecided;" that is, we should have to fight or give up the possibility of agreement on common action or common limitations on action.

It is cases of common action (in which I include common recognition of limitations on private or individual action) that matter for this argument. In many everyday cases, we can ignore disagreement. We need not agree in our calculations if your calculations affect only you and my calculations affect only me: If our golf balls lie side by side on the fairway (or, more plausibly, in the rough) and we differ in our judgments of the distance to the pin so that you choose a seven-iron and I choose a six-iron, there is no great problem. The game can go on. It is when we are, for example, summing an account so that we can sort out what I owe you for services rendered that agreement must be reached. Purely private actions that affect only the agent are not touched by this argument; judgments concerning public actions — public in the sense that they affect others — are the ones on which the argument bears.

There might, of course, be argument about the sense in which others must be affected by the action if the right reason argument is to be brought to bear: All the arguments we have grown used to about the applicability of J. S. Mill's principles about liberty[23] could be employed for this purpose. Such disputes must be resolved if we are to know how we can act, so *those* disputes and judgments are certainly ones to which the argument is applicable. They must be submitted to an arbitrator or artificial right reason.

The argument is designed to demonstrate that a necessary condition of (relatively) peaceful life together, of life in a community, is the recognition of rights and duties that do not depend simply on the private judgments of those affected.[24] Such a peaceful life is possible only for people who are prepared to recognize the public judgment of the arbitrator as binding on them despite their own private judgments.[25] They must recognize that the one favored by the decision has a right that the other comply, and that the other has a duty to comply. So it is an argument designed to show that life in a society necessarily has some pattern of rights and duties: It necessarily has properties that might have been produced by the making of a contract. And that is just the sort of argument we should expect Hobbes to produce if he is taking the passage about the circle as his model.

As I have said, the argument does make empirical assumptions. It assumes, for a start, that people disagree. But such an assumption might have a privileged status, being treated as something like a presupposition of raising the question rather than simply as an empirical assumption that might not have been true, because questions about morals and politics might not be capable of being raised for people or other beings who immediately agreed in all of their judgments.[26]

The operation of this argument quite clearly does not presuppose psychological egoism or any claim that everybody is unpleasantly or excessively devoted to his own interests. The problem that Hobbes has pointed out could arise for a group of altruistic saints provided they differed in their opinions. What selfishness does is make it more difficult for us to get around the problem of our disagreement. The Hobbesian story, clearly, depends on our having enough people who are capable of reaching some accommodation with other people with whom they disagree. There must be enough people with enough of that capability for them to form a community large enough to protect themselves against the others or force them to fit in. They will be people who are prepared to follow the first law of nature: "That every man, ought to endeavour Peace, as farre as he has hope of obtaining it; and when he cannot obtain it, that he may seek, and use, all helps, and advantages of Warre."[27]

In dealing with somebody who refuses to accommodate himself at all to others in cases of disagreement but insists on having everything his own way,[28] we might, out of our own desire for peace, simply play our games of cards with somebody else who does recognize as trumps whatever suit was turned up on the pack; if that cannot reasonably be done, then we may properly fight to defend our own views and interests. As part of following the first clause of the first law of nature, we must be prepared to follow the explication that comes in the second law of nature: "That a man be willing, when others are so too, as farre-forth, as for Peace, and defence of himselfe he shall think it necessary, to lay down this right to all things; and be contented with so much liberty against other men, as he would allow other men against himselfe."[29] But how are the limits on that liberty to be set? It will not serve the purpose if each insists on being private judge of that liberty and its limits: One might say, "I am happy if I am allowed to drink wine, so you may drink wine, but beer is a crass, working-class drink and must be made illegal." People have differing tastes and views, which is where the problem Hobbes deals with in the right reason argument began. If the problem is allowed to rise again here, nothing has been gained. We must go to a public judgment for the second law of nature to have any effect: Each agrees to subject himself to some sort of arbitrating procedure, tossing a coin or whatever it might be, and to abide by the result of that procedure so that we get an impartial setting of the limits of the liberty each allows the others. A different standard is set up from the private ones that lead to dispute — it is the standard of the arbitrator or sovereign. And that is why the second law of nature leads to the third: "That men performe their Covenants made."[30]

Seeking peace, as the first law of nature requires us to do, is not necessarily a matter of looking for a quiet life so that we have to give up bungee jumping[31] and football games. It is a matter of being prepared to go to arbitration,[32] to submit one's private judgment and recognize a public judgment as binding and taking precedence over the private judgment. It means being prepared to toss a coin or recognize the sovereign's edict provided that the other person is prepared to do so too; it means being prepared to accommodate oneself to what makes life together possible.[33] How selfish people are, and how insistent they are on their own judgments, how many people there are of each sort, and generally how often and how seriously the problem comes up, are questions of fact, and what must be done to counteract the problems that they cause is also a question of fact to which the answer will not be a logical truth of the sort that Hobbes's science of politics was designed to produce.

Hobbes's point is that there are, or at least can be, more reasons to be given in cases of disagreement, but they will be reasons of a different kind from those that have been given in the earlier part of the debate. We may assume the first part of the debate to have been exhaustive, each having presented all the reasons for his views, objections to other views, replies to objections to his own views, and so on. In that part of the debate, concern for the truth was the guiding principle.[34] To stick with that principle at the later stage is to insist on having one's own way, to insist that truth-as-I-see-it be imposed on everybody else even if they see things differently.[35] It is to insist that trumps are whatever *I* hold most of no matter what, by chance in accordance with convention, was turned up on the deck. And if my reasons did not persuade the others that my view was true, they will not persuade the others that truth-as-I-see-it should be imposed on them. If I see my reasons for my belief as justifying me in imposing my views on others, the others will, with as much right, see their reasons for their beliefs as justifying them in imposing their beliefs on me. "For such is the nature of men, that howsoever they may acknowledge many others to be more witty, or more eloquent, or more learned; Yet they will hardly believe there be many so wise as themselves: For they see their own wit at hand, and other mens at a distance."[36]

Following this line and insisting on private judgment means either that there will be no common policy or that what the common policy is will be determined simply by greater force, enabling one to have his way and impose his views on the others, whatever they think of it. So we must move away from concern for truth and right reason as our guiding principle, though we may still be concerned with honesty. As Hobbes makes clear with his image of cheating at cards when he sets out the right reason argument, honesty is not simply a matter of telling the truth; it is a matter of fairness. We must concentrate on the need for common action and shift to consideration of a different sort of reason: that we agreed to decide the issue by the toss of a coin and the coin came down heads, for example, or that you have to take the responsibility for the decision and therefore get to make the decision, or that you won the election. None of these reasons tends to show that your views are true, but they do give a reason for the rest of us to go along with your views given that common action is necessary. We shift from concerning ourselves only with the truth of what is in contention

to concerning ourselves with the use of some decision-procedure that will bind us all, a decision-procedure that is fair. (Hence Hobbes's contemptuous pointing out that those who insist that the dispute be settled in terms of right reason are insisting that they be judges in their own dispute, which he took to be plainly unfair.) So, in the absence of a right reason that does wear an identifying lapel badge, we can have common action among people who disagree only by calling on a conventional decision-procedure: "Seeing right reason is not existent, the reason of some man, or men, must supply the place thereof; and that man, or men, is he or they, that have the sovereign power."[37]
Though I have stressed the role of a decision-procedure, a person or group of people is needed, according to Hobbes:[38] Tossing a coin, for example, does nothing unless the result can be definitively interpreted as heads or tails, so having such a procedure does not do away with the need to have people who operate it. Thus do we have the sovereign introduced simply in terms of arguments about reason, with no reference to the passions. Whatever might be true in the dispute between Kavka[39] and Bernard Gert[40] about whether egoistic assumptions play any role in Hobbes's moral and political theory, they certainly play no role in this central argument.

Hobbes had plenty of people to argue with about this point. George Lawson, for example, a good and intelligent man, could not see the point at all and kept insisting on the truth: "There is no Power to punish the good and protect the bad. For the Sword must execute according to Judgement, and that must pass according to Laws: and both Judgement and Laws must be regulated by Divine Wisdom and Justice."[41] And then Lawson says that "the subject hath not only liberty, but a command to examine the Laws of his Soveraign, and judge within himself, and for himself, whether they be not contrary to the Laws of his God."[42]

That Hobbes's point was an original one is suggested by the fact that Lawson and so many others missed it by so wide a margin, insisting that the truth must prevail and not dealing with Hobbes's arguments at all. Hobbes was not arguing that a sovereign was entitled to destroy moral virtue, but that a sovereign was necessary to peaceful life together and therefore, as I shall try to show, to the flourishing and even, as emerges from consideration of the effectiveness of the laws of nature in our natural condition, the possibility of exhibiting at all the moral virtues.[43] Without the context of the rights that come with a sovereign or with a binding decision-procedure, there can be no other sort of morality; the virtues cannot flourish, or, indeed, be exhibited. Lawson leaves coercion as the only way of dealing with disagreement, and that way lies our natural condition. Hobbes's point at this stage is about the importance of getting over the problem of disagreement.

Modern commentators, too, have failed to recognize Hobbes's point about the role of reason. C.A.J. Coady[44] takes it that a fairly simple distinction can be drawn between the right to self-preservation and other natural rights in the Hobbesian natural condition in terms of the content of the rights. He has overlooked the significance of Hobbes's point about reason and right reason: Whatever my reason tells me is what I shall take to be right reason, and in our natural condition I am not bound to submit to anybody else's judgment of the matter; hence, my right to self-preservation becomes a right to anything I believe to be necessary to my preservation even if, in the judgment of others, my belief is false or even stupid. My right to self-preservation thus becomes materially equivalent to a right to all things: There is nothing of which it can definitively be said that, whatever my beliefs may be, I have no right to do it, and the fact that everybody else believes my belief to be false and me to be a lunatic is irrelevant.[45] In the natural condition, *my* judgment of what is reasonable (whether or not that judgment is that I should accept somebody else's advice) is what properly determines my action. In that situation, I am not bound by any other standard.

Gregory S. Kavka[46] makes the same mistake when he suggests that the reference to reason in Hobbes's definition of the right of nature might charitably be taken as implying that the agent's belief in the necessity of the act must be reasonable. The only judge of reasonableness in the natural condition is the agent. If I sincerely believe that you are attacking me and that my shooting you is in defense of my life, then I am in my natural condition with respect to you and my judgment of what is reasonable prevails.[47] There is no impersonal test of reason to be applied in our natural condition, and your views, or those of any onlooker, are irrelevant to my judgment.

Later, Kavka says:

> Hobbes uses the term "right reason" (sometimes "natural reason" or simply "reason") to refer to a certain kind of reasoning process, or its conclusions, or the mental faculty that enables us to engage in such a process. Right reason(ing) viewed as a process has three defining characteristics: it is sound, it is about kinds of acts that affect others' interests, and it concerns such acts insofar as they secure and advance the agent's own preservation. In short, it is correct prudential reasoning about interpersonal conduct.[48]

This again misses Hobbes's point. Whether the reasoning, prudential or otherwise, is correct is a matter about which people can disagree. Disputes about the truth might consist of the protagonists' pointing out to each other what (they believe) is true, but they are not settled by that procedure. The relevant passage in Hobbes is the following: "Yet being without this civil government, in which state no man can know right reason from false, but by comparing it with his own, every man's own reason is to be accounted, not only the rule of his own actions, which are done at his own peril, but also for the measure of another man's reason, in such things as do concern him."[49] And what is being overlooked here by Kavka is no small thing: It is the driving force of Hobbes's first argument about sovereignty. As isolated atoms, people would be locked into their own private judgments. We need a conventional decision-procedure, something that can act as an arbitrator, if we are to be able to resolve our disputes peacefully.

Again, Kavka suggests that Hobbesian philosophy (that is, Kavka's reconstruction; the claim is not one directly about Hobbes) might suggest that "our intuitions imply limits on the right of self-preservation, for we may hold that the right of self-preservation is initially unlimited in a pure state-of-nature situation but can be limited by one's own actions and commitments, and is so limited — by explicit or tacit consent — upon entering civil society."[50] However, as I have already pointed out, what makes the right to self-preservation spread so uncontrollably is that it is applied in terms of the agent's judgment.[51] My actions and commitments to limit that right, provided that it is still applied in terms of my judgment, will not succeed in limiting it one whit. Failure to recognize the force of Hobbes's argument about right reason means that Kavka misconstrues the problem about the right to self-preservation. My right to self-preservation gives me no guard against the sovereign if the judgment of what it allows and when it comes into play is handed over to the sovereign, but if I retain that judgment it is not clear that anything at all has been handed over to the sovereign or laid down. I take up this point again later.

Contrary to the possibility that Jean Hampton considers,[52] what Hobbes requires here is not a matter of converting to a new standard of rationality and becoming a new kind of reasoner. Rather, the exigencies of a situation in which common action is required lead one to *change the question*. It is not a matter of converting to a new standard of rationality and becoming a new kind of reasoner in order to get an answer to the old question; it is a matter of recognizing the priority of a different question. The question "What is true?" is left behind in favor of the question "What are we to do?" That is the issue with which the sovereign deals. He cannot give us the certainty of truth any more than any other person or body of people; his being sovereign makes his reason an *artificial* right reason, but not a natural right reason. What he can do is resolve disputes if his decision is taken as binding.

Hampton says of Hobbes that "in all of his political writings he maintains that it was *bad reasoning* that had plunged England and other European political societies into chaos during the seventeenth century, so that the only effective cure for this disorder was to give members of these societies a sound, rational argument for the correct political structure of a state as rigorous as any of Euclid's proofs."[53] But the issue is: What is Hobbes concerned to produce the right reasons *about?* His views on right reason certainly do not require that he ignore the fact that (he thinks that) he has the truth. Nor do they require that he refrain from trying to persuade other people to agree with him. Nevertheless, he does not argue about "*the* correct political structure of a state." The sovereign might be one man or a body of men,[54] and so on. Hobbes's point is much more about form than about content: As I have suggested, he is less concerned about arguing that a certain answer is true than about arguing that a different question should be asked. The truth might not change with a change in government, but one's allegiances, on Hobbes's account, should. Perhaps God's truth is that the Stuarts still rule, but the British of today are nevertheless bound in this world to obey the elected government.

The right reason argument is a forceful argument for the necessity of giving primacy to public judgment in social life. Insistence on private judgment makes it impossible for us to play a game of cards, because we would all be playing with different suits as trumps and no common outcome would, therefore, be possible. The same point applies on the larger scale in our communal life together. If we want to live peacefully together and avoid the calamity of solitude,[55] let alone the greater calamity of constant conflict, then we must be prepared to go to arbitration and to have the result of that arbitration take precedence over our initial private judgments. We must be prepared to make covenants and to keep our covenants made; that is, to recognize the public judgment as binding.

There might still be questions about the extent to which public judgment must be given precedence over private judgment. Suppose the arbitrator decides that the smoking of marijuana is to be illegal because it is addictive, dangerous, and generally a bad thing. Suppose that I, as one who has devoted his whole life to the study of this subject, know that marijuana is not addictive, not dangerous, and that my smoking it affects nobody but me. Surely, in such a case, I do not have to give precedence to the public judgment? And one can certainly find passages in Hobbes supportive of such a view. Nor, as emerges later in this book, do I want to play down their importance.

But one would expect the writ of public judgment, as argued for by Hobbes in his right reason argument, to run a long way. That argument suggests that public judgment should take precedence over private judgment whenever the two come into conflict. To say that public judgment should take precedence when it is correct, and not otherwise, for example, simply gives private judgment precedence all the time and means that public judgment will be unable to serve its function of making common action or common policy possible: If public judgment comes into play because of a dispute between private judgments, then at least one of the holders of those private judgments must be of the view that the public judgment, even if binding, is mistaken. The public judgment cannot agree with both of two conflicting views.

If we cannot, in that way, *sometimes* subject public judgment to the private judgment of the subjects, then public judgment must *always* take precedence if the right reason argument carries force. People who hold their views with sufficient fervor might refuse to accept the decision in some cases, but that does not go against the argument; it simply means that those people in those cases are a problem and that the public judgment must be enforced on them. The bailiffs must be put in, or a restraining order served on them, or whatever.

Nor does the fact that the sovereignty that most immediately emerges from the right reason argument is a matter of arbitration limit it in any significant way. If there had been complete agreement, so that arbitration did not come into the matter, then nobody would have tried to stop the subject from what he was doing anyway. And if other people do not like what the sovereign is doing, that is a disagreement between him and them to be arbitrated by the sovereign. And, Hobbes argues in chapter 18 of *Leviathan*, the arbitrator for peace must have all the other attributes of sovereignty as well: If one of the disputants, not liking the decision that is reached, can then insist that a different procedure be used for the arbitration, the arbitration will not succeed in doing its job, so the disputants cannot change the form of arbitration.[56] The arbitrator must have enforcement powers[57] so that each disputant knows that a decision in his favor will be observed, so that the arbitration does replace fighting. And so on. So we should expect Hobbes's argument to lead to the conclusion that public judgment takes precedence in every case with which it deals and that it can deal with any case with which it wants to deal.[58]

In chapter 21 of *Leviathan*, Hobbes lists those cases in which a subject may, without injustice, refuse to obey the command of the sovereign. His most general statement on the matter is that "when . . . our refusall to obey, frustrates the End for which the Soveraignty was ordained;

then there is no Liberty to refuse: otherwise there is."[59] But this gives the subject much less protection against the sovereign's caprice than might at first glance appear. In chapter 18 of *Leviathan*, Hobbes sets out in some detail the rights of the sovereign.[60] The relevant passage is:

> And because the End of this Institution, is the Peace and Defence of them all; and whosoever has the right to the End, has the right to the Means; it belongeth of Right, to whatsoever Man, or Assembly that hath the Soveraignty, to be Judge both of the meanes of Peace and Defence; and also of hindrances, and disturbances of the same; and to do whatsoever he shall think necessary to be done, both before hand, for the preserving of Peace and Security, by prevention of Discord at home and Hostility from abroad.[61]

Perhaps the subject need not obey if obedience to the sovereign's command is not necessary to the preservation of peace and security, but the judgment of whether obedience is necessary to that end lies with the sovereign. It does not, in any relevant way that might limit what the sovereign can properly do, lie with the subject: "A man that is commanded as a Souldier to fight against the enemy, though his Soveraign have Right enough to punish his refusall with death, may nevertheless in many cases refuse, without Injustice."[62] The sovereign may require obedience and enforce obedience; the subject will be bound by the law without consideration of whether he *feels* bound by it, and no other subject has liberty to come to his aid.[63] That he could refuse to obey without injustice will be little comfort and no protection against coercion and, furthermore, against coercion applied by the sovereign with no injustice on his side, either.

The subject may justly disobey the command of the sovereign to kill himself, or to maim himself, or to incriminate himself (which might lead to his being killed or maimed).[64] But again, the justice of this disobedience does not imply any lack of right on the part of the sovereign to give the command and to support it with punishment, including death. When the sovereign puts himself in that sort of relationship with his subject, he is putting the subject into the natural condition with respect to him. Hence the subject (or, more accurately, former subject) may justly resist, but at the expense of putting himself into his natural condition with his sovereign, and a more unfortunate natural condition for him than the one usually referred to in that it consists of a war of many against one rather than of each against all. He may properly resist the sovereign's demands, but by doing so he puts himself outside the community, as is suggested by Hobbes's tale, of the institution of the sovereign and the part of the potential subject in that institution: "And whether he be of the Congregation, or not; and whether his consent be asked, or not, he must either submit to their decrees, or be left in the condition of warre he was in before; wherein he might without injustice be destroyed by any man whatsoever."[65]

Hobbes suggests other limitations on what the sovereign can do. Laws, he says, must be promulgated; it is of their essence to be made known to all those who are to be obliged to obey them,[66] which appears to mean that a sovereign is restricted in that he cannot make retrospective legislation. But any restriction of that sort is a merely logical restriction, amounting to no more than saying that when a sovereign does what might be objected to as legislating retrospectively, it should be redescribed in some other way. Certainly Hobbes allows for the sovereign to act retrospectively: If no law has been made, then the sovereign shall deal with actions people have performed by punishing or rewarding them, if he sees fit to do so, in such a way as will best encourage men to serve the commonwealth and discourage them from disserving it.[67]

The sovereign is legally unlimited.[68] Public judgment may intrude into any case at all, and it takes precedence over private judgment in that it may properly be imposed even if particular citizens may, without injustice, resist its imposition on them. The sovereign is subject to natural law, but that is no joy to the subjects: For his obedience to the natural law, the sovereign is answerable to God and to nobody else.[69] Disobedience to the natural law, in Hobbes's view, was quite likely to lead to "natural" penalties. Nevertheless, all that the subject could properly do was sit back and wait for the sovereign to be visited with a plague of boils or to suffer in some other way for his improper behavior.

Hobbes sets out the argument about legal limitation on the sovereign[70] as an argument about logical necessity: It is not merely that sovereigns are not legally limited; it is absurd to suppose that they could be, and that follows from the function in terms of which the sovereign is defined. The lack of legal limitation on the sovereign means that public judgment rules everywhere that it goes. The right reason argument is an argument designed to show that every community must have a sovereign. Put them together and we have an argument that life in a community must have certain features that could be modeled by people's making a contract of the sort that Hobbes describes even if those features did not arise from such a contract.

If we are to live peacefully together despite our disagreements, then we must be prepared to accommodate ourselves to others to the required extent. We are not required to become slaves, as Hobbes makes clear in his discussion of sovereignty by conquest,[71] because slaves have no obligations at all; we are required to accommodate ourselves to others within certain limits, and the requirement is a fair one in that it depends on others' accommodating themselves to the same extent. Right reason is the obvious candidate to set those limits, but it cannot do the job because there is no natural right reason; each man takes for right reason what is his own.[72] Hence, attempts to set the limits by reference to right reason simply lead to conflict. The idea that the limits should be set by right reason must, therefore, be false, because "Doctrine repugnant to Peace, can no more be True, than Peace and Concord can be against the Law of Nature."[73] So we must have recourse to an artificial right reason; we must turn to conventional decision-procedures that will give us a binding public judgment.

The right reason argument is also an argument about liberty. It is, specifically, an argument about the necessity of toleration if we are to live peacefully together, but also, as part of that, an argument about the proper limits of the citizen's liberty. The liberty that is worth bothering about, Hobbes argues, is created by the sovereign; it is made up of civil rights, not protected by natural rights. Natural right turns into a right to all things, and "for so long as every man holdeth this Right, of doing anything he liketh; so long are all men in the condition of Warre."[74] The rights that matter, on Hobbes's account, are positive rights.

Deborah Baumgold claims that Hobbes has a very weak theory of politically inconsequential rights that might not qualify as a theory of rights at all.[75] Her argument is a solid one. Nevertheless, the rights about which she has been arguing at that stage are *natural* rights; positive rights, and especially those of the sovereign, are crucial to Hobbes's theory. Because she overlooks the importance of positive rights in Hobbes's theory, she takes Hobbes to be arguing consequentially[76] in saying that citizens may disobey the sovereign when their doing so will not frustrate the end for which sovereignty was ordained, and otherwise they must obey. It would be more straightforward here to read Hobbes as making a point about the presuppositions of having any rights at all: The point is one about what rights and duties may or must be in the framework that is necessary if citizens are to have any rights at all.

The alternative to conventional authority (or to the sovereign, in Hobbes's account) is natural right, and natural right leads us to, or keeps us in, our natural condition. With respect to natural right, each is, and must be, his own judge: Were anybody else the judge, natural right could not protect us against the intrusions from authority against which it is its point to protect us. The point of natural right is that it does not depend on the say-so of any sovereign or other authority but can be used as a reference point from which to criticize what that authority does. Natural right goes with private judgment.

This returns us to the right reason argument that Hobbes set out in chapter 5 of *Leviathan*. Natural rights theorists were among Hobbes's targets. He employed a *reductio* argument against them, showing that what followed from natural right was not a civil society in which the citizens had the maximum of liberty, but the radical form of man's natural condition.[77]

The problem about natural rights can be overcome only with full-blown notions of *right* and *obligation*. Mere force will not do the job. Fear, whether of God or the sovereign or a roving mugger, will do the job only when I *submit* to the force and take on a proper obligation,[78] acknowledging the right of the other to determine what is to be done, whether what is to be done in general or what is to be done in a particular limited sphere. Doing something only because I have been hit or am afraid of being hit is not leaving our natural condition of a war of each against all, but it is acting in that condition. We are in our natural condition not only when we battle but when willingness to fight is known,[79] as it is when I act from fear of being hit. We are out of that condition only when we obey the orders of others because we recognize their authority, even if we recognize their authority only because of their superior force. It is clear that submission, and not *merely* coercion, is necessary to obligation on Hobbes's account[80] when he says that "it is not therefore the Victory, that giveth the right of Dominion over the Vanquished, but his own Covenant"[81] and when he makes other remarks about sovereignty by acquisition: "As when a man maketh his children, to submit themselves, and their children to his government, as being able to destroy them if they refuse; or by Warre subdueth his enemies to his will, giving them their lives on that condition."[82] The children must submit; it is the submission that matters, because, by the time they are old enough to have their own children, their own parents might not be able to destroy them, especially in anything like our natural condition. And the conquered must make a bargain with their conqueror; that, and not merely possession of force, is what creates the obligation. On Hobbes's account, authority and the concomitant notions of *right* and *obligation* are necessary to communal life; the sovereign is one of the conditions that enable us to generate rights and obligations.

We have already seen some of the important consequences that Hobbes draws from the fact that people differ, and especially his conclusion about the need for a conventional decision-procedure. Of course, the people might simply refuse, out of bloody-mindedness or selfishness or a deep conviction of the rightness of their cause, to toss a coin or to submit to an arbitrator or to do anything of that sort, but then they cannot have common action or peaceful life in a community. They would be breaking the first part of Hobbes's first law of nature, which requires them to seek peace insofar as they have any hope of attaining it.[83] Each could simply fight for his own way, in which case we have a war of each against all. Something approaching this, perhaps, can be seen in recent times between groups, though not between each person and each other person, in Ireland or in parts of the Middle East. If one should subdue the others, then we should have sovereignty by acquisition with its underlying agreement: The war ends only when one submits to the other, even if the submission is only because of superior force. Until that submission, the war continues.

That outcome, though, is unlikely, as is pointed out in Hobbes's argument about equality in chapter 13 of *Leviathan:* If there are, say, 1,000 people involved in a war of each against all, and if they are roughly equal, then the odds against a final victory by any one of them are 999 to 1 against, and only a fool would take those odds with his life as the stake. Inequality between the people would need to be very great indeed to change those odds enough to make the bet a reasonable one.

It is clear from that point that empirical assumptions do come into Hobbes's arguments, though those involved at this stage seem to be fairly plainly true. It is assumed, for example, that people do disagree, that they are vulnerable to hurt, and so on. And one notices that Hobbes does call on a probability argument, which seems not to sit well with the method of mathematically tight deductive argument that he set out. One can simply note that fact. The Great Tew Circle, of whose work Hobbes must have been aware, discussed the theory of mathematical probability, and Hobbes might, given his devotion to mathematics, have accepted a mathematical theory as sufficiently tight for his purposes. He was not, after all, working with a philosophy of philosophy as restrictive as some of those accepted today. Or he might have thought, quite plausibly, that it is pretty close to a necessary truth that odds of 999 to 1 against (especially with one's life at stake) constitute a bad bet, that is, that backing such an outsider with so much at stake would be irrational. The latter seems to be the more likely interpretation.

Nevertheless, it should be said that the sort of mathematical probability theory that is available today was not available in Hobbes's time; he did not use such arguments, and because they were not available, he could not have intended them. Interpretations of him as having intended complex arguments based on the Prisoners' Dilemma and calling on sophisticated theories in mathematical probability, for example, are certainly false interpretations of him, though they might deal in a different way with a point that concerned him. Both Jean Hampton[84] and David Gauthier,[85] for example, construct interesting theories in this way, but the issue I am raising here is whether those theories can capture *Hobbes's* arguments. Attempts to set out what Hobbes would have said had twentieth-century tools been available to him can be valuable exercises, but they cannot be taken to be attempts to set out what Hobbes did say. Hampton claims[86] that use of modern games theory in elucidating Hobbes is not anachronistic, but she presents no serious defense of that claim: Perhaps it is true that, as Hampton says, "Euclid would feel himself vindicated rather than violated if his faulty proofs were corrected so that his conclusions could be derived from his axioms, and Hobbes would feel the same,"[87] but better arguments are not the same arguments as the arguments they are better than. Nor are they clarifications of those arguments; they are different arguments, and they must be if they are to be better arguments. Games theory was not available, so Hobbes did not intend such arguments. There is a good deal of power and interest in the arguments that he actually used.

There is a side to Hobbes's argument that is often overlooked because of the emphasis placed on the fact that Hobbes's theory would countenance some very repressive governments: One aspect of Hobbes's argument is about toleration. It is often overlooked because what he tells me about toleration is not that it must be *of* me, but that it must be *by* me. This, of course, applies to everybody, and that is how there comes to be toleration *of* me *by* others. There can be common action in the face of disagreement only if somebody gives way, so each of us must be tolerant in that each of us must be prepared to give way if the coin comes down tails or the other side wins the election or, generally, if a fair decision-procedure decides against us. As the story is set up, it is clear that this will involve each of us in a willingness to tolerate what we see as falsity or a failure to act in accordance with right reason.

Here, and not in natural right, is where Hobbes locates the liberty of the subject, so we should note here something about private consciences. It is a point that has bearing on present-day disputes. Private consciences should be tolerant, and they should be tolerant in just the way that has been explained. A decent person, whenever the decision-procedure goes against him or her, will think that a mistake has been made, and in the relevant cases will think that a moral mistake has been made. The idea of private conscience is sometimes called on these days in ways suggesting that in any such case one should oppose the decision and refuse to abide by it. Hobbes's argument shows the simplistic nature of any such view: A private conscience with even a minimum of subtlety would question the propriety of simply forcing its own views on others in any and every case of disagreement and would wonder about the justice of refusing to accept the decision of a fair procedure when other decent people had taken their chances with it. Public procedure and private conscience are not as simply opposed as is sometimes suggested. Whether or not the public decision-procedure should always be able to overrule the first-off judgment of a private conscience (that is, the view held by that conscience as one of the differing views that went before the decision-procedure), the operation of a fair procedure is surely something that a private conscience ought to consider when finally deciding on action.

Hobbes, apart from being read as a psychological egoist, is often read as espousing some sort of egoistic moral theory, but this is, in fact, a misreading of him: It takes for remarks about morality as such what are really remarks about the problems of morality in man's natural condition. David Gauthier,[88] for example, gives a definition of what he takes to be Hobbes's account of the meaning of "good" in terms of the desire of the person using the word. He quotes Hobbes's "But whatsoever is the object of any man's Appetite or Desire, that is it which he for his part calleth *good*."[89] This is Hobbes's account of the way in which value terms will operate in our natural condition, and Hobbes is quite clear that this is a bad condition in which to be: The doctrine that private appetite is the measure of good is "Pernicious to the Publique State,"[90] and "so long a man is in the condition of meer Nature . . . as private Appetite is the measure of Good, and Evill."[91] There are, indeed, problems about morality in the condition of mere nature. Those problems help to show that the home of morality is civil society: Morality is, in some respects, inescapably conventional.[92] That is to say, the problems about morality in our natural condition are solved by the introduction of the sovereign.

> Aristotle, and other Heathen Philosophers, define Good, and Evill, by the Appetite of men; and well enough, as long as we consider them governed every one by his own Law: For in the condition of men that have no other Law but their own Appetites, there can be no generall Rule of Good and Evill Actions. But in a Common-wealth this measure is false: Not the Appetite of Private men, but the Law, which is the Will and Appetite of the State is the measure.[93]

More important than the misreading of Hobbes as espousing an egoistic theory in either morals or psychology is the fact that his argument about the role of convention in morality can be shown to stand up without any assumption of egoism. The role of convention, as it appears in Hobbes's argument, is the role of the sovereign as set up by the right reason argument.

Hobbes's point about right reason is that the notion is of no use for any purpose but the stirring up of trouble. Insistence on right reason as I believe it to be is intolerable; that is to say, that sort of thing is incompatible with people's living together as a community.[94] Hence Hobbes's important distinction between conscience and private conscience:

> For the conscience being nothing else but a man's settled judgment and opinion, when he hath once transferred his right of judging to another, that which shall be commanded, is no less his judgment, than the judgment of that other; so that in obedience to laws, a man doth still according to his own conscience, but not his private conscience. And whatsoever is done contrary to private conscience, is then a sin, when the laws have left him to his own liberty, and never else. And then whatsoever a man doth, not only believing it is ill done, but doubting whether it be ill or not, is done ill, in case he may lawfully omit the doing.[95]

Hobbes also writes that "in every commonwealth, every subject should in all things to the uttermost of his power obey the commands of him or them that is the sovereign thereof; and that a man in so obeying, doth according to his conscience and judgment, as having deposited his judgment in all controversies in the hands of the sovereign power."[96]

These passages, especially the second, look as though Hobbes was taking just the position to which R. P. Wolff has objected so vehemently in his *In Defense of Anarchism*,[97] but Wolff seems not really to have seen the point about distinguishing conscience from private conscience. In fact, I do not think that Hobbes is talking about slavishly turning all one's judging over to somebody else. We can make sense of Hobbes without reading him in that way, and we should do so: His insistence that not even subjects by conquest are slaves[98] and his retention of the natural right to self-preservation suggest that we should, if possible, avoid reading him as making subjects into slaves. He has a proper distinction to make between conscience and private conscience.

One can think of this as being the exercise of conscience at two different stages of proceedings: before and after the election or the toss of a coin or the judgment from a court. The court (or whatever procedure we choose) might have to settle a dispute between us in which each of us believes quite sincerely in the justice of his cause. Imagine that the court decides in your favor.

The court might not have succeeded in persuading me that my initial judgment was mistaken, so my private conscience might not have shifted, but my full-blown conscience (still mine, not handed over to somebody else) should lead me to behave in a manner different from that in which I could properly have done had the court ruled in my favor or had there been no conventional decision-procedure to use. The distinction is not between my acting in terms of my conscience and my acting in terms of somebody else's conscience or handing over all my moral decisions and responsibility to somebody else; it is between my having only a very crude conscience and my having a conscience sufficiently subtle to consider fairness in the resolution of disputes when I disagree with somebody else about justice.

If I were to go ahead and act on the basis of private conscience after the court has ruled in your favor, I would be breaking Hobbes's third law of nature, which requires that I keep my covenants made.[99] Recognizing that, I might refuse to go to court (or to toss a coin, or to consult the elders, or whatever procedure is suggested). But that does not protect my private conscience. I would then be breaking Hobbes's first law of nature, which requires that I seek peace insofar as I can find it.[100] These are the basic laws of nature, the real fundamentals of social life; a private conscience that leads me to break them is nothing to be proud of. It is, in fact, something that makes me unfit for social life, a person with whom others cannot enter truly cooperative relationships: Those who will not accommodate themselves to others, Hobbes says, are to be "cast out of Society, as cumbersome thereunto."[101] Conscience, Hobbes says in the passage quoted earlier, is the same thing as a man's settled judgment, and a settled judgment should consider the significance of the conventional means by which we resolve our disputes. Conscience should not simply be set over and against such procedures when they happen not to favor us. This point, and the distinction between private and public judgment, is, I think, fundamental to Hobbes's moral theory.

To resolve cases of disagreement while living together and not resorting to violence, we must go to arbitration, as Hobbes's sixteenth law of nature[102] requires, and put our case before a judge. The judge is not committed to getting things right,[103] but that he did not even try to get things right might be a quite different matter. Mistaken judgments on the part of the ruler (or mistaken judgments as I take them to be) are one thing; the sorts of abuses by government (as opposed to sloppy thinking by citizens) that undermine political life on Hobbes's account will be concerned with procedure. The procedure that resolves our disputes must be one to which we "will both stand."[104] That is to say, Hobbes's claim is that the procedure must be one on the fairness of which we can agree. Equity is a law of nature,[105] and thus it is required of the sovereign. The eleventh law of nature requires that "if *a man be trusted to judge between man and man*, it is a precept of the Law of Nature, *that he deale Equally between them*. For without that, the Controversies of men cannot be determined but by Warre."[106] In other words, it is only if the disputants see the decision-procedure as a fair one that they have any reason to go along with it; if they see it as unfair, they therein see it as favoring the other party and thus as no more than an instrument he uses in the battle to assert his will. The battle continues, and the decision-procedure, instead of being a means to peace, becomes no more than a weapon. There is, in such a case, no reason why the party who feels disadvantaged should submit to the procedure and its outcome: "If other men will not lay down their Right, as well as he; then there is no Reason for any one, to devest himselfe of his."[107] That the sovereignty, or the decision-procedure, is perceived as fair is a necessary part of its serving its function of allowing domestic politics to replace civil strife. But it is also a necessary part of the sovereign's serving his function that he cannot be taken to have contracted to do justice in everybody's eyes,[108] because one of his functions is to resolve disputes about justice.

Sometimes, of course, the truth really does matter: It does matter whether some policy will produce dramatic famine or whether thousands of people sail over the edge of a flat earth. But that is something that can be said only with hindsight. At the time of the dispute we have to argue from the premise that we disagree, because the discussion will get nowhere if we insist on starting from the premise that we are right and our opponents are wrong. Doing that would be breaking the second law of nature, trying to reserve to ourselves rights that we were not prepared to allow to others. And disputes about whether the issue at hand is one of those where truth really does matter are merely other disputes that must be resolved. The community might eventually collapse if the wrong decision is made, but it will certainly collapse if no decision can be made in cases of dispute so that common action is not possible.

The basic point here is that we must move away from considering evidence for or against the claim in dispute when consideration of such evidence has failed to do the job of resolving the dispute.[109] We must turn to something different: At that stage we must be prepared to accept the relevance of such claims as "I am taking responsibility for the outcome" or "You were elected to decide this sort of thing." These considerations do nothing to show that the person to whom the decision is left is right in that decision, as Hobbes does not require that the judge be right, but they do resolve the dispute. In each case, we have moved to add a political premise to the argument.

The idea that there must be a moral element in politics (in one sense, anyway) is fairly widely recognized. The idea that there must be this political element in morality, though, is less widely recognized. This political element in morality is toleration. Others sometimes differ from us, and we must be prepared to tolerate their views' prevailing when the dispute has been fairly resolved in their favor.

What we have seen so far is an argument that Hobbes sets up simply on the basis of what right reasoning is and the idea that there is no natural mark of right reason. No reference has been necessary to claims about the passions or assumptions of egoism or a belief that people are ineluctably nasty. What sorts of moral or political conclusions might be drawn from such a spare starting point?

One conclusion we might draw is that though we might respect, and even demand, honesty, and though we might think highly of a disinterested search after truth and require that of a judge, a citizen's insisting too strongly on the truth is equivalent to his insisting on having his own way even when his way conflicts with the ways of others in the community. The truth on which he insists is, necessarily, the truth as he sees it, and, if that varies from the truth as others see it, then there is no reason in that story as it is told so far why his view should be given precedence and the other people required to fit in with him. Searching for the truth is all very well, but insisting on (one's private judgment of) the truth is an injustice to others whose views must be taken to be, in the absence of public standards, as worthy as one's own. And, in the absence of a mutually binding procedure to determine worth, one must recognize that the fact that the other person's views are different from one's own does not by itself make them less worthy in any way that explains to the other person why he should give way. Criminals and lunatics must be publicly judged to be so.

Another version of the same point, a version that Hobbes pressed very forcefully, is that no simple opposition of conscience to the law carries great weight: Insofar as my conscience is my private judgment, insisting that my conscience be satisfied is insisting that I have my way where we disagree.

> When two, or more men, know of one and the same fact, they are said to be CONSCIOUS of it one to another; which is as much as to know it together. And because such are fittest witnesses of the facts of one

another, or of a third; it was, and ever will be reputed a very Evill act, for any man to speak against his *conscience;* or to corrupt or force another so to do: Insomuch that the plea of Conscience, has been alwayes hearkened unto very diligently in all times. Afterwards, men made use of the same word metaphorically, for the knowledge of their own secret facts, and secret thoughts; and therefore it is Rhetorically said, that the Conscience is a thousand witnesses. And last of all, men, vehemently in love with their own new opinions, (though never so absurd,) and obstinately bent to maintain them, gave those opinions also that reverenced name of Conscience, as if they would have it seem unlawfull, to change or speak against them; and so pretend to know they are true, when they know at most, but that they think so.[110]

That sort of individualism is incompatible with life in a community, and, given Hobbes's declared views on life outside a community (that is, in the natural condition), one might consider it unlikely that he gave an account of human nature that was individualistic in that way rather than an account of people as communal beings.[111]

In fact, he gave an account of people as communal beings: "The Lawes of Nature, which consist in Equity, Justice, Gratitude, and other morall Vertues on these depending, in the condition of meer Nature . . . are not properly Lawes, but qualities that dispose men to peace, and to obedience."[112]   Hobbes's moral theory is a theory of virtues and vices,[113] and the laws of nature are his account of a part of human nature.   The story of the laws of nature as policies that rational people consciously reflect on and agree on emerges from the application to the virtues of the model of explanation set out in Hobbes's account of the circle.   The use of that model in the case of the virtues, as will emerge, is seriously misleading in a way that leads to some of the objectionable features of Hobbes's theory of sovereignty.

The infallibility of somebody would not undermine Hobbes's argument about the need for an arbitrator.   If somebody is often right about a certain sort of matter, much more often than the rest of us, then we might come to place considerable weight on his opinion.   That he believes any particular claim and that he is usually right about these things is a point that each of us might consider as evidence in reaching our own opinions about the matter.   But that does not touch Hobbes's point, even though it might remove some disputes.   Each of us has then formed his own private judgment considering that piece of evidence, but that piece of evidence is in no way naturally compelling.   If somebody is infallible, but the rest of us do not believe that she is, then her infallibility is just one more matter over which we differ in our private judgments; it is simply one more case for the argument to work on.   In the same way, if we believe that somebody is infallible, even if she is not, then we shall agree; there will be no disputes to cause trouble. But actual infallibility is irrelevant; it is as irrelevant as the truth.

Appealing to God's word will not solve the problem: In the absence of direct revelation from God, we would be trusting those who told us that this was God's word, or that they have had revelations.[114] (We might consider what limitations this imposes on the roles available to God in Hobbes's theory of obligation.[115]) That is to say, appeals to God, like appeals to right reason, come down to appeals to the private judgments of people making claims about God or about right reason. This point applies even when I am the one claiming direct revelation, which brings out the hard point that Hobbes's views about toleration require that I be tolerant and not simply that I insist that others tolerate me. Even if I am the one who claims to have had direct revelation, the disagreement is still between my private judgment and the private judgment of others who, because they believe that I am wrong, will not believe that I have had direct revelation. My conviction does not, just because it is mine, turn the dispute into one between God and the benighted.

To summarize the points so far: If discussion and argument do not resolve a matter about which we disagree, then right reason and truth are inadequate to the task. *If common or corporate action is required* — and we might need to consider how often it is required — then we must have recourse to one or more of three methods: We must persuade, coerce, or have an exercise of authority. In the sort of case that matters to us here, persuasion has failed. Coercion will put us into our natural condition, which is at best unpleasant and more likely impossible. That leaves authority and emphasis on positive rights at the expense of natural rights as a condition of common action where there are disputes. Hobbes says that we must *agree* to set up an arbitrator or judge. Is he right?

Many people agree very readily that consent is a condition of authority, but in more particular cases we seem to accept equally readily that it is not. Parents cannot bring up children without having authority over them, and by the time the child is old enough for his consent to have any significance, the need for a parent to have authority is disappearing. We do not usually regard the consent of an intending murderer to the law against murder as a necessary condition of that law's being binding on him. Certainly Hobbes did not regard such a person's consent as a necessary condition of the law's being properly enforced on him: "Whether his consent be asked, or not, he must either submit to their decrees, or be left in the condition of warre he was in before; wherein he might without injustice be destroyed by any man whatsoever."[116]

I do not determine just by myself what rules are binding on me, or at least not simply by saying so. That I say yes to something counts as my consent only if the consent is mine to give, and the consent is mine to give only if I have the authority to give it,[117] so at least *one* kind of authority, the sort that makes consent mine to give, cannot be founded on consent. In certain situations, and with respect to certain actions, I am bound quite apart from my giving or withholding consent. If I live here, make use of the hospitals, educational facilities, and so on, call on the police when somebody threatens to take my bicycle, collect welfare payments, and generally insist on being given the benefits of membership in the community, then the others can properly treat me as a member of the community when it comes to my paying taxes or trying to take somebody else's car because it is raining and I don't want to get wet riding my bike.

Whether I am a member of the community, insofar as that is a matter of whether its rules or public judgments are binding on me, is not solely a matter of my consent. Once the community is there, I can find myself in situations in which I am bound by the rules whether or not I feel bound by them and whether or not I want to be bound by them. But that is a point concerning what can happen once the community is there: If there were no community, no cooperation generating rights and obligations of the sort called on in the previous argument, could it be that we all suddenly found ourselves bound to obey?

In such a situation, there are no rules of the community to obey; it would simply be a matter of going along with somebody else's judgment, and, as we have seen, Hobbes is clear that there is no rational compulsion on me to do that. One can be a member of a community without feeling that one is a member of that community, but only if the community is already there; the basis of community must be that people feel that they are members of the community; that is to say, it is something about each individual person and the way in which he voluntarily relates to other people making up the community.

This, I think, is the point that Hobbes is getting at: Community and the authority that community creates depend on people's identifying themselves with the community. It may not be specifically an agreement that we reached, but it is a matter of an attitude that people willingly take: Perhaps I do not agree to all the provisions of the Australian Constitution, for example, but, in appropriate circumstances, I think of myself as Australian. Once that enterprise is in operation, other people may be bound against their wills and I may be bound against mine. The point seems to apply to communities as they are, and not merely in setting them up: If somebody is bound by the rules, there must be some explanation of the propriety of treating him or her as a member of the community. The explanation cannot be that each person is bound against his or her will by the rights and obligations set up by the cooperation of others because if nobody is voluntarily going along with the plan, then there will be no cooperation of others. In other words, the point does not seem to commit Hobbes to a theory about an actual contract; the contract is merely a model, as is suggested in his statement of his method.

There remains a further problem about whether Hobbes can put private judgment quite as far out of the picture as he tries to do. Can the sovereign's authority stretch as far as Hobbes claims it does? The problem is best brought out by a discussion of inalienable rights and what Hobbes has to say about them, and especially about what he has to say on the subject of a right to self-preservation.

Notes

1. Richard Tuck, *Hobbes* (Oxford: Oxford University Press, 1989), pp. 57-58, does not overlook it, though he takes the version of the argument presented in *The Elements of Law*. Tuck describes this argument as "the vision at the heart of Hobbes's moral and political philosophy."

2. This is a point well made by Paul J. Johnson in "Hobbes and the Wolf-man" and by Brian F. Stoffell in "Hobbes's *Conatus* and the Roots of Character," both papers in C. Walton and P. J. Johnson (eds.), *Hobbes's `Science of Natural Justice´* (Dordrecht: Martinus Nijhoff, 1987). See also Bernard Gert's Introduction to his edition of *Man and Citizen* (Brighton: Harvester Press, 1978), *passim*, and his "Hobbes and Psychological Egoism," *Journal of the History of Ideas*, vol. XXVIII, 4 (December 1967), reprinted in Bernard H. Baumrin (ed.), *Hobbes's Leviathan: Interpretation and Criticism* (Belmont, CA: Wadsworth, 1969).

3. Cf. Tuck, *Hobbes*, p. 56: "It was conflict over what to *praise*, or morally approve, which Hobbes . . . isolated as the cause of discord, rather than simple conflict over *wants*. What he was frightened of, it is reasonable to assume, were such things as the Wars of Religion, or other ideological wars; not (say) class wars, in which the clash of wants could more clearly be seen."

4. *The Elements of Law* 2.5.2, p. 139.

5. *Leviathan*, chapter 17, pp. 224-225.

6. *Leviathan*, chapter 17, p. 226.

7. *The Elements of Law* 1.17.10, p. 92.

8. Sir Robert Filmer, "Observations on Mr. Hobbes's *Leviathan,*" in Peter Laslett (ed.), *Patriarcha and Other Political Works of Sir Robert Filmer* (Oxford: Basil Blackwell, 1949), p. 243.

9. Cf. Sheldon S. Wolin, *Politics and Vision: Continuity and Innovation in Western Political Thought* (Boston: Little, Brown & Company, 1960), p. 241. The problem of union and unity, he says, was the starting point for Hobbes. Wolin expresses the point thus: "Translated into political terms, the issue read: on what basis could the practice of government be conducted once the society was no longer a community?" The Civil Wars made this question one at the forefront of Hobbes's mind. His concern was with the *construction* of a unity given that disagreement in judgments, as well as clashing interests, ruled out a natural unity.

10. Cf. *The Elements of Law* 2.1.2, p. 108, and 2.2.11, p. 124; *Leviathan*, chapter 16, p. 220; *De Cive* 6.1, pp. 174-175.

11. John Eachard, *Mr. Hobbs's State of Nature Considered in a Dialogue Between Philautus and Timothy,* edited by Peter Ure (Liverpool: Liverpool University Press, 1958), p. 89.

12. *Leviathan*, chapter 14, p. 200.

13. *Leviathan*, chapter 5, pp. 111-112. Cf. also chapter 26, pp. 316-317: "That Law can never be against Reason, our Lawyers are agreed; . . . but the doubt is, of whose Reason it is, that shall be received for Law. It is not meant of any private Reason; . . . but the Reason of this our Artificiall Man the Common-wealth, and his Command, that maketh Law." Compare also the philosopher's response to the lawyers's reference to natural reason, *A Dialogue,* p. 67: "Would you have every Man to every other Man alledge for Law his own particular Reason? There is not amongst Men an Universal Reason agreed upon in any Nation, besides the Reason of him that hath the Soveraign Power; yet though his Reason be but the Reason of one Man, yet it is set up to supply the place of that Universal Reason, which is expounded to us by our Saviour in the Gospel, and consequently our King is to us the legislator both of Statute-Law, and of Common-Law."

Deborah Baumgold, in *Hobbes's Political Theory* (Cambridge: Cambridge University Press, 1988), p. 27, says: "Legitimation arguments answer the question of who to follow, as contrasted to the obligation question of whether to follow at all." Hobbes's right reason argument deals with the question of whether to follow at all with some implications about how one might pick out whom to follow in terms of his or her function, but the legitimation argument remains to be given.

14. Cf. J.W.N. Watkins, *Hobbes's System of Ideas: A Study in the Political Significance of Philosophical Theories* (London: Hutchinson University Library, 1965), p. 177: "Behind Hobbes's legal positivism is the idea that private moral judgements are utterly subjective." Hobbes's argument does not require that they be any more subjective than are claims made in accountancy or engineering. The problem is about our access to what might be, in some sense, a quite objective truth.

15. *Leviathan*, chapter 15, p. 209.

16. His target today, I think, would be those who foment civil unrest in the name of conscientiously held private views.

17. David Gauthier, *The Logic of Leviathan* (Oxford: Oxford University Press, 1969), p. 13.

18. He means that it is less important for the resolution of potentially destructive disputes, but there are sometimes suggestions that his own rhetoric carried him on to the idea that it is less important for every purpose. That second position is false. It is less important, for example, in the scientific endeavor: The edict of the sovereign, or a vote of the legislature, does not determine whether or not smoking causes lung cancer, though it does determine whether cigarette packets must carry a statement that smoking causes lung cancer. Cf. *Leviathan*, chapter 32, pp. 410-411.

19. Cf. Wolin, *Politics and Vision*, p. 245: "In an age where men called not only for peace, but also for truth,´ Hobbes believed that for the first time political philosophy was genuinely in a position to bring both truth and peace." But the truth it brought was that we should concentrate on a different question. Cf. Tuck, *Hobbes*, p. 57: "The traditional moralist's response to ethical disagreement had been to hope that sooner or later everyone would come to see the moral *facts* clearly and rationally, but Hobbes of course could not resort to pious hopes of this kind. Instead, he proposed that the route to agreement must lie through *politics*, and this must count as Hobbes's most distinctive contribution to political theory."

20. *The Elements of Law* 1.17.7, p. 91.

21. *Leviathan*, chapter 26, p. 323.

22. See *Leviathan*, chapter 15, p. 209, for Hobbes's claim that those who will not accommodate themselves to others are to be cast out of society as cumbersome thereunto.

23. J. S. Mill, "On Liberty," in *Utilitarianism, Liberty, and Representative Government* (London: J. M. Dent and Sons Ltd, 1957).

24. In the terms used by Howard Warrender, *The Political Philosophy of Hobbes: His Theory of Obligation* (Oxford: Clarendon Press, 1957), the ground of obligation will be the necessity to social life of there being instruments of obligation. No more is needed. The idea of an obligation preexisting civil law sounds dubious when Warrender recognizes (p. 30n and pp. 237-242) that the state of nature is a logical and not a historical postulate. Despite Warrender's claims that "a moral obligation . . . to obey the law cannot be extracted from a system in which man has *no* moral obligations before or apart from the law" (p. 6) and that "the civil sovereign can never himself provide the moral foundation which is used in his own justification" (p. 7), it seems that, given that Hobbes is not telling a historical story, he can argue that the sovereign is a necessary part of any social world in which people can live, because rights and duties are necessary to any such world and can be made actual only with a sovereign. One might argue (as I shall do, later) that a Hobbesian sovereign is not necessary to make rights and duties actual, but, clearly, Warrender's argument does not succeed.

25. Cf. the sixteenth law of nature (*Leviathan*, chapter 15, p. 213) and the third law of nature (*Leviathan*, chapter 15, p. 201).

26. Cf. the claim that in heaven there will be no laws: *De Cive* 17.8, p. 340.

27. *Leviathan*, chapter 14, p. 190.

28. Cf. *Leviathan*, chapter 15, p. 209.

29. *Leviathan*, chapter 14, p. 190.

30. *Leviathan*, chapter 15, p. 201.

31. I should explain, for the benefit of anybody who has not come across this activity, that it consists of tying a rubber band around one's ankles and leaping off a bridge or other tall structure. The activity is said to have been introduced by New Zealanders.

32. Cf. Hobbes's sixteenth law of nature: *"That they that are at controversie, submit their Right to the judgement of an Arbitrator"* (*Leviathan*, chapter 15, p. 213).

33. Cf. Hobbes's fifth law of nature: *"That every man strive to accommodate himselfe to the rest"* (*Leviathan*, chapter 15, p. 209).

34. Cf. note 18 of this chapter. The sovereign does not, by his edict, make it the case that smoking causes lung cancer, even if he does, by his edict, make it the case that cigarette packets must carry a statement that smoking causes lung cancer. In some contexts we never get beyond the first stage of the debate that I am describing here: Good physics is not what the editors of *Nature* decide, even though what gets to be published in *Nature* is what the editors decide.

35. Cf. Watkins, *System of Ideas*, p. 151: "If moralising talk in the state of nature makes any difference, it *worsens* men's condition." In our natural condition, where we have the right of private judgment and disagree, such moralizing talk will merely lead to dispute.

36. *Leviathan*, chapter 13, p. 184.

37. *The Elements of Law* 2.10.8, p. 188.

38. *Leviathan*, chapter 46, p. 699.

39. Gregory S. Kavka, *Hobbesian Moral and Political Theory* (Princeton: Princeton University Press, 1986), pp. 49-50.

40. Gert, Introduction to *Man and Citizen*, *passim*, and "Hobbes and Psychological Egoism."

41. George Lawson, *An Examination of the Political Part of Mr. Hobbs his Leviathan* (London: Francis Tyton, 1657), p. 8. Contrast Hobbes's claim that exercising private judgment about the justice of a war is a sin: *De Cive* 12.2, pp. 245-246.

42. Lawson, *Examination*, p. 127.

43. This is a point that I shall take up in greater detail later.

44. C.A.J. Coady, "The Peculiarity of Hobbes's Concept of Natural Right," in Walton and Johnson, *Science of Natural Justice*, p. 167.

45. Cf. Warrender, *Political Philosophy of Hobbes*, p. 61: "A specific action cannot be prescribed that *could* not be a bona-fide means to preservation for some man in some circumstances." The case is made that much stronger when the claim is simply that any act could be *believed* to be a bona fide means to preservation.

46. Kavka, *Hobbesian Theory*, p. 316n.

47. If I do not think that you are attacking me or are likely to do so and I nevertheless attack you, then I am in breach of the laws of nature, not being bound by them even *in foro interno*.

48. Kavka, *Hobbesian Theory*, pp. 338-339.

49. *De Cive* 2.1, p. 123n.

50. Kavka, *Hobbesian Theory*, p. 318.

51. Cf. Warrender, *Political Philosophy of Hobbes*, p. 139: "Consistency requires Hobbes to take the view that the right of the subject to preserve his life does involve a right of the subject to decide for himself when a crisis has been reached."

52. Jean Hampton, *Hobbes and the Social Contract Tradition* (London: Cambridge University Press, 1986), pp. 209ff.

53. Hampton, *Contract Tradition*, p. 1.

54. Hobbes, given his historical context, would not have been unaware of the possibility that the sovereign might be a woman. Presumably one should take the word "man" as meaning person, a point nicely made by Hampton with her references to the sovereign as "she."

55. *E. W.*, vol. 1, p. 8.

56. Cf. *Leviathan*, chapter 18, p. 229.

57. Cf. *Leviathan*, chapter 18, p. 235.

58. Cf., on the other hand, Warrender, *Political Philosophy of Hobbes*, p. 165 and pp. 188-195. My argument over the next few pages suggests that Warrender has not provided a very solid grounding for the liberty of the subject against the sovereign.

59. *Leviathan*, chapter 21, p. 269.

60. He summarized them in a later chapter, *Leviathan*, chapter 20, pp. 252-253: "His Power cannot, without his consent, be Transferred to another: He cannot Forfeit it: He cannot be Accused by any of his Subjects, of Injury: He cannot be Punished by them: He is Judge of what is necessary for Peace; and Judge of Doctrines: He is Sole Legislator; and Supreme Judge of Controversies; and of the Times, and Occasions of Warre, and Peace: to him it belongeth to choose Magistrates, Counsellors, Commanders, and all other Officers, and Ministers; and to determine of Rewards, and Punishments, Honour, and Order."

61. *Leviathan*, chapter 18, pp. 232-233.

62. *Leviathan*, chapter 21, p. 269.

63. *Leviathan*, chapter 21, p. 270.

64. *Leviathan*, chapter 21, pp. 268-269.

65. *Leviathan*, chapter 18, p. 232. Earlier in the paragraph, Hobbes refers to a tacit covenant; that reference needs to be read in light of the passage quoted.

66. *Leviathan*, chapter 26, p. 319.

67. *Leviathan*, chapter 18, p. 235.

68. *Leviathan*, chapter 29, p. 367.

69. *Leviathan*, chapter 30, p. 376.

70. *Leviathan*, chapter 29, p. 367.

71. *Leviathan*, chapter 20, p. 255.

72. *Leviathan*, chapter 5, p. 111.

73. *Leviathan*, chapter 18, p. 233.

74. *Leviathan*, chapter 14, p. 190. Hobbes sometimes describes the right as that of doing whatever one judges to be necessary for one's preservation, but it is clear from the formulation in the quoted passage just how far he sees that as expanding.

75. Baumgold, *Hobbes's Political Theory*, p. 35.

76. Baumgold, *Hobbes's Political Theory*, pp. 32 and 34.

77. I discuss man's natural condition, and the radical form thereof, in chapter 4.

78. Cf. the distinction between being obliged and being obligated, drawn by H.L.A. Hart, *The Concept of Law* (London: Oxford University Press, 1961), pp. 80-81.

79. *Leviathan*, chapter 13, pp. 185-186.

80. But coercion is appropriate when people do not willingly submit: See *Leviathan*, chapter 18, p. 232.

81. *Leviathan*, chapter 20, pp. 255-256.

82. *Leviathan*, chapter 17, p. 228.

83. *Leviathan*, chapter 14, p. 190.

84. Hampton, *Contract Tradition, passim.*

85. David Gauthier, *Morals by Agreement* (Oxford: Oxford University Press, 1986), especially chapter 6.

86. Hampton, *Contract Tradition, passim.*

87. Hampton, *Contract Tradition*, p. 137.

88. Gauthier, *The Logic of Leviathan*, pp. 7-8.

89. *Leviathan*, chapter 6, p. 120.

90. *Leviathan*, chapter 46, p. 697.

91. *Leviathan*, chapter 15, p. 216.

92. Cf. the discussion in chapter 5 of the conditions necessary for the laws of nature to be effective.

93. *Leviathan*, chapter 46, p. 697.

94. *Leviathan*, chapter 15, p. 209.

95. *The Elements of Law* 2.6.12, pp. 157-158.

96. *The Elements of Law* 2.8.5, p. 171.

97. R. P. Wolff, *In Defense of Anarchism* (New York: Harper Torchbooks, 1970).

98. *Leviathan*, chapter 20, p. 255.

99. *Leviathan*, chapter 15, p. 201.

100. *Leviathan*, chapter 14, p. 190.

101. *Leviathan*, chapter 15, p. 209.

102. *Leviathan*, chapter 15, p. 213.

103. *The Elements of Law* 1.17.7, p. 91.

104. *Leviathan*, chapter 5, p. 111.

105. *Leviathan*, chapter 15, p. 212.

106. *Leviathan*, chapter 15, p. 212.

107. *Leviathan*, chapter 14, p. 190.

108. *The Elements of Law* 1.17.7, p. 91.

109. Hobbes's insistence that disputes be settled by reference to the counting of witnesses when all else is equal (his nineteenth law of nature, *Leviathan*, chapter 15, p. 214) suggests that an attempt to get at the truth wherever possible still lies behind this procedure, but success in that search cannot be required. The sovereign cannot be taken to have contracted to do justice (*The Elements of Law* 1.17.7, p. 91). And Hobbes emphasizes the practical point about resolution of disputes again at the end of the nineteenth law of nature when he gives the reason for it: "For else the question is undecided, and left to force, contrary to the Laws of Nature."

110. *Leviathan*, chapter 7, pp. 131-132. If Hobbes is right in his etymology, then the whole idea of private conscience is nonsense.

111. Cf. Gert, Introduction to *Man and Citizen*, pp. 11-12. The point might be made by saying that man is, by nature, a convention-making animal.

112. *Leviathan*, chapter 26, p. 314.

113. I argue this point in chapter 7.

114. See *Leviathan*, chapter 15, pp. 205-206.

115. See, for example, Warrender, *The Political Philosophy of Hobbes, passim*. See also the discussion in Michael Oakeshott, *Hobbes on Civil Association* (Oxford: Basil Blackwell, 1975), pp. 104-110.

116. *Leviathan*, chapter 18, p. 232.

117. See E. D. Watt, *Authority* (London: Croom Helm, 1982), p. 79.

3

The Inalienable Right
to Self-Preservation

Hobbes was opposed to, and argued strongly against, that form of individualism that amounts to a raw assertion of self-as-arbitrator.[1] Historically, in Hobbes's eyes, that description would have been true of the behavior of the Puritans, who set conscience and private scriptural interpretation against a sovereign political body. If it is true that these same men were also those who most frequently employed contractarian arguments modeled on Old Testament accounts of covenants between God and the Jews, then one might conjecture that Hobbes used the contract model, at least in part, as a *reductio:* Taking the preferred model of his opponents, he was able to reach the negation of their rejection of a legally unlimited civil sovereign.[2]

Hobbes takes it that natural rights are something about which one must be one's own judge. He is right. A lot of people in Hobbes's time talked about natural rights (just as a lot of people nowadays talk about human rights, which are, in at least a number of significant respects, similar). Hobbes took the notion that they employed and showed that it could not do the job that they wanted it to do — that of providing a contrasting standard against which could be judged the positive rights awarded by the state or any other body. These rights can protect me from such subjection to the views of others in that way only if the judgment is kept in my hands. But if natural rights go with private judgments, they are useless: They cannot act interpersonally to resolve disputes. Concern about natural rights, with its reliance on private judgment, plunges us into man's natural condition rather than giving us the liberty and noninterference that claimants to natural rights are looking for.

Nevertheless, remnants of natural rights remain in Hobbes's theory: For Hobbes, the right to defend one's life is inalienable, for example. Why this should be so is worth thinking about. It is usually read as somehow following from the fact that people cannot help defending themselves when they are under attack, but it is by no means obvious that this is the correct reading of Hobbes. No claim about a right goes anywhere near following from that claim about the nature of people, and Hobbes says only that people must have the right to defend their lives, not that they cannot help but exercise it: "Most men choose rather to hazard their life, than not to be revenged."[3] Hobbes clearly did not believe that people cannot help refusing to put their lives at risk,[4] or at least he did not believe it as a universal truth about people even though he did believe that some could do nothing but run in the face of danger. And Hobbes did believe that people could be bound to *risk* their lives:

> To the Laws of Nature . . . I would have this added, *That every man is bound by Nature, as much as in him lieth, to protect in Warre, the Authority, by which he is himself protected in time of Peace.* For he that pretendeth a Right of Nature to preserve his owne body, cannot pretend a Right of Nature, to destroy him, by whose strength he is preserved: It is a manifest contradiction of himselfe.[5]

Perhaps not much does lie in some people, but those who are capable of doing so — and Hobbes clearly thinks that some are — must be prepared to hazard their lives to defend the sovereign in war. Hobbes knew and admired men who were prepared to risk their lives in defense of their sovereign. That fact makes clear either that something is seriously wrong with a reading of Hobbes that makes such risk-taking psychologically impossible, or that Hobbes thought that most of those whom he admired were insane.

This fact about Hobbes makes clear Jean Hampton's misinterpretation of the following quotation from Hobbes: "For (as I have shewed before) no man can transferre, or lay down his Right to save himselfe from Death, Wounds and Imprisonment, (the avoyding whereof is the onely End of laying down any Right,) and therefore the promise of not resisting force, in no Covenant transferreth any right; nor is obliging."[6] In response to this passage, Hampton writes:

> This means that, according to Hobbes, *contractual obligations exist only insofar as it is in our interest to perform them.* To be precise, Hobbes defines two conditions that must be met in order for an obligation to exist: First, there must be a renunciation or transfer of a right to another; second, it must be in the interest of the renouncer or

transferrer to respect that renunciation or transfer. So Hobbes defines the nature and extent of our obligations such that our performance of them can never conflict with self-interest.[7]

On the very toughest of interpretations, that passage from Hobbes implies nothing anywhere near as strong as Hampton's claim: Many things other than death, wounds, and imprisonment can be contrary to my interest, but those other things are not covered in that passage from Hobbes. And the claim that when it comes to the crunch, I have the right to protect myself against the immediate threat of death, wounds, and imprisonment does not mean that I cannot be obligated to do something that puts my life at risk: Perhaps I have the right to run when the enemy throws a hand-grenade into my trench, but Hobbes is very clear that I am morally bound in time of war to accept conscription and do my best to protect the authority that protects me in time of peace.[8] That is to say, I can be morally bound to enter situations that put my life at risk even though it would be in my immediate interest to avoid them. Hence Hobbes's belief that people were bound to fight on the side of the king in the civil war as long as there was some chance of winning, even though, as he explained to John Aubrey,[9] the final defeat of the Royalist cause changed the sovereignty and freed people from that obligation so that they could compound with Oliver.[10]

Hobbes's general position on natural rights is that they are pointless: Those who use the notion want to use it to criticize positive rights, but the idea of a natural right cannot be used to set up a properly organized society, he argues, because it leads to people's living in the radical form of their natural condition, which is one of war of each against all because disputes cannot be resolved peacefully. We must have a civil law the purpose of which is specifically the restraint of natural right[11] so that we can avoid this terrible condition. The sovereign remains in his natural condition, though certainly not in a war of each against all with respect to his citizens, because he is the only one who retains his private judgment in all things and is not subject to a higher power in the commonwealth. His private judgment takes on a special significance because of his office and becomes not merely private judgment but public judgment. The arbitrator cannot be merely one more party to the dispute.[12]

Private judgment rules in the natural condition, so what I may do in that condition is properly a matter for my judgment. Hence Kavka's claim[13] that Hobbes never argued that we have a natural right to self-defense is misleading. Hobbes never sets out a nice, neat argument leading to that conclusion at the end of the paragraph, but the reasoning is clear. My rights in the natural condition are determined by my judgment, which means, substantively, that I have a right to all things: Nobody can overrule my judgment and determine that, whatever my judgment may be, I have no right to X. There is a limitation on this right to all things, though, in the form of natural law[14] (I might knowingly break natural law, but could not claim a right to do so[15]), but that limitation is itself limited: What matters is *my* judgment of natural law and how it applies.[16] I shall not exceed the limits of natural law in my judgment, provided that my action is intentionally directed toward my preservation. Hence I have a natural right to defend myself (which, again, substantively extends itself to a right to all things because I am the judge of what it is against which I must defend myself).[17] The *postulate* in Hobbes's moral theory is not about a right to self-defense, but about the primacy of private judgment in the absence of binding conventions.

This use of private judgment is the core of man's natural condition, as is clear from the references to will, judgment, and reason in the following quotation and from Hobbes's summary of the laws of nature: "The sum whereof consisteth in forbidding us to be our own judges."[18] In the natural condition, one has, substantively, a right to all things, but the logic of the right is somewhat more limited: "The Right of Nature, which Writers commonly call *Jus Naturale,* is the Liberty each man hath, to use his own power, as he will himselfe, for the preservation of his own Nature; that is to say, of his own Life; and consequently, of doing any thing, which in his own Judgement, and Reason, hee shall conceive to be the aptest means thereunto."[19]

The *logic* of the right is that it is a right to self-preservation; it becomes, substantively, a right to all things because it depends on private judgment. There is no way of ruling out somebody's private judgment, no matter how bizarre it might seem to me, that something constituted some sort of long-term or short-term threat. I may judge that person's views to be bizarre and give them no weight in my own calculations except as showing the person to be a threat, but he is not bound to take notice of my judgment. In the absence of a sovereign, nobody is bound to take notice of anybody's judgment but their own. Not everybody is mentally stable, and even those who are mentally stable can have unusual ideas about what constitutes a threat, especially a threat in the long term.

The right that we have in our natural condition is a right to preserve ourselves, and it causes problems because the judgment of what threat it is that each of us needs to preserve himself against is simply the private judgment of the person involved.[20] Given that we know that some people are irrational, some people are jumpy, and some people are moody, and, perhaps, given that we know that at least most people are capable of exhibiting any of those traits some of the time, and that we do not know everybody and cannot always know who will exhibit which trait at what time, even those who are sober and conservative in their judgment of what is necessary to their conservation will find that the range of threats is fairly wide. The preemptive defensive actions that they quite properly take will only increase the range of threats to others and thus, in the end, to themselves.[21] When private judgment rules, it is hard to see how to stop the increase in what are *properly* seen as threats, never mind what are improperly seen as threats.[22]

It is clear to each of us that some people are silly: Some people are timid and react far too readily to minor threats; others invent threats where there are none; and so on. But my certainty that somebody else is like that is not the crucial point: That is merely *my* judgment, and what matters for that person is his judgment. We know who would be ignored or locked away or denied the vote in civil society where we have agreed-upon and enforceable standards for such things, but in the natural condition each is his own judge. Even those people I believe to be below standard are their own judges, and that includes their being their own judges of my reason. As Hobbes writes,

> Although in a civil government the reason of the supreme, that is, the civil law, is to be received by each single subject for the right; yet being without this civil government, in which state no man can know right reason from false, but by comparing it with his own, every man's own reason is to be accounted, not only the rule of his own actions, which are done at his own peril, but also for the measure of another man's reason, in such things as do concern him.[23]

I might think that the other person is being silly, and if he agrees with me or otherwise decides to take my word, then he will no doubt change his ways. Nevertheless, if he disagrees with me, he will think that I am mistaken, and a *mistaken* view gives him no reason to change his ways. His is the judgment that counts when it comes to his actions, and that includes his judgment of my judgment. If I can persuade him, well and good. If I cannot persuade him, then, in the absence of a sovereign, *he* cannot see any reason why he should do other than what his reason suggests to him is best. It certainly would be irrational of him to act contrary to reason as he saw it. A public mark of right reason is required if he is to be bound.

Private judgment rules when people will not submit to public judgment. This fact is part of the problem that the bad behavior of some annoys the others: Lack of reciprocity removes obligation,[24] so if nobody else obeys the rules, I shall not be bound to do so. Hobbes insists that it is a *mutual* laying down of rights that is worthwhile, not a unilateral one.[25] If others will not submit to public judgment, I am not bound to submit. Hence Hobbes's belief that, given that there are at least *some* untrustworthy people around, the conventions that we use to resolve our disputes must be coercive conventions. But Hobbes is wrong about that, as I shall show later. If Fred breaks his promise to me, that does not release me from my promise to you. I may not be bound to submit to the conventional decision-procedures when dealing with those who ignore them, but it does not follow that I can properly ignore the decision-procedures when dealing with those who will submit. The considerations of how many people break the rules, how often they do so, what sort and degree of temptation is required to make them do so, and whether we can identify and isolate the rule-breakers determine whether there is general insecurity of the sort that makes obligation impossible. These matters are empirical. It is not a logical truth that we must have coercive conventions, and if it is a matter of fact that we must have them, then it is also a question of fact how much coercion is needed, and of what sort.

The move from our natural condition to civil society is the laying down of our right to all things. Hobbes sets this out in his second law of nature: "That a man be willing, when others are so too, as farre-forth, as for Peace, and defense of himselfe he shall think it necessary, to lay down this right to all things."[26] This appears to mean one of two things: Either we lay down our right to preserve ourselves or we lay down the right to judge for ourselves what it is that we need to defend ourselves against. These rights, formally, are the only ones that we have in our natural condition. Filmer picked up this point and the problems that follow from it: "To authorize and give up his right of governing himself, to confer all his power and strength, and to submit his will to another, is to lay down his right of resisting: for if right of nature be a liberty to use power for preservation of life, laying down of that power must be a relinquishing of power to preserve or defend life, otherwise a man relinquisheth nothing."[27] The distinction between giving up the right to self-preservation and giving up the right to judge for ourselves is by no means a clear one, and Hobbes does not distinguish them in his account of our natural condition: If the sovereign is the judge of what it is that I need to defend myself against, my right to defend myself is nugatory. If the sovereign judges that the evil are better off going to heaven before they get too much evil on their records, he might judge that I do not need to defend myself even when he comes after me with the executioner's ax. If I give up the right to judge such matters for myself, then to all intents and purposes, I give up the right to defend myself as well. At least, any right that I have to defend myself in such circumstances is a positive right, determined by the sovereign, not a natural right; the sovereign can give it, and the sovereign can take it away. He might allow me to defend myself against the executioner or against the manufacturer of chemicals who sets up a plant next to my house and subjects me to fumes that I believe to be poisonous, or he might allow me to decline military service in a dangerous theater. On the other hand, he might not.[28]

Nor is it obvious that everybody must always retain such a right to self-defense. There is a lot of plausibility in what Lawson says:

> *Paul* pleading before *Festus* saith, If I be an offender, or have committed any thing worthy of death, I refuse not to die. *Acts 25.118.* How this can stand with what this Author saith, when he affirmeth that its lawful for a man guilty and condemned to save himself if he can, I leave to others to examine. From the Apostles words its evident, he desires no protection, even of himself, as worthy of death, neither hath God given any power to man to save in such a case. And though any person by the Law of nature may defend himself, yet this must be done *cum moderamine tutelae inculpatae.* In case a subject hath made himself capitally guilty, he hath forfeited his life to his Soveraign as Gods Vice[reg]ent, whom he must not resist in the execution of Justice, though he be not bound to kill himself: neither doth the multitude or strength of any such capital offenders, any waies give them the right to resist their Soveraign in their own defense, as the Author would have it. For they cannot defend themselves as men, but they must defend themselves in this case as guilty men, which is not lawful.[29]

Hobbes's idea *might* be that my reliance on private judgment is severely restricted. The war of each against all is plainly terrible, and in such a situation I must expect my life to be solitary, poor, nasty, brutish, and short. Perhaps I am to exercise my private judgment with that in mind: Self-defense will be impossible in the medium or long run of those circumstances, and submission to a sovereign is the only way to avoid those circumstances. So perhaps I am to fall back on my private judgment and my right to self-preservation only when I believe that I would not be better off submitting to the sovereign's judgment, and the threat of the natural condition will keep me from being frivolous in my judgment of when that is. In the absence of an immediate and severe threat, I should be extremely foolish to make such a move. Or, consider another version of the same thing. Perhaps my right to self-preservation and my right to judge for myself come into play when I find that I *must* defend myself against the sovereign because he is after me with the executioner's ax. But neither of these fits the Hobbesian requirements, because the question of whether it is appropriate for me to call on my private judgment and my right to self-defense is left as a matter for my private judgment. I would be judging the sovereign's every act, even if usually judging it favorably, and Hobbes is perfectly clear that the citizen has no business judging the sovereign. The point of the right reason argument (and of much of Hobbes's argument about the need for a sovereign) is that private judgment must be subordinated to public judgment. And that is no accident. If I retain my right to self-preservation, and if the story depends on my constantly exercising (even favorable) private judgment on the sovereign's acts, then I have given up no right that I had in my natural condition and therefore have managed to make no move into civil society. To escape my natural condition and enter civil society, I have to lay down rights. In my natural condition I have, formally, only two rights: The right to self-preservation and the right to judge for myself. If I retain those two rights, then I have not made the move that I need to make to enter civil society.

Filmer picked up this general problem, too — a problem that, in the end, undercuts the stronger conclusions that Hobbes wants to draw:

> Mr Hobbes saith . . . "No man is bound by the words of his submission to kill himself, or any other man: and consequently that the obligation a man may sometimes have upon the command of the sovereign to execute any dangerous or dishonourable office, dependeth not on the words of our submission, but on the intention which is to be understood by the end thereof. When therefore our refusal to obey, frustrates the end for which the sovereignty was ordained, then there is no liberty to refuse: otherwise there is." If no man be bound by the words of his subjection to kill any other man, then a sovereign may be denied the benefit of war, and be rendered unable to defend his people, and so the end of government frustrated. If the obligation upon the commands of the sovereign to execute a dangerous or dishonourable office, dependeth not on the words of our submission, but on the intention, which is to be understood by the end thereof; no man, by Mr. Hobbes's rule, is bound but by the words of his submission, the intention of the command binds not, if the words do not: if the intention should bind, it is necessary the sovereign must discover it, and the people must dispute and judge it; which how well it may consist with the rights of sovereignty, Mr. Hobbes may consider: whereas Master Hobbes saith the intention is to be understood by the ends, I

take it he means the end by effect, for the end and the intention are one and the same thing; and if he mean the effect, the obedience must go before, and not depend on the understanding of the effect, which can never be, if the obedience do not precede it: in fine, he resolves refusal to obey, may depend upon the judging of what frustrates the end of sovereignty, and what not, of which he cannot mean any other judge but the people.[30]

The main thrust of Hobbes's argument throughout his moral and political writings is the necessity of making private judgment take second place to public judgment wherever the two come into conflict.[31] Yet he is, in this way, always forced back to private judgment. The right to self-preservation appears to be an insurmountable problem for him as long as it is part of his theory because it means that private judgment does not always give way to public judgment. In fact, retention of the right to self-preservation seems to completely undermine the claims he makes for public judgment and the authority of the sovereign.

Hobbes's claims about giving up rights on entering civil society cannot be taken to mean that I must, insofar as I am psychologically capable of not defending my life, attempt to submit to any waiting mugger and try to let him succeed in his attempt to kill me. If the sovereign is not immediately present, then I must exercise my own private judgment of the threat, and I must exercise my own private judgment of the proximity of the sovereign. If the sovereign himself is the threat, his immediate presence only makes things worse. Hobbes is clear on both points. At any time, questions can be raised about whether the sovereign is threatening me or whether he is capable of coming to my aid in time if I think that other people are threatening me; those are matters for my private judgment. I must again, even if I do so favorably, exercise my private judgment with respect to the sovereign all the time.

To make the bind of this problem tighter, Hobbes is clear that not all rights are alienable: "There be some Rights, which no man can be understood by any words, or other signes, to have abandoned, or transferred. As first a man cannot lay down the right of resisting them, that assault him by force, to take away his life; because he cannot be understood to ayme thereby, at any Good to himselfe."[32] Anybody who appears to alienate the right to self-preservation — and that appears here to encompass the right to judge for oneself what is a threat and what is necessary to meet the threat — is not to be taken seriously; we are to take it that he "was ignorant of how such words and actions were to be interpreted." If entering civil society requires that we lay down an inalienable right, then entering civil society will be a very difficult job indeed. Is there any way out of this problem?

In our natural condition we have, substantively, a right to all things; in civil society we have not. Could the point of Hobbes's argument lie in that? Could it be that we lay something down that leaves us with the same formal right but changes the way that it applies? There is a suggestion of this in chapter 15 of *Leviathan:* "As it is necessary for all men that seek peace, to lay down certain rights of nature; that is to say, not to have liberty to do all they list: so it is necessary for man's life, to retain some; as right to govern their own bodies; enjoy air, water, motion, ways to go from place to place; and all things else, without which a man cannot live, or not live well."[33] Hobbes seems to shift his ground about this. Here he suggests that in our natural condition we have a right to do whatever we list. Elsewhere he is clear that there are limits to what we may do or have a natural right to do: In chapter 27 of *Leviathan* he says that where there is no law but the law of nature, "there is no place for Accusation; every man being his own Judge, and accused onely by his own Conscience, and cleared by the Uprightnesse of his own Intention. When therefore his Intention is Right, his fact is no Sinne: if otherwise, his fact is Sinne; but not Crime."[34] Here it seems clear that Hobbes is saying that we have no right to do whatever we wish, or whatever the mood takes us to do, but only what we really believe to be necessary to our own preservation or the maintenance of a reasonable standard of living. And given that limitation, it is far from clear what rights we had in our natural condition other than those that he says we retain in civil society, which means that it is far from clear what rights are given up in moving from our natural condition into civil society. But that is one possibility for us to consider.

Another possibility is that talk of retaining the right to self-preservation in civil society is simply a way of saying that people cannot keep from defending themselves when faced with a clear and present danger.[35] To say that they retain a right to defend themselves would then be to say that it would be pointless to impose a duty on them not to resist, because they would be incapable of carrying out the duty.[36] If one cannot have a duty to do what one cannot do, and if one cannot but resist when one's life (or ease of life) is threatened by force, then one cannot have a duty not so to resist; not to have such a duty is to have a right, or liberty, to resist.[37] Hobbes suggests this sort of approach in several places. In chapter 27 of *Leviathan* he says: "If a man, by the terror of present death, be compelled to do a fact against the law, he is totally excused; because no law can oblige a man to abandon his own preservation. And supposing such a law were obligatory; yet a man would reason thus, If *I do it not, I die presently; if I do it, I die afterwards;*

therefore by doing it there is time of life gained; nature therefore compels him to the fact."[38] And in chapter 14 of *Leviathan* he says: "Though a man may covenant thus, *Unlesse I do so, or so, kill me;* he cannot Covenant thus, *Unlesse I do so, or so, I will not resist you, when you come to kill me.* For man by nature chooseth the lesser evil, which is danger of death in resisting; rather than the greater, which is certain and present death in not resisting."[39] Both passages suggest that the reason we retain a right of self-preservation is simply because our psychological compulsion makes it impossible for us to have an effective duty not to defend ourselves.

There are certain fairly obvious problems about this claim as a matter of fact. History presents us with a long list of martyrs, and not all of those who have given their lives have done so simply because of an expectation of a better life after death. However rare heroism might be, it does at times appear, and one of its forms is in giving one's life for another, either in war or in peace. And Hobbes, despite his often-quoted claim that death is the chiefest of natural evils, did not regard it as an evil that could not be outweighed: Courage, he said, is "the Contempt of Wounds, and violent Death,"[40] and he made clear that he thought that there are instances of such courage in the world. He also made clear that he thought that people might die for their honor,[41] or to avoid having to suffer slander,[42] or because they found that their lives were insufficiently commodious[43] (which might not mean that the television set has been repossessed, but that one is suffering from a painful and incurable disease or is facing hanging drawing and quartering on the morrow), or because things worse than death are required of one,[44] or possibly because of a religious belief that eternal life, not promised to the reprobate, is a greater good than the life present.[45] And he did prescribe, as a law of nature, a willingness to take the risks of going to war,[46] as well as admiring some of those who risked and lost their lives in the civil war.

Hobbes certainly did not hold the view that nobody is ever psychologically capable of knowingly facing death. He did subscribe to the obviously true view that at least most people, other things being equal, will try to avoid death. Somebody who *simply* wants to die (that is, wants to die, but for no particular reason — does not want to die because it is a necessary means to avoiding pain or dishonor, to saving comrades, or to going to a better world, or whatever) is probably incomprehensible. But that is a long way short of the claim that people who have some reason to die or to risk death are, necessarily, psychologically incapable of facing death. Indeed, Hobbes pointed out in *De Homine*[47] that, in some circumstances, people may number death among the goods.

Hence the oddity of Jean Hampton's claim that "it seems implausible for Hobbes to insist that this desire [for self-preservation] is *always* prior to *all* other desires in *everyone*."[48] Hobbes does not so insist. Moreover, as Hampton goes on to soften the position that she has attributed to Hobbes, she brings up the point that Hobbes recognized the importance of the commodiousness of a life. His point seems to be the entirely plausible one that we cannot understand somebody who wants death simply for its own sake, and we expect people not to desire death unless they have a reason that we will see moves them strongly. Seeking death is not just another incident in life, like having a cup of coffee.

Another possible line is that we retain only a limited right to self-defense.[49] Hobbes suggests this in chapter 27 of *Leviathan*:

> A man is assaulted, fears present death, from which he sees not how to escape, but by wounding him that assaulteth him: if he wound him to death, this is no crime; because no man is supposed at the making of a commonwealth, to have abandoned the defense of his life, or limbs, where the law cannot arrive time enough to his assistance. But to kill a man, because from his actions, or his threatenings, I may argue he will kill me when he can, seeing I have time, and means to demand protection, from the sovereign power, is a crime.[50]

We might, then, retain a right to defend ourselves only against a clear and present danger so immediate that the sovereign cannot be called on. There are problems remaining if this line is taken: There is never a sovereign around when I want one, and the judgment of how soon he will be along to help me is a private judgment of mine. And what if I take a less immediate threat along to the sovereign to be dealt with, but the sovereign's judgment of the seriousness of the threat differs from mine so that he refuses to take any action? But the line is one to be considered, both on its own and in partnership with the idea that in leaving our natural condition we lay something down that leaves us with the same formal right but changes its content.

And then there is the idea that Hobbes is not claiming that we give up anything to do with a right to self-preservation, but rather we give up something altogether different. This sounds bizarre, but the claim is to be found expressed by Hobbes in so many words: "In the making of a Common-wealth, every man giveth away the right of defending another; but not of defending himselfe."[51] The idea that it was the right to defend others that kept us in our natural condition does indeed sound odd, but we shall investigate this idea, too, returning to further discussion of it in considering Hobbes's account of man's natural condition in chapter 4.

If we give up the right to defend others except when called on to do so by the sovereign, then we give up the right to form factions.[52] The barons or other factional leaders would thus lose their power, and the threat to the good order of the society posed by their power struggle would be removed. This account of what is given up in entering civil society would, perhaps, make sense if Hobbes were dealing with families as the basic units in our natural condition rather than with individual people, though then this account would run into trouble because that line seems to assume that Hobbes was telling a sort of historical story about how the state arose, requiring an actual state of nature and an actual contract. This is a possibility with which I shall deal in the next chapter.

Hobbes suggests different things about natural right, as we have already seen. He sometimes says that we have a right to everything in our natural condition and sometimes that we have a right to everything in our judgment necessary for our own preservation, and he gives a list of particular rights that he says we have in our natural condition. But he points out that it is necessary that our natural right, or rights, be limited: "Civill, and Naturall Law are not different kinds, but different parts of Law; whereof one part being written, is called Civill, the other unwritten, Naturall. But the Right of Nature, that is, the naturall Liberty of man, may by the Civill Law be abridged and restrained: nay, the end of making Lawes, is no other, but such Restraint; without the which there cannot possibly be any Peace."[53]

How might the civil law limit our right to defend ourselves without alienating that right from us? In order to leave behind us the extreme case of our natural condition, each of us contracts with each other person, though not with the sovereign. It is "as if every man should say to every man, *I Authorise and give up my Right of Governing my selfe, to this Man, or to this Assembly of men, on this condition, that thou give up thy Right to him, and Authorise all his actions in like manner.*"[54] Each of us does this, not simply to pass the time, but in order to avoid that natural condition in which our lives are constantly under threat. By having an arbiter to resolve our disputes — one with sufficient power to enforce the resolution — we remove, or at least reduce, that threat. Disputes that I may have with those with whom I have contracted can now be resolved without actual resort to violence, and those with whom I have not contracted are less likely to threaten me because my contract increases my strength in that it gives me a powerful sovereign to defend me. My contracting, therefore, deals with my right to defend myself, not by giving it up *simpliciter*, but by exercising it in a particular way: I employ the most powerful bodyguard that I can find. Though the most powerful that I can find, he is not perfect or, at least, cannot be guaranteed to be so; at some time he may not be present in the appropriate place when I am threatened, in which case I am thrown on my own resources and must exercise them as I should have done had I never contracted but instead remained in my natural condition.[55] When my bodyguard is not there or otherwise cannot protect me (when, for example, he has the daylights beaten out of him by the threatening party), I revert to the immediate dependence on my natural right to defend myself; I strike out with my own fists instead of depending on somebody else, or in some cases I might seek to employ the conqueror of my old bodyguard. If the bodyguard is not doing his job for any reason (that is, if the sovereign is not providing security), then all bets are off and I am back on my own resources. The bodyguard cannot defend me against the bodyguard; I am always on my own resources when it comes to attacks from the sovereign. If the sovereign attacks me, or if he fails to defend me or to do so adequately when somebody else attacks me, then I am not being provided with security, and, consequently, all contracts that I have made lapse.

So, we might say, the inalienable right to self-defense is not given up in the contract; it is merely exercised in a particular way. Just what is it that is given up in leaving our natural condition in favor of life under Leviathan? And what effect does retention of the inalienable right to self-defense have on Hobbes's claims about the subjection of private judgment to public judgment?

If the sovereign does not provide me with protection, then I have only my own resources. It is not merely that I exercise private judgment in deciding that it would be more efficient to have a sovereign than to have a war of each against all, because it is only *after* such a decision that I am required to subordinate my judgment to the sovereign's. The problem is that the general rationale requires that I constantly judge whether the sovereign is providing protection. When a mugger attacks me with an iron bar and there are no police at hand, I judge that the sovereign is not providing me with security and I go for my life. In both cases, both in judging that I am attacked and in judging that no police are at hand, I exercise my private judgment. If somebody threatens me and there is time to let the police handle the matter, then I do so, but that involves my private judgment that it is that sort of case rather than one in which there is not enough time to wait for the police. And what if my neighbor, in my judgment, poses a threat that plainly leaves me time to call on the sovereign (say my neighbor sets up a chemical plant that releases fumes that, in my informed or uninformed judgment will poison everybody within a one-mile radius) but the sovereign says that my fears are poppycock? Such cases, along with others such as views I might hold about the likely long-term consequences of the sovereign's economic and foreign policies, bring out the difficulties remaining because of the role played in this account by private judgment. The sovereign's function, in Hobbes's theory, is to supplant private judgment where the sovereign judges, but this account of the retention of the inalienable right to self-defense depends heavily on private judgment's being exercised in those cases.

The intervention of the civil law is the intervention of the sovereign and of public judgment, but we have seen that such intervention is not enough to get around the problem. This limiting of natural right by civil law takes us no further than we have already gone. It means that I must not act where the law determines what I must or may do in my own defense, but that point applies only where I am being provided with security. It never applies when I am threatened by the sovereign; the civil law can say until it is blue in the face that I may not resist the sovereign's attempts to kill me, but Hobbes is clear that I retain the right to resist nevertheless. The civil law limits my natural right only if I am given security, and whether I am given security is a matter for my private judgment.

The basis of Hobbes's views about inalienable rights, and particularly the right to self-defense, is set out in chapter 14 of *Leviathan:*

> Whensoever a man Transferreth his Right, or Renounceth it; it is either in consideration of some Right reciprocally transferred to himselfe; or for some other good he hopeth for thereby. For it is a voluntary act: and of the voluntary acts of every man, the object is some *Good to himselfe.* And therefore there be some Rights, which no man can be understood by any words, or other signes, to have abandoned, or transferred. As first a man cannot lay down the right of resisting them, that assault him by force, to take away his life; because he cannot be understood to ayme thereby, at any Good to himself. The same may be said of Wounds, and Chaynes, and Imprisonment; both because there is no benefit consequent to such patience; as there is to the patience of suffering another to be wounded, or imprisoned: as also because a man cannot tell, when he seeth men proceeding against him by violence, whether they intend his death or not. And lastly the motive, and end for which this renouncing, and transferring of Right is introduced, is nothing else but the security of a mans person, in his life, and in the means of so preserving life, as not to be weary of it. And therefore if a man by words, or other signes, seem to despoyle himselfe of the End, for which those signes were intended; he is not to be understood as if he meant it, or that it was his will; but that he was ignorant of how such words and actions were to be interpreted.[56]

There are two points about this passage that we should notice immediately, if only to set aside. One is that a man need not hope for some immediate material good from his renouncing of a right, but he might hope only for the reciprocal transfer to himself of another's right. Hobbes's use of the word "other" at the beginning of the quoted passage shows that he regarded the transfer to oneself of another's right as itself a good even without accompanying material gain. The other point is that the argument that we must be able to defend ourselves against wounds, chains, and imprisonment because we cannot tell, when somebody approaches us with force, whether he intends to take our lives, does not apply outside our natural condition — if I am charged with parking my car in a no-parking zone and am taken before a court, I know perfectly well that I shall not be executed for that offense. Insofar as my inalienable right to resist the sovereign's attempts to punish me depends on *that* argument, it is no good. *Particular* sovereigns might be arbitrary and untrustworthy, but not all need be: If the sovereign's record is good, the fact that he charges me with parking in a prohibited area gives me no reason at all to fear for my life. To say that one never can tell, that even a sovereign with a perfect past record might now go berserk, is not a good answer; it is an answer that applies just as well when the sovereign is not approaching me with force, so it does not allow for the distinction that Hobbes wants to draw.

As was suggested earlier in this chapter and will be argued further in chapter 5, Hobbes did not believe that my contracts are binding on me only if it is in my interest to carry them out. Nevertheless, there is a related point that he might have in mind — one about consideration, the idea that there is no contract unless each party stands to gain something by it. One might, of course, be bound in some other way, and what one gained might be no more than the other person's giving up some previously held right. Hobbes clearly regarded that as a good, and there is no requirement that one give up anything material. The idea is that if I decide to give something up, you need some special reason if you are to be in a position to insist that I cannot change my mind.[57] One possible reason is that I have been paid to give it up: I received consideration, so the right to do whatever is in question if I change my mind is no longer a right that is mine. The consideration might be no more than membership in a group, or an opportunity; I might fail to realize the opportunity, and there might be no material gain. And certainly Hobbes stresses the idea of reciprocity and the idea that it is only *mutual* transfer of rights that is worthwhile in entering civil society.

If the contract threatens my life, he might say, then it threatens everything for me; the contract offers me no consideration, and hence it cannot be binding on me. But that argument is not clearly good. For a start, I might care about things that survive my death: I might care about my children, for example, and my death might benefit them by giving them time to escape the danger or by helping them in some other way. The benefit to them might be my consideration. And, if I contract to obey various rules because I believe that I shall benefit from our community's having those rules, then I might still be right even if I am threatened with punishment for parking illegally: I still get all the benefits of others' obedience to those rules, including future obedience, only if they are enforced on the refractory (including, at the moment, me).

The point goes further: If the death penalty is required for some of those rules to be effective, and if I am threatened with the death penalty for breaking one of the relevant rules, then a similar line can be followed. It might not be true that I can continue to reap the benefits of having those rules only if the punishment is imposed on me because I shall fail to reap any benefits from my death (setting aside benefits to my children, and so on), but because I have *already* reaped those benefits. That I have taken what benefits I can from the contract means that I have received my consideration; that I am now faced with the prospect of paying my share is no reason for saying that the contract is no longer binding on me.[58] If Hobbes is right, then I have already received great benefits from the contract: I would not have lasted nearly so long in my natural condition, so, instead of complaining that the death penalty is shortening my life, I should be grateful to that system of rules with the death penalty for prolonging my life.

One needs to be clear about the role of receipt of benefits in this argument. It is, perhaps, quite clear that I have a lot to gain from living in a society in which these rules are enforced, even if the death penalty is attached to infringement of the rules, but it is at least equally clear that I have nothing personally to gain from dying in such a society. Considering only my personal interests, I have no reason to submit to the penalty; my interests, however, are not the only things to be considered. Rights and duties are parts of the context in which the question arises, quite apart from the right to self-defense being the focus of consideration. The benefits I have had are those of living in a community with a certain pattern of rights and duties. Arguments about rights and duties do not work in the same way as arguments about interests: That I shall never in the future receive any more benefits from a particular policy goes a long way toward showing that the policy is not in my interest now even if I have, in the past, received many benefits from it. But that I have taken benefit in the past (that I have had you mow my lawn, for example) can show, in the appropriate circumstances, that I have a present duty (to pay you, for example). That you have done nothing for me today does not remove or lessen my obligation to you if I have not paid you for the work you did last week.

The role of the sovereign's sword in explaining obligation in Hobbes's theory is not merely that of running obligation and self-interest together or showing or making sure that they always coincide in their requirements. As Hobbes writes, "faith only is the bond of contracts";[59] coercion from the sovereign does not in any direct way create obligation in the person coerced. He says that "the Validity of Covenants begins not but with the Constitution of a Civill Power, sufficient to compell men to keep them,"[60] but the sovereign does not impose obligation on me by making sure that I shall do what is required of me. The sovereign does that by making sure that the person with whom I have made the arrangement will do what is required of him. When the sovereign sets about doing the relevant part of his job — "to compell men equally to the performance of their Covenants"[61] — the significance of my being forced to perform (if I need to be forced) is not that it places me under an obligation, but that it places the other person under an obligation. If I shall be forced to perform (should that be necessary), then the other party to the agreement is secure that I shall perform, and that places an obligation on him. It does not place an obligation on me. What places an obligation on me is my security of their performance. That security can take a number of different forms: One form is force, the sovereign's sword, but another is prior performance.[62] Hobbes puts these two side by side, making their equivalence clear: It is not against reason to perform "where one of the parties has performed already; or where there is a Power to make him performe."[63] And he says, "because Covenants of mutuall trust, where there is a feare of not performance on either part . . . are invalid; though the Originall of Justice be the making of Covenants; yet Injustice actually there can be none, till the cause of such feare be taken away."[64]

The sovereign's function in the generation of obligation is to remove that fear by giving each party a guarantee of the other's compliance. The significant point is the security, and if I have already received the benefits, then I have the best security possible. It is not at all clear, therefore, why I should be freed from my obligation when the time comes for me to pay up. If the only way we can have security is to have a system of punishment (the death penalty, the lash, forcibly locking people up), then I have already drawn benefit from that system; the sovereign who approaches me to punish me when I break the rules is not attacking me but is calling in debts on behalf of the community. I have taken the benefits, and now I have an obligation to pay the price. The sovereign's approaching me in that way does not show that I receive no consideration under the contract and am therefore freed from obligation; I have already received my consideration. The claim that a contract that threatens my life cannot be binding because it fails to give me consideration, then, will not adequately defend Hobbes's claim that nobody can be understood to have made a contract that might require giving up or risking his life.

One other possibility is that Hobbes is making a psychological claim about people: People are so constituted that they cannot contract unless they see some advantage to themselves in it. But, for the reasons given earlier, people might see advantage in giving up their rights to self-defense in return for others' doing the same. And if they did not, that fact would explain only why they could not make contracts. It would explain to us why people, with the appropriate contract before them and pens in their hands, groaned, sweated, took up unusual religious observances concerned with the worship of shoes, and so on, but could not bring themselves to sign their names. It would not explain why the contracts that they did make were not to be interpreted in plain terms and held to be binding.

There is another way of taking this point, a way that does not deal directly with obligation or duty not to resist but does so indirectly.

> No man is obligated by any contracts whatsoever not to resist him who shall offer to kill, wound, or any other way hurt his body. For there is in every man a certain high degree of fear, through which he apprehends that evil which is done to him to be the greatest; and therefore by natural necessity he shuns it all he can, and it is supposed he can do no otherwise. When a man is arrived to this degree of fear, we cannot expect but he will provide for himself either by flight or fight. Since therefore no man is tied to impossibilities, they who are threatened either with death (which is the greatest evil to nature), or wounds, or some other bodily hurts, and are not stout enough to bear them, are not obligated to endure them. Furthermore, he that is tied by contract is trusted; for faith only is the bond of contracts; but they who are brought to punishment, either capital or more gentle, are fettered or strongly guarded; which is a most certain sign that they seemed not sufficiently bound from non-resistance by their contracts.[65]

There is no suggestion here that everybody crumples at the slightest sign of a threat, or that everybody crumples at the same point, though it is suggested that for each person (or perhaps only for most people, given the behavior of some martyrs) there is a point at which the threat becomes too great and one succumbs to temptation by flying or fighting. That one can, in this way, give in to temptation does not show that one is unjust or pays too little attention to Hobbes's third law of nature. Injustice is *willfully* breaking contracts, not merely breaking them under insupportable temptation to do something such as save one's life. This is suggested by Hobbes's remark about flight in battle: "And there is allowance to be made for naturall timorousnesse, not onely to women, (of whom no such dangerous duty is expected,) but also to men of feminine courage. When Armies fight, there is on one side, or both, a running away; yet when they do it not out of trechery, but fear, they are not esteemed to do it unjustly, but dishonourably."[66]

If somebody regularly gives in when faced with only the slightest of threats, such as the threat of the pain and frustration of having to wait for five minutes, then we might well think that they are unjust; that is because we should doubt their motivation and would suspect that they could have resisted the threat but just did not care about the rights of others. Once we recognize that the person concerned could not have resisted the temptation to save his life, or to avoid torture, or whatever might have been the threat he was tempted to avoid, then we recognize that his failure to perform was not a sign of injustice. If the threat before which they succumb is too slight, then they may be shown to be a wimp or a coward or to have some moral failing (that one did not exhibit the vice of injustice does not mean that one exhibited no vice), but the vice they display is not that of willfully ignoring the rights of others. Those who are stout enough to bear it must do so; those who are not stout enough to bear it are excused from their obligation on the ground of impossibility of performance. But if Hobbes is right, they then take on an obligation to do whatever they can to make up the difference that their nonperformance made to the other party in the arrangement.[67]

The point here is not one about the conditions generating obligations; it is, rather, a point about when people may properly be held to blame for what they do. Nevertheless, the point might, in a misleading way, be put by saying that people who acted with that motivation, because they did not display the vice of injustice, did nothing they had no right to do, and therefore they must have had a right to do what they did. This does, indeed, seem to make the most sense of what Hobbes says about the inalienable right to self-defense. But it is a point about what follows when people cannot help what they do, so it does not fit into arguments about what people have a right to do in the way in which consideration of the conditions generating obligations will fit in. It is not a point that would in any way help somebody trying to work out whether he had the right to resist the sovereign in these conditions or was still obligated to obey the law. If one's consideration of this point could be relevant to one's actions, that is to say, if one is *choosing* one's actions, then this right could not justify one's resisting the sovereign. That I was not to blame for something because I could not help doing it does not mean that my doing it was an exercise of my liberty.[68]

In fact, if one were to read Hobbes that way, he would best be taken as giving me advice about how to expect others to act, and only in that way giving me advice about how to act myself. I should not trust people to stick to their duties in real extremities such as when their lives are in danger, so I should bind the felon before sending him on his way to the gallows. When they are faced with serious loss, Hobbes might be telling us, we cannot reasonably expect people to concern themselves with the consideration that they have already received even if it does mean that they are bound to keep their side of the bargain. Therefore we should not expect them so to concern themselves. In effective terms, in other words, we should work as though there were no such obligation on them to give up their lives. But this does not amount to any serious claim that they have a right to do whatever is necessary for their self-preservation; it is very much a remark addressed to other people.

It might be thought that Hobbes's real position is that there is, in fact, no natural right to self-defense: We have the positive rights to defend ourselves that we are allowed by the sovereign, but beyond those, there is only the fact that we are not to blame for what we cannot help doing. And that would be no proper right at all; it is an excusing condition. That I cannot help doing something is not a consideration I can put on the scales when deciding what to do; if I act because of my decision, that shows that I *could* help it. But Hobbes does seem to mean a genuine right that we can consider in deciding what to do: Protecting that natural right and making it effective is the point of the contract.[69] Natural laws are effective only when they are made into civil laws,[70] so it might be thought that a natural right to self-defense is effective only when made into positive rights by the sovereign's edicts and that it has no existence beyond those positive rights. But that will not do, because the natural right to self-defense is one that is called on against the sovereign. One may, indeed, call upon it in deciding what to do. One might well consider it, for example, when deciding whether to disobey an order from the sovereign,[71] or in deciding to run because this particular battle has been lost.[72]

There is another point that we might notice, which brings

psychological necessity into the argument in a different way. The connection between infringing on rights and giving up rights is, at least usually, conventional and determined by the public decision-procedure. It is not simply a matter of my giving up my right to X if I infringe on your right to X. If I infringe on your rights by parking my automobile in your driveway, the state is licensed to take some money away from me; my misbehavior does not license you to park your automobile in my driveway, which would result in your being fined, too. The connection between my action infringing on your rights and the rights that I give up by that action is as conventional as the relationship between my employing you to mow my lawn and my paying you for it: What I am obligated to do for you depends on the terms of the contract, and if you are a professional mower of lawns it is unlikely that the requirement will be that I do for you what you did for me and mow your lawn. I shall have to pay you in the usual way, with money.

Self-defense at least seems to call on the idea that somebody who attacks another unprovoked thereby gives up various rights, failing to meet the condition of reciprocity and thereby licensing the person attacked to respond by treating the attacker in ways that would otherwise be improper. But the manner in which rights are given up by attacking somebody in a way that made it appropriate for them to call on the right to self-defense might be different from the way rights are given up by parking in somebody else's driveway. Self-defense might be special in that any set of conventions that did not allow me to kill you when you were unjustly attacking me — and when killing you was the only way in which I could stop you from killing me — would be ineffective. People would not obey those conventions, perhaps as a matter of psychological necessity, *and they would neither expect others to obey them nor help to enforce them.* This goes beyond the first point about psychological necessity and on to a point about the possibility of having any such set of conventions (including the Hobbesian sovereign) establishing rights, because conventions that nobody follows, expects others to follow, or tries to enforce are simply not effective conventions. It does allow us to make some distinctions that we might want to make, too. If in some community that retained the death penalty, the public hangman was attacked by the condemned person when he tried to do his gruesome job, the people probably would come to the aid of the hangman and thus show that the conventional right to self-defense did not extend that far. So a set of rules that did not allow a right to self-defense might be inoperable in a political community, which would mean that a right to self-defense was a necessary condition of anybody's having any positive rights.

That suggestion can be developed by considering a couple of other possibilities, which might, in fact, amount to one possibility, in reading what Hobbes has to say about inalienable rights. One possibility is that we have not one right but innumerable rights in our natural condition, so we can lay down some rights without affecting others. The other possibility is that we retain the one formal right that we have in our natural condition, the right to defend ourselves, but that it is restructured because of the change of circumstances when we move into civil society and substantively amounts to a lot less if we translate it into a set of particular actions that we have a right to do, though it gives us a lot more effective protection of our lives. This latter interpretation is suggested by Hobbes's remark[73] that the civil law can limit natural right. The former is suggested by Hobbes's willingness to list rights:

> As it is necessary for all men that seek peace, to lay down certaine Rights of Nature; that is to say, not to have libertie to do all they list: so is it necessarie for mans life, to retaine some; as right to governe their owne bodies; enjoy aire, water, motion, waies to go from place to place; and all things else without which a man cannot live, or not live well. If in this case, at the making of Peace, men require for themselves, that which they would not have to be granted to others, they do contrary to the [natural] law, that commandeth the acknowledgment of naturall equalitie.[74]

One notices in that passage the use of the plural form "rights," but one can, nevertheless, see how the two possibilities currently being examined might amount to the same thing: A right to do whatever I judge necessary to preserve myself might also be described as a right to seek water if I judge that to be necessary to my preservation, *and* a right to seek food if I judge that to be necessary to my preservation, *and* a right to use you as fishbait if I judge that to be necessary to my preservation, and so on.

Could Hobbes's point be this: I made a contract to preserve my life; I paid a certain price, in agreeing to refrain from certain actions and agreeing to submit to the judgment of the sovereign; and the other side of the bargain was that I have security of my life. If I do not have security of my life, then I am not getting what I paid for and, therefore, am no longer under any obligation to pay. If the gardener decides that he would rather go surfing than garden this week, and acts on that decision, then he is not entitled to be paid for doing the gardening this week even if he has done the gardening, and been paid for it, in previous weeks. If I am to be under any obligation to pay the price laid down in the covenant, therefore, and if I am to be obligated to submit to the judgment of the sovereign, then I must have those things that are necessary to my life: water, food, freedom from vicious attack, and so on. Whether it is a matter of retaining some rights from a list, or of restructuring the one formal right to do what I judge necessary for my preservation (restructuring it in terms of some sort of dependence on what the sovereign judges), not to allow me to retain a right to food, water, and those other things necessary for my life means that the other party to the covenant is not doing his part, which means that the conditions necessary to impose on me an obligation to keep my side of the bargain are not met.

This is like a point about a right to one's body, a "right" sometimes called on, though rarely supported by reasons, in arguments about the propriety of abortion at the mother's request. We do not always recognize such a right. In times of war, for example, it is sometimes accepted that it is proper to conscript young men and send them off in the knowledge that they are likely to be killed or injured; there is no suggestion then that the young men may not be conscripted because they have a right to their bodies. If I attack you for no good reason, you may lambast my body as necessary for your own defense. If I sell my body to science, it is still my body even though science has a right to it. But my body is special to me; I need it if I am to exercise any rights at all. It is necessary to any structure of rights in which I am to live that I have some *rights* to do with my body, and especially that I have rights that my body not be wantonly attacked.

The similarity of this to the point about consideration is clear, and it leaves us with similar problems. One might also notice that whether or not the gardener is entitled to be paid for the week he takes off, the conditions that must be met if I am to be able to fire him is a matter of positive law.

This account of the inalienability of rights still leaves us heavily dependent on private judgment, which is just what Hobbes wanted to get away from. I must retain a right to those things necessary *in whose judgment* to my preservation? If the relevant judgment is mine, then I am untrammeled; I am limited only by my judgment of what is necessary to my preservation, which is the position in which I was in my natural condition. That the circumstances are different (if they are: everybody else would be in the position I was in, and it is not at all clear that any of us can have left our natural condition if each of us retains that wide-ranging right) means only that I might feel less threatened and might, therefore, exercise my judgment differently; it does not change the fact that I am exercising my judgment all the time and am not submitting my judgment in any general way to that of the sovereign. If the relevant judgment is the sovereign's, then I have retained nothing of any worth. The worthlessness of what I have retained is most obvious when it is the sovereign who threatens my preservation, and Hobbes is quite clear that my right is supposed to be effective in that case.

The dependence on private judgment is stronger than might appear at first glance. When the sovereign has not kept his side of the bargain (or, strictly speaking, has not carried out the function that was created for him by the bargaining among the citizens), that is, he has not preserved my life, I am dead and can do nothing; any *action* that I took in exercise of my right would have to be based on the prospect of the sovereign's not keeping his side of the bargain and not be a response to his actually having failed.

And the detail of what Hobbes says makes the dependence stronger still: Whether I am living *well*, if the issue matters, would have to be a matter for my private judgment. This issue of how well I live widens the area in which I can use my private judgment with propriety beyond that in which I see my life as threatened (and that area is determined as much by how timid, silly, or wise I am as by whether there is any threat to me; I am limited only by my own judgment) and into that in which, though I am perfectly clear that my life is not threatened, I believe that present tax rates threaten to restrict me to one overseas holiday this year. The list of retained rights given by Hobbes in the passage quoted previously is enough to put me in the position of judging constantly whether the sovereign is doing a good job. So this interpretation is unsuccessful, too, in explaining how Hobbes can have inalienable rights without making the sovereign's job impossible. The conceptual problems about private and public judgment in Hobbes's theory still arise even if, as Deborah Baumgold has persuasively argued,[75] the right to self-preservation is a politically irrelevant right. The natural right to self-preservation is still theoretically relevant and undermines Hobbes's claims about the necessity of giving supremacy to public judgment in our communal life. Given his argument about right reason, he seems to be stuck in the position of saying that we can live in civil society only if we alienate an inalienable right.

Notes

1. Cf. Deborah Baumgold, *Hobbes's Political Theory* (Cambridge: Cambridge University Press, 1988), pp. 21ff.

2. Hobbes argues that absolute sovereignty is necessary in any civil society, so attempts to remove it by limiting the sovereign will do no more than shift the absolute power to another seat. See *De Cive* 6.13, p. 182.

3. *Leviathan*, chapter 15, pp. 210-211.

4. He is often read as claiming that people are incapable of willingly facing death. See, for example, David Gauthier, *The Logic of Leviathan* (Oxford: Oxford University Press, 1969), pp. 23-24; J.W.N. Watkins, *Hobbes's System of Ideas: A Study in the Political Significance of Philosophical Theories* (London: Hutchinson University Library, 1965), pp. 166-168; and Howard Warrender, *The Political Philosophy of Hobbes: His Theory of Obligation* (Oxford: Clarendon Press, 1957), p. 91. For the opposite view, see Don Herzog, *Happy Slaves: A Critique of Consent Theory* (Chicago: University of Chicago Press, 1989), pp. 74-77.

5. *Leviathan*, "A Review, and Conclusion," pp. 718-719.

6. *Leviathan*, chapter 14, p. 199.

7. Jean Hampton, *Hobbes and the Social Contract Tradition* (London: Cambridge University Press, 1986), p. 56.

8. *Leviathan*, "A Review, and Conclusion," pp. 718-719.

9. John Aubrey (ed. Andrew Clark), *Brief Lives* (Oxford: Oxford University Press, 1898), vol. 1, p. 335.

10. In chapter 5 I take up the issue of the conditions for obligation.

11. *Leviathan*, chapter 26, p. 315.

12. See the discussion of the natural and political capacities of the sovereign in *A Dialogue*, pp. 160-162.

13. Gregory S. Kavka, *Hobbesian Moral and Political Theory* (Princeton: Princeton University Press, 1986), p. 315.

14. Cf. Bernard Gert, Introduction to *Man and Citizen* (Brighton: Harvester Press, 1978), pp. 19-20, on the limitation imposed on natural right by reason.

15. Even an action in conformity with the laws of nature is a breach of it if the agent believes it to be contrary to them (*The Elements of Law* 1.17.13, p. 93).

16. Kavka, in *Hobbesian Theory*, p. 354, assumes that sincerity is enough to avoid the problem. Each of us might be perfectly sincere, but differing private judgments will still raise the problem. We *do* disagree about the application of the natural or moral law: We might all agree that justice should be done, but there are plenty of differing opinions about what that means when applied to the Middle East, or Ireland, or the issue of Aboriginal land rights in Australia. Hobbes points out (*Leviathan*, chapter 26, p. 314) that the differences of private men about what is equity, justice, or moral virtue make necessary the ordinances of a sovereign.

17. Baumgold, in *Hobbes's Political Theory*, especially pp. 22ff, suggests an interpretation of Hobbes that would have him using a *reductio* argument again to show that a right to self-defense cannot be a right of resistance that limits tyrannous kings. Inalienable rights, she argues persuasively, are always politically inconsequential on Hobbes's account. She also suggests (pp. 26ff) that Hobbes found the idea of a nonresistance contract implausible.

18. *The Elements of Law* 2.5.2, p. 139.

19. *Leviathan*, chapter 14, p. 189.

20. Cf. Warrender, *Political Philosophy of Hobbes*, p. 118: "For each man the comprehensive test for `sufficient security´ is always to some extent subjective, in that both in the State of nature and in civil society it depends in part upon the individual's estimate of his own safety." In the end, it depends *completely* on his estimate of his own safety.

21. Cf. *De Cive* 3.27, pp. 148-149.

22. Gert, in *Man and Citizen*, pp. 10-11, sees this problem of how trouble can spread from a few troublemakers in a large group, though he skips over the role of private judgment in setting the problem up.

23. *De Cive* 23.2.2n, p. 123.

24. See the further discussion in chapter 5 of the conditions under which contracts are binding.

25. *Leviathan*, chapter 14, p. 190.

26. *Leviathan*, chapter 14, p. 190.

27. Sir Robert Filmer, "Observations on Mr. Hobbes's Leviathan" in Peter Laslett (ed.), *Patriarcha and Other Political Writings of Sir Robert Filmer* (Oxford: Basil Blackwell, 1949), p. 243.

28. Cf. the discussion in chapter 2 of what protection the citizen gets from the right to disobey as allowed by Hobbes.

29. George Lawson, *An Examination of the Political Part of Mr. Hobbs his Leviathan* (London: Francis Tyton, 1657), p. 71. There are sometimes suggestions that Hobbes might go at least part of the way with this point. Insofar as psychological impossibility of obeying the law is the excuse for fighting back when the police come to take one away, we might bear in mind his statement (*Leviathan*, chapter 26, p. 318) that any man who, through accident *not proceeding from his own default,* lacks the means to obey the law is excused obedience to that law. This suggests that Hobbes would not accept drunkenness as a defense if somebody were charged with dangerous driving, but he never develops the point in terms of there being no excuse for those who fight back when they are responsible for the situation that provoked others to attack them. The only suggestion that he might take that path is his remark (*Leviathan*, chapter 21, p. 270) that becoming a soldier takes away a man's right to run in fear unless he has his captain's leave.

30. Filmer, "Observations," p. 247.

31. See, for example, the preface of *De Cive*, p. 97: "How many rebellions hath this opinion been the cause of, which teacheth that the knowledge whether the commands of kings be just or unjust, belongs to private men; and that before they yield obedience, they not only may, but ought to dispute them! . . . Before such questions began to be moved, princes did not sue for, but already exercised the supreme power. They kept their empire entire, not by arguments, but by punishing the wicked and protecting the good. Likewise subjects did not measure what was just by the sayings and judgments of private men, but by the laws of the realm; nor were they kept in peace by disputations, but by power and authority. Yea, they reverenced the supreme power, whether residing in one man or in a council, as a certain visible divinity."

32. *Leviathan*, chapter 14, p. 192.

33. *Leviathan*, chapter 15, pp. 211-212.

34. *Leviathan*, chapter 27, p. 337.

35. In *De Cive*, "Epistle Dedicatory," p. 90, Hobbes says that the right of self-preservation is something "which we all receive from the uncontrollable dictates of necessity." Also in *De Cive*, the preface, p. 99, Hobbes says of man that in conditions of distrust and dread, "as by natural right he may, so by necessity he will be forced to make use of the strength he hath, toward the preservation of himself."

36. Cf. *De Cive* 2.18, p. 130.

37. This follows on at least some accounts of rights. See, for example, W. N. Hohfeld, *Fundamental Legal Conceptions* (New Haven: Yale University Press, 1964); and Carl Wellman, *A Theory of Rights* (Totowa: Rowman and Allanheld, 1985). For this sort of interpretation of Hobbes, see Warrender, *Political Philosophy of Hobbes*, pp. 33, 91-96, and 214.

38. *Leviathan*, chapter 27, pp. 345-346.

39. *Leviathan*, chapter 14, p. 199.

40. *Leviathan*, "A Review, and Conclusion," p. 717.

41. *Leviathan*, chapter 11, p. 164.

42. *De Cive* 3.12, p. 142.

43. *Leviathan*, chapter 15, pp. 211-212, suggests that it is not worth leaving our natural condition if life in civil society is insufficiently commodious.

44. *De Cive* 6.13, pp. 182-183.

45. *Leviathan*, chapter 38, p. 478.

46. *Leviathan*, "A Review, and Conclusion," pp. 718-719.

47. *De Homine*, pp. 48-49.

48. Hampton, *Contract Tradition*, p. 15.

49. For a suggestion of this interpretation, see Warrender, *Political Philosophy of Hobbes*, p. 115: "The effect of the political covenant is not to restrain the individual from action in the face of patent mortal danger, but to restrain him from action on *suspicion* of danger, or to put the matter more precisely, it narrows the field of `just suspicion.´"

50. *Leviathan*, chapter 27, p. 343.

51. *Leviathan*, chapter 28, p. 353.

52. Cf. Baumgold, *Hobbes's Political Theory*, chapter 2.

53. *Leviathan*, chapter 26, pp. 314-315.

54. *Leviathan*, chapter 17, p. 227.

55. Cf. *Leviathan*, chapter 27, p. 343.

56. *Leviathan*, chapter 14, p. 192.

57. Cf. *De Cive* 2.16, p. 129: "It holds universally true, that promises do oblige when there is some benefit received."

58. See *Leviathan*, chapter 15, p. 204.

59. *De Cive* 2.18, p. 130.

60. *Leviathan*, chapter 15, p. 203.

61. *Leviathan*, chapter 15, p. 202.

62. Warrender, *Political Philosophy of Hobbes*, p. 42, notices that prior performance and the sovereign's sword serve the same function here.

63. *Leviathan*, chapter 15, p. 204.

64. *Leviathan*, chapter 15, p. 202.

65. *De Cive* 2.18, p. 130.

66. *Leviathan*, chapter 21, p. 270.

67. *Leviathan*, chapter 14, pp. 197-198.

68. Kavka, in *Hobbesian Theory*, pp. 329-333, sets out and disposes of a Hobbesian argument that attempts to derive a genuine right from psychological necessity.

69. *Leviathan*, chapter 13, *passim*.

70. *Leviathan*, chapter 26, p. 314.

71. *Leviathan*, chapter 21, pp. 268-269.

72. *Leviathan*, chapter 20, p. 257.

73. *Leviathan*, chapter 26, pp. 315 and 335.

74. *Leviathan*, chapter 15, pp. 211-212.

75. Baumgold, *Hobbes's Political Theory*, chapter 2.

4

The Natural Condition of Mankind

It is clear that Hobbes's account of the natural condition of mankind plays an important part in his argument. It is sometimes less clear just what that important part is, and it is not clear that he gives only one account of the condition of mere nature. He gives no formal definition of it, but a number of descriptions: It is a war of each against all;[1] a condition in which each person has a right to all things;[2] the condition that obtains between sovereign states;[3] a condition in which each is his own judge;[4] and so on. It is not always clear, even given Hobbes's explanation that a war of each against all does not require actual fighting, that anything satisfies all of these descriptions, let alone that anything that satisfies one of them must also satisfy the others. In the light of the right reason argument[5] it might seem plausible, for example, that in the absence of a common power over people, each will be his own judge, and we might agree that there is no earthly common power over sovereigns. But it is by no means clear that it follows that every person has a right to all things or that there will be a war of each against all.

If the natural condition of mankind is the relationship that holds between sovereign states, then we could learn what it is by observing relationships between sovereign states. We would learn, among other things, that alliances are possible, that cooperation in trade for mutual gain is possible, and that unpleasantness sometimes flares up. We would learn different things about different relationships between different sovereign states: The history of the relationship between France and Germany, for instance, is quite different from that between Australia and New Zealand. Such observations of history would not give us knowledge of the relationship between universals and is not Hobbes's favored method. He distinguished sharply between history and science.[6]

What Hobbes says about man's natural condition, I think, is often misread as an account of an actual state about which we might speculate. And indeed it can be an actual state, but in the theoretically important way, it is not.[7] The natural condition is a relationship between terms, and different sorts of terms can stand in that relationship. What follows from the relationship depends on the nature of the terms.

Hobbes took the expression "state of nature" from other writers of his time, and a large part of his point is that if they wanted to show something about the nature of authority and its role in social life, they chose the wrong terms for the relationship: When they wrote about families and things of that sort, they chose terms that already involved relationships of authority. The state of nature that they wrote about was not one that when compared with civil society provided a comparison between a condition in which there was authority based on convention and a condition in which there was no such authority. Authority was already present, so the story that those people told could not provide us with an account of the basis of authority. When, on the other hand, we take individual people, each his own judge, and make them the terms of the relationship, we get something from which social life cannot be constructed. We have, in fact, a *reductio* argument to show the necessity of authority relationships in any social life. When it is put together with the right reason argument, we have an argument to show the necessity of conventional authority relationships, among other things,[8] to social life. Those who argue for natural right as the basis for and limitation on all authority, he thinks, are arguing for a nonsense — a dangerous nonsense that will lead to a life of strife and violence.

The speculative nature of much discussion of Hobbes's natural condition often seems to assume that he was telling a sort of historical story about how the state arose, and that it required an actual state of nature and an actual contract. Apart from not fitting with his model of explanation, this story runs counter to his assertion that men never did live in their natural condition all over the world:

> It may peradventure be thought, there was never such a time, nor condition of warre as this; and I believe it was never generally so, over all the world: but there are many places, where they live so now. For the savage people in many places of *America*, except the government of small Families, the concord whereof dependeth on naturall lust, have no government at all; and live at this day in that brutish manner, as I said before. Howsoever, it may be perceived what manner of life there would be, where there were no common Power to feare; by the manner

of life, which men that have formerly lived under a peacefull government, use to degenerate into, in a civill Warre.[9]

It also seems to run counter to his claim that all kinds of law are of the same age as mankind.[10] If civil law is of the same age as mankind, as Hobbes's remark clearly implies and clearly is meant to imply, then there can never have been a time when everybody lived without the benefit of civil law.

There is certainly at least a suggestion in Hobbes's remark about the American Indians that the state of nature can be actual, and that its units are families rather than individual people. An actual natural condition certainly looks more plausible if it is imagined as populated by families rather than by individual people sprung from the earth full-grown like mushrooms,[11] but then it is much harder to make any sense of the natural condition as a war of each against all while interpreting "each against all" literally.

On the other hand, Hobbes might not have wanted to claim that the American Indians actually lived in man's natural condition. Instead, he might have wanted to suggest that those people were nearer to the natural condition, or absence of government, than we are, and that his thesis is supported by what he believed to be the fact that their lives were singularly nasty and brutish. (In elucidating Hobbes's argument, knowing what Hobbes believed is more important than knowing whether what he believed was true.) Because they lived in smaller groups, they might give some indication of the changes that take place as we get nearer to the radical individualism of the natural condition in which we can readily make sense of the idea of a war of each against all. There are oddities whichever way Hobbes is taken.

If Hobbes is to be taken at face value when he says that it never was the case that men lived in their natural condition all over the world, then at least one state did not begin in the way Hobbes describes — by a contract made by individual people who were in their natural condition. In fact, Hobbes is quite clear that at least many states did not arise in that way:

> Great Monarchies have proceeded from small Families. First, by War, wherein the Victor not only enlarged his Territory, but also the number and riches of his Subjects. As for other forms of Common-wealths, they have been enlarged otherways. First, by a voluntary conjunction of many Lords of Families into one great Aristocracie. Secondly, by Rebellion proceeded first, *Anarchy*, and from *Anarchy* proceeded any

form that the Calamities of them that lived therein did prompt them to; whether it were that they chose an Hereditary King, or an elective King for life, or that they agreed upon a Council of certain Persons (which is *Aristocracy*) or a Council of the whole People to have the Soveraign Power, which is *Democracy*.

After the first manner which is by War, grew up all the greatest Kingdoms in the World, *viz.* the *Ægyptian, Assyrian, Persian* and the *Macedonian Monarchy*; and so did the great Kingdoms of *England, France,* and *Spain*.

The second manner was the original of the *Venetian Aristocracy*, the third way which is Rebellion, grew up divers great Monarchies, perpetually changing from one form to another; as in *Rome* rebellion against Kings produced *Democracy*, upon which the Senate usurped under *Sylla*, and the People again upon the Senate under *Marius*, and the Emperor usurped upon the People under *Cæsar* and his Successors.[12]

This passage does not suggest that all states arose from people contracting to emerge from an individualist war of each against all; it suggests fairly strongly that Hobbes believed that the origin of states was in amalgamations among families, each family having already constituted a small social unit. That being so, we should have to read Hobbes's political works as being quite specifically accounts of how the state arose in England if we took them as some sort of historical tale. He would be carrying out a historical study, rather as Selden did, which is a task that does not seem to fit his general style of argument in, say, *Leviathan*, and he would not at all be setting up a science of politics, as he claimed to be doing.

It was common among Hobbes's contemporaries to take him as making historical claims about an actual state of nature and an actual contract, because other writers of the period who wrote in those terms were, indeed, making historical claims. Lawson, for example, took Hobbes to be making historical claims, and therefore wrote:

His Covenant of every one with every one for to design a Soveraign, is but an Utopian fancy. For by the best Histories we may understand that many States have attained to a settled form of Regular Government by degrees in a long tract of time, and that by several alterations intervening, so that the Laws of their constitution are rather customs th[a]n any written Charter. Some Communities come under a form of Government more suddenly, and by a way fortuitous unto man, though not so to God. And in this point the practise of former times, not the fancies and speculations of men must instruct us.[13]

Filmer, likewise, takes Hobbes to be making claims about an actual state of nature (Hobbes eschewed the term "state of nature" in his later writings, possibly because it does suggest that what is at issue is a general condition that people are either in or not in, whereas it is actually a matter of relationships that somebody might have with some people but not with others) and spends time arguing that there never was, nor could have been, such a general condition, a conclusion which Hobbes would cheerfully accept. Filmer writes, "Mr. Hobbes confesseth and believes it was never generally so, that there was such a *jus naturae:* and if not generally, then not at all, for one exception bars all if he mark it well; whereas he imagines such a right of nature may be now practised in America, he confesseth a government there of families, which government how small or brutish soever (as he calls it) is sufficient to destroy his *jus naturale.*"[14]

In fact, Hobbes was taking over prevailing models and turning them to his own ends, making the point that these existing theories (not only about the natural condition, but also about natural law, natural right, and the contract) can work only if they are developed into his theories, which then lead to conclusions different from those derived from the original theories. Hobbes fairly frequently did this sort of thing, taking the models that others had used and showing that they had misused their own models or designed them poorly and misunderstood their significance. Hobbes moved from the history that Selden and others did to his own science of politics; that move changed the model and thus changed the significance of the term "state of nature." Others tried to illuminate the nature and justification of authority by anthropological speculation about the earliest stages of humankind's existence, but Hobbes's point in reply is that even families and small communities already have authority and therefore cannot properly be used as a contrast to show the nature of authority. Human life with no authority or conventional decision-procedures at all, even in the form of families or other small groups, is the radical form of the natural condition in which each person is in the natural condition with respect to each other person, and, as Hobbes made clear, that is not a possible continuing existence for humankind.

I gave an account of Hobbes's method of argument in chapter 1. If that is his method, and if the point of it is to set up a science, then we should expect that his attempt to set up a science of politics was not merely a matter-of-fact account of how England came into being as a political entity. We should not, that is to say, read him as telling a story that requires an actual state of nature and the making of an actual contract; the contract, rather, would be no more than a model, playing the part in the story of the making of a state that the moving point plays in the story of the making of a circle. Empirical examinations of states of nature, if there be such things, would not help much. It would be their necessary features that mattered, not the contingent features that such examination would reveal.

Hence, speculation about how people would behave in such a natural condition — speculation of the sort undertaken by those who analyze the natural condition in terms of games theory — is not relevant to the point that Hobbes is dealing with, especially if such a state of nature is an impossibility for people. That Hobbes does intend it to be an impossibility and is using a *reductio* argument is something that we should consider, given his known admiration for geometry.

Gregory S. Kavka, after quoting Hobbes's misleading example of the dismantling of a watch, says,

> Hobbes's plan is to break the commonwealth up into its constituent elements, human individuals, and examine the operations and interactions of these elements in the absence of the commonwealth, that is, in the state of nature. The primary purpose of doing this is to determine what the proper *function* of the State is, what undesirable conditions or features of the state of nature it serves to ameliorate. This, in turn, can provide guidance for improving existing States, by indicating what purposes they should be serving and by providing a contrasting model of a situation (the state of nature) in which these purposes are not being served. In addition, to the extent that existing States are carrying out the proper function of States, we thereby provide a potential *justification* for them and legitimize some of the powers exercised by their officials. . . . It is essentially a *hypothetical* theory concerning what (counterfactually) would happen if the social and political ties between persons were suddenly dissolved. Such a theory is called for because actually dissolving society to observe the result would likely be disastrous and irreversible, if not impossible.[15]

This interpretation simply has Hobbes doing what we should regard now as very poor speculative science. (Even thought experiments in science are tied down to other experiments in the thoughts that go into them.) Had Hobbes wanted to see what happened when states did not serve their proper functions, he would have done better to observe those states that were not serving their proper functions and which, for that reason, needed to be improved. Considering the state of nature would not tell him what the proper function of a state is; it would simply tell him the difference between having a state, whether serving its proper function or not, and not having one. And the idea that Hobbes was simply speculating for want of the chance to carry out the experiment of dissolving society into individual people with no social or political ties will not do: Speculation about that would not fit any better with Hobbes's expressed ideas about the nature of science and what distinguishes it from history than would actually carrying out the experiment. Hobbes was looking for necessary truths of the sort that are found in geometry.

Jean Hampton,[16] too, discusses Hobbes's views on man's natural condition in a way that fails to distinguish different types of natural condition and hence fails to recognize the significance of the radical form of that condition. She, too, begins with discussion of the Hobbesian example of the watch. This is not the correct example to take because, as I pointed out in chapter 1, it is an example of the resolutive method in action and Hobbes makes clear that even though civil philosophy is available to the less philosophically adept by the resolutive or analytical method,[17] the whole method of demonstration and of teaching, which are, presumably, the activities that Hobbes is involved in, is compositive or synthetical,[18] in which case the model of the circle[19] would be more appropriate. But, setting that aside, when we take a watch apart we get things that, if they are to explain the watch, are conceptually *parts* of the watch, not conceptually individualist. Hobbes's position, for all his rejection of Aristotle, is much more like the Aristotelian position that Hampton goes on to set out. The sort of people that Hampton attributes to Hobbes's theory would indeed live (very briefly) in the radical form of our natural condition. People need not do so because of the part of Hobbes's account of human nature that is yet to come: People have those qualities of character that are set out in the laws of nature,[20] or, at least, enough people have those qualities of character to a sufficient degree. The question to be raised at the end is: When the resolutive job has been done, can *these* parts be put back together to make the whole? In the Hobbesian natural condition, we have man the mere animal (or machine); life for him is solitary, poor, nasty, brutish, and short. Such beings cannot simply be herded together to form a community.[21] They must be combined in terms of certain principles — the laws of nature — which, as Hobbes points out, are qualities of character[22] and are thus part of Hobbes's full-blown account of human nature. Those who lack the laws of nature in any effective form therefore lack qualities that Hobbes regarded as essential to communal life. In an important sense, such "people" are incomplete.[23]

Hobbes's full-blown account of human nature is of people as social beings, as citizens, people who are part of a people and not merely part of a multitude. Hobbes argues that were that not their nature, they could not live in communities. What is in the radical form of the natural condition is not a person; that is why those "people", unlike real people, cannot avoid the radical form of the natural condition by being prepared to keep their covenants made, and so on. Our natural condition, far from being something that we have contracted out of in a single move, is something that we have with us still at some levels. But its radical form is something that people never were in, never could be in, and never could leave for want of those qualities that constitute the laws of nature, if they were in it. Hobbes's seeing this is the originality that took him beyond the other thinkers who puzzled about a state of nature. He considered what a genuine natural condition without any political relationships at all would be and showed it to be impossible as a starting point for the state. The state may have grown as time went by and families amalgamated, but authority, Hobbes set about showing us, has always been with us.

Did Hobbes regard the American Indians as living in a state of nature? If he did, then clearly families could be the units in man's natural condition and it might be important that we give up the right to defend ourselves in family units or, generally, the right to defend others.[24]

One way of arguing that Hobbes could not take the Indians as an example of an actual state of nature would be to argue, as Filmer did, that they had government. If they have no government, then they have no commonwealth; and if they have no commonwealth, then they are in man's natural condition. But, we might argue, they have commonwealths and governments, even if only on a small scale: They have them in their families. Hobbes is at best equivocal about this. He says that "the beginning of all Dominion amongst Men was in Families."[25] He also says that "Cities and Kingdoms . . . are but greater Families."[26] "[A] family is a little city."[27] The greater weight of his view, though, seems to go the other way:

> A great family, if it be not part of some commonwealth, is of itself, as to the rights of sovereignty, a little monarchy: whether that family consist of a man and his children; or of a man and his servants; or of a man, and his children, and servants together: wherein the father or master is the sovereign. But yet a family is not properly a commonwealth; unless it be of that power by its own number, or by other opportunities, as not to be subdued without the hazard of war. For where a number of men are manifestly too weak to defend themselves united, every one may use his own reason in time of danger, to save his own life, either by flight, or by submission to the enemy, as he shall think best; in the same manner as a very small company of soldiers, surprised by an army,

may cast down their arms, and demand quarter, or run away, rather than be put to the sword.[28]

And again:

Nor is it the joining together of a small number of men, that gives them this security; because in small numbers, small additions on the one side or the other, make the advantage of strength so great, as is sufficient to carry the victory; and therefore gives encouragement to an invasion. The multitude sufficient to confide in for our security, is not determined by any certain number, but by comparison with the enemy we fear; and is then sufficient, when the odds of the enemy is not of so visible and conspicuous moment, to determine the event of war, as to move him to attempt.[29]

So families, it seems, will not remove us from the war of each against all, because they will not provide us with a *settled* peace. We may not actually be fighting all the time, but we will be in constant fear that our neighbors will somehow increase their numbers by enough to give them the odds over us and enable them to secure themselves against us by taking us over.[30] With the numbers so small, that will always be a practical possibility. The example of the American Indians, in short, might well have been intended by Hobbes as one of people actually living in their natural condition.

But, even if the state of nature could be populated by families, that does not seem to get us far. Giving up our right to defend others, as Hobbes says that we do in making a commonwealth,[31] might well break up the family unit and would certainly break up the family as a unit of coercive power, but all that this does is thrust us into an alternative state of nature in which each individual person is at war with all other people. Giving up the right to defend others would not get us from our natural condition into civil society but would plunge us into a worse situation than we had been in before. In a family, we can make sure that there is always somebody awake and on guard; left to myself, I must sleep sometime and am then easy prey to anybody.

This possibility of an actual state of nature is important in the context of my argument, because I want to suggest that Hobbes in fact employs a *reductio* argument about authority: He argues that authority (and the concomitant concepts of *oughts* and *duties*) is necessary to human life, and he argues this by showing that authority is what distinguishes the radical form of man's natural condition from life in civil society and by showing that the radical form of man's natural condition is an impossibility. If Hobbes thought that there were people actually living in their natural condition, then he cannot have thought that the natural condition was impossible. In fact, he makes clear that the relevant form of our natural condition is an impossible one for humans. Human life can continue only if we are out of that condition.

The solution to this problem is that Hobbes did not, in his thinking, restrict himself to philosophy in our narrow sense of that term even though his conception of philosophy was similar to ours. Hobbes was interested in what we would now call anthropology, and he was prepared to speculate about how states actually arose. This speculation is separate from his philosophical arguments about the justification of political authority. Reference to man's natural condition, or to the state of nature, crops up in both contexts because it is a movable concept: It is the concept of a relationship that can hold between different terms.[32] Three people, 1, 2, and 3, might make a contract or an alliance so that they are not in their natural condition with respect to each other. They are, therefore, able to live a life with some amenities; they are able to have around-the-clock security because the group, unlike a particular person, need not sleep and thus make itself vulnerable to attack; and so on. Three other people, I, II, and III, might make a similar arrangement among themselves. Person 1 will then be in his natural condition with respect to I, though not with respect to 2 or 3, and similar truths hold for each of the other five people. The Romans will be in their natural condition with respect to the Arabs. There is no simple answer to the question whether the natural condition obtains; what relationship one finds will depend on what terms one examines. What Hobbes thought was impossible, though, the impossibility that he used as the basis for his *reductio* argument about the justification of political authority, was the extreme natural condition holding between each person and each other person in the world.[33] Once we have some social relationships we might be able to survive, because the laws of nature can then be effective[34] and we can see them in action, but we cannot live without any social relationships at all.

This idea is suggested by what Hobbes says in his comparison of the relationships between people considered one by one, though living together in community, and between cities:

> To speak impartially, both sayings are very true: that *man to man is a kind of God*; and that *man to man is an arrant wolf*. The first is true, if we compare citizens amongst themselves; and the second, if we compare cities. In the one, there is some analogy of similitude with the Deity; to wit, justice and charity, the twin sisters of peace. But in the other, good men must defend themselves by taking to them for a sanctuary the two daughters of war, deceit and violence: that is, in plain terms, a mere brutal rapacity.[35]

Consider people as they actually are — living together in communities, genuine people and not the constructs of parts of people with which Hobbes populates the radical form of the state of nature — and we see social inclinations and relations that are exercised and set up in the context of the conventions of that society. To see an example of an actual state of nature we have to look not at relationships between particular people (relationships between people who know each other and spend much time together are usually fairly civilized) but at relationships between cities or states, which relationships have a different quality from those between neighbors in a community. Between cities we find more willingness to distrust and be defensive.[36] But this sort of relationship between cities is not the radical form of our natural condition. It might be a war of some against others, but it is not a war of each against all, and that is the war on which Hobbes bases his argument. Each city provides its citizens with enough security for the laws of nature to be effective.

This question about whether the state of nature was inhabited by individual people or by families, though, is the wrong question. It takes it that the state of nature was actual in the sense that there was a time, unlike now, when people lived in the state of nature, and that we can somehow investigate or speculate about that time and come up with answers. Those who believe this misread the state of nature and ignore the examples that Hobbes gives: That sovereign states are in a state of nature even now.

> But though there had never been any time, wherein particular men were in a condition of warre one against another; yet in all times, Kings, and Persons of Soveraigne authority, because of their Independency, are in continuall jealousies, and in the state and posture of Gladiators; having their weapons pointing, and their eyes fixed on one another; that is, their Forts, Garrisons, and Guns upon the Frontier of their Kingdomes; and continuall Spyes upon their neighbors; which is a posture of Warre. But because they uphold thereby, the Industry of their Subjects; there does not follow from it, that misery, which accompanies the Liberty of particular men.[37]

It is not that there was a state of nature that we have somehow left, with all the traditional problems about how we might have left it; there still is a state of nature in which we live as well as a civil society in which we live. The state of nature is not simply a condition of the world; it is a sort of relationship, and a relationship in which the terms can change.

Particular people might be in their natural condition with respect to each other, or families might be in that relationship to each other, or sovereign states might be in that relationship to each other. We shall never completely escape the state of nature short of world government, if then.

So speculating about the state of nature as an actual condition in our history, and asking whether it was populated by individual people or by families, is improper. But if our natural condition is something in which we still live now in some of our relationships, then there must have been something very special about the natural condition from which Hobbes drew his dramatic conclusions. We need to look for what is peculiar to the radical form of the Hobbesian natural condition. Were there not something very special about that form of our natural condition, then, if we are still in our natural condition, we could have no tale about the great advantages we have gained by leaving it or by not being in it.

The point is worthy of reiteration: Our natural condition is not something that we are simply either in or out of. We shall be in it with respect to some people or groups and are likely to be, at the same time, out of it with respect to other people or groups. (Establishing a common power over everybody in the world would see to it that there was nobody with whom I was in my natural condition, but that would be a fact about the political state of the world and not about what the natural condition of mankind is.) Asking of me on my own whether I am in my natural condition or not is like asking whether I am north of or south of — no proper question has been asked until we know what the other term is to which I might or might not stand in the relationship in question. Hobbes made this clear: Within our own communities we are not in our natural condition with respect to the other citizens, but the relationships between sovereign states, and thus between the members of those different sovereign states, are at the same time those of our natural condition. Hobbes certainly did not think of the natural condition as something that we were simply either in or out of.

The idea that the state of nature is something about which we can speculate is widespread. Kavka[38] considers the possibility that if it were wrong to attack innocent people in the state of nature, even out of defensive motives, many people might refrain from attacking them so that the violence that Hobbes associated with our natural condition would be minimized. This idea has us imagine that we take people as we know them and somehow plunge them into the radical form of our natural condition, but that is an impossibility. The "people" with whom Hobbes populates the natural condition are in reality only aspects of people; they lack the qualities of character that are the laws of nature, and part of the point of the description of the radical form of our natural condition is to show the significance in social life of those qualities of character. Those qualities of character are crucial aspects of people as we know them. If all of our political institutions were somehow destroyed at once, we would not be plunged into the radical form of the Hobbesian natural condition: We would be dealing with people who *are* inclined to keep their covenants made, and so on, and we should know that fact about a lot of those with whom we must deal immediately. We might lack a sovereign, but we should still have traditions and established expectations in terms of which we could resolve at least many of our disputes. And we should still have the laws of nature, as well as having people with whom those laws of nature could be effective. (Development of Hobbes's account of what is required if the laws of nature are to be effective, and development of his argument to show that his account of the laws of nature is a virtues theory, are necessary to complete this argument. Those developments will be presented in the next two chapters.)

I am in my natural condition with respect to somebody else if the pair of us have no common power over us and if each of us therefore submits everything to the test of his own reason. If we have a common power over us (say, our father), then we form a unit and are not in our natural condition with respect to each other; however, our unit will be in its natural condition with respect to other such units if those units and ours have no common power over them. Some sizes of units will not provide much security; we leave the state of nature by degrees, moving into larger and larger units that provide more and more security. Hobbes's speculation about anthropology seems to have been that families were the original units, and that states were formed by federations of families, made by the heads of the families, or so children are to be taught:

> They are to be taught, that originally the Father of every man was also his Soveraign Lord, with power over him of life and death; and that the Fathers of families, when by instituting a Common-wealth, they resigned that absolute Power, yet it was never intended, they should lose the honour due unto them [from the children] for their education. For to relinquish such right, was not necessary to the Institution of Soveraign Power.[39]

The forming of commonwealths, Hobbes suggests in this passage, is like the amalgamation of smaller states to form a larger one for the purposes of improving security. We are not simply either in the state of nature or not in it; there is a whole range of states of nature, with different terms to the relationships that constitute the state of nature. Smaller units do not provide much security, so people looked for larger units to improve security, that coming only with numbers, and thus states were formed. But we never can have complete security; we shall be to some degree insecure and to some degree in our natural condition.

Hobbes was clearly happy with this idea of amalgamations of smaller units, despite what he says about the relationship between social units in their natural condition with respect to each other being a war of each against all. Actual fighting was not required for that war of each against all, and Hobbes clearly thought amalgamation a better way of dealing with the situation. That is to say, where there was a choice between the two, he would clearly have regarded sovereignty by institution as morally preferable to sovereignty by acquisition. Somebody concerned about following the first law of nature and seeking peace where it could be found would try to work things out peacefully rather than try to establish sovereignty by acquisition. Hobbes seems not to have thought much about the possibility of there being a choice between the two methods of establishing sovereignty, but such cases can arise. One practical conclusion that might be drawn from what he says, for example, is that in such a situation as the arrival of Europeans in New South Wales in 1788, it would have been morally preferable for the Europeans to have tried to sort things out cooperatively with the Aborigines than for them to have simply used superior force in the years following to establish sovereignty. That remains true on Hobbes's account even if the two groups were in their natural condition with respect to each other.

But, apart from this anthropological suggestion, Hobbes has a logical point to make, an argument about what is necessarily the case, the sort of argument one would expect of somebody trying to set up a science of politics of the sort that was Hobbes's aim. The natural condition between individual people, which Hobbes says did not exist all over the world, is quite special. Where we have a social unit, such as the family, we have the relationships of a social unit, notably relationships of authority, as well as the relationships that constitute the state of nature between the social units. Where we have the natural condition holding between each particular person and each other particular person, there are only the relationships that constitute the state of nature and none of the social relationships, notably relationships of authority. We are thus cast onto our own judgment, dependent on right reason and excluded from use of an artificial right reason in the form of an arbitrator or conventional decision-procedure. In cases of disagreement, therefore, when recourse to a conventional decision-procedure is thus precluded,[40] there is nothing for it but isolation, the use of force, or submission to force, and Hobbes makes clear[41] that submission to force works as a case of consent and thus is the introduction of a conventional decision-procedure.

This extreme case, then, can be used by Hobbes to make points about the necessity and conventional nature of authority even if the extreme case never existed, and even if the extreme case never could have existed. It could never have existed as the source of civil society because such a life would cease with one generation. Even if rape, which would be a distracting and dangerous activity for all concerned in circumstances in which everybody's life was constantly threatened, explained the birth of children whose parents were constantly trying to kill each other, there could be no explanation of why the children, despite the extra inconvenience and consequent danger that they constituted in their youth, should be brought up simply to be additional enemies — one's children, in such circumstances, will be no less one's enemies than anybody else. More generally, it could not have existed as the source of civil society because there could be no way of escaping from such a condition for reasons too widely known to be worth rehearsing here and almost certainly too obvious for Hobbes not to have recognized them. And, more accurately, it could not have existed because it is not complete people who populate such a condition. Hobbes makes clear that we must be out of our natural condition or we shall perish. It is an impossible condition for continuing human life, so Hobbes has a sort of *reductio* argument to show the necessity of submission to absolute authority of a conventional kind. The alternative interpretation, that Hobbes was not using a *reductio* but was simply offering us a choice between life in civil society and the terrors of our natural condition, is one that could fit into the required slot in his theory only if he were committed to the actual existence of the radical form of our natural condition as the setting in which the choice was made. As I have shown, he is not committed to that.

The old and obvious argument — that if there can be no covenants without the sovereign's sword and there can be no sovereign without covenants, then we cannot escape our natural condition — can be turned around to tighten Hobbes's argument about the necessity of authority. That a state of nature can be actual does not mean that the relevant state of nature cannot be an impossibility and used to make this sort of point. Hobbes's original and significant move beyond where others had been in discussions of a state of nature was, clearly, going beyond speculation about anthropology or history in setting up his science and beyond actual early social units to set up the extreme case of the state of nature in which there are no social relationships. It is because of this that

Paul J. Johnson says,

> We can see that for Hobbes there can be no practical problem of how
> men get out of the state of nature. It is clear enough that if men ever
> fell into such a state, they would never get out of it, for their lives there
> would not only be poor, nasty, brutish and short. They would also be
> *solitary*. And not just in the sense that they would not live in cities, but
> more radically in that they would be isolated from one another by the
> individuality of their conceptions and speech. For while men in such
> a state might have words to use as markers for the things they wished
> to remember by themselves, there would be no community of meaning
> or reference on which the use of signs for communication could be
> founded.[42]

Johnson has seen just how different the "people" in the natural condition
would be, and just how impossible it is as a starting point for the life of
people in communities. He has seen, therefore, what is required if the
radical form of our natural condition is to be used as part of a *reductio*
argument. But he does not take it to be part of a *reductio*; he takes it to
be "an ideal limiting case as are the concepts of a pure inertial state or
a frictionless plane in physics."[43] He does not distinguish the different
sorts of state of nature in Hobbes, the anthropological and the logical,
and hence does not recognize the significance of the fact that we *are* still
in a state of nature in some of our relationships; what we are not in, and
could not be in, is the radical form of our natural condition. Johnson,
therefore, misses an important point in Hobbes's argument about the
radical form of our natural condition: The method of argument set out
in Hobbes's discussion of the circle, given that Hobbes is not claiming
that every society was *in fact* formed by the making of a contract,
requires that he produce a proof independent of any contract that social
relations between people *must* involve rights and duties of the sort for
which a contract, "though not perhaps that [method] by which it was
made, [is] yet that by which it might have been made."[44] Hobbes's
discussion of the radical form of our natural condition, an impossibility,
shows the necessity of rights and duties determined by public judgment
in the (social) lives of people.

Notes

1. *Leviathan,* chapter 13, p. 185; chapter 14, p. 189; chapter 31, p. 395; *De Cive* 5.2, p. 166.

2. *Leviathan,* chapter 14, p. 189; chapter 28, p. 354; chapter 31, p. 397; *De Cive* 1.12, p. 117.

3. *Leviathan,* chapter 13, p. 187.

4. *Leviathan,* chapter 14, p. 189; chapter 29, p. 365; *The Elements of Law* 1.19.1, p. 100.

5. *Leviathan,* chapter 5, pp. 111-112.

6. *E. W.,* vol. 1, p. 10.

7. Sheldon S. Wolin, in *Politics and Vision: Continuity and Innovation in Western Political Thought* (Boston: Little, Brown & Company, 1960), pp. 262-263, says that this form of the natural condition "was logically absurd because the right of everyone to everything contradicted the right of anyone to anything; an absolute right was at war with itself."

8. The other things will include whatever must be true of people if they are to enter conventional authority relationships. Notably, they will include the laws of nature.

9. *Leviathan,* chapter 13, p. 187.

10. *De Cive* 14.14, p. 281.

11. *De Cive* 8.1, p. 205.

12. *A Dialogue,* p. 161.

13. George Lawson, *An Examination of the Political Part of Mr. Hobbs his Leviathan* (London: Francis Tyton, 1657), p. 14.

14. Sir Robert Filmer, "Observations on Mr. Hobbes's *Leviathan*" in Peter Laslett (d.), *Patriarcha and Other Political Writings of Sir Robert Filmer* (Oxford: Basil Blackw ll, 1949), p. 241.

15. Gregory S. Kavka, *Hobbesian Moral and Political Theory* (Princeton: Princet n University Press, 1986), pp. 83-84.

16. Jean Hampton, *Hobbes and the Social Contract Tradition* (London: Cambridge University Press, 1986), pp. 7-8; see also p. 269.

17. *E. W.,* vol. 1, pp. 73-74.

18. *E. W.,* vol. 1, pp. 81-82.

19. *E. W.,* vol. 1, p. 6.

20. I shall argue in chapter 6 that Hobbes's laws of nature should be understood as a virtues theory of morality.

21. See *Leviathan,* chapter 17, p. 227, and *De Cive* 6.1, pp. 174-175.

22. *Leviathan,* chapter 26, p. 314.

23. J.W.N. Watkins, in *Hobbes's System of Ideas: A Study in the Political Significance of Philosophical Theories* (London: Hutchinson University Library, 1965), p. 163, says that "[Hobbes's] civil philosophy will set out from an account of men

as they would be if civil society were entirely dissolved" (see also p. 72). This is misleading. As I pointed out in chapter 1, Hobbes's resolutive method does not involve that sort of dismantling into physical parts (see *E. W.*, vol. 1, p. 67). Also, people in that condition would know each other, and residual trust would allow the immediate formation of at least small groups; they would retain the benefits of having been in civil society. Hobbes's question is: How much of people could have been achieved had there never been civil society? Contrary to the claim made by Michael Oakeshott (*Hobbes on Civil Association* [Oxford: Basil Blackwell, 1975], p. 28), in this case it clearly *does* make a difference whether the argument starts from art and goes to nature or starts from nature and goes to art, that is, whether the method is resolutive or compositive. Whether the people have been civilized changes how they are likely to behave.

24. *Leviathan*, chapter 28, p. 353.

25. *A Dialogue*, p. 159.

26. *Leviathan*, chapter 17, p. 224.

27. *De Cive* 6.15, p. 184n.

28. *Leviathan*, chapter 20, p. 257.

29. *Leviathan*, chapter 17, p. 224.

30. Cf. the cold war and the arms race, but also consider recent signs that it might be possible to get by without them.

31. *Leviathan*, chapter 28, p. 353.

32. Kavka (*Hobbesian Theory*, p. 88) recognizes that the natural condition is a relational concept, but he takes it (p. 89) to be *defined* in terms of the absence of a sovereign. Hobbes (for example, *Leviathan*, p. 185) rather suggests that it is a clear truth (one that he has established) that the sovereign (and only the sovereign) can keep us from the natural condition; this does not suggest that it is a matter of straightforward definition. Working out the implications of the definitions or the names is a complex task; it is what Hobbes took demonstration to be, not simply a stipulation of a definition. Man's natural condition is to be understood in terms of private judgment's holding sway (see *The Elements of Law* 1.17.10, pp. 92-93), and working out what it would be like is not a matter of speculating about how people would behave but of seeing what follows logically about the resolution of disputes and hence about relationships between people.

33. Wolin, in *Politics and Vision*, pp. 263-264, says: "Ironical overtones rule out interpreting the state of nature as belonging to the remote past, or as a strictly logical device designed to demonstrate the logical necessity of absolute sovereignty. Instead, it represented an imaginative reconstruction of a recurrent human possibility, a reconstruction intended to illumine the meaning of human events and to point out the desirable path of human actions." This might be true of one form of our natural condition, but the radical form is used as a device in an attempt to show the logical necessity of absolute sovereignty. The radical form must be used in that way if Hobbes is to produce demonstrations and not merely arguments about what is desirable, which he thought he had done in all cases except his argument about the merits of monarchy as a form of sovereignty.

34. I shall discuss in chapter 5 the conditions required for the laws of nature to be effective.

35. *De Cive*, "Epistle Dedicatory," pp. 89-90.

36. Any problem about a *real* state of nature is about the likelihood of war between groups, which is an empirical matter. In that context, Hobbes comes out as a balance of power theorist.

37. *Leviathan*, chapter 13, pp. 187-188.

38. Kavka, *Hobbesian Theory*, p. 320.

39. *Leviathan*, chapter 30, p. 382.

40. There is a lack of recourse because these "people" in their natural condition lack those important qualities that are the laws of nature: They are not willing to keep their covenants made, and so on. If they have those qualities of character in conditions in which they can be effective, they will soon sort out a conventional decision-procedure to resolve their disagreement.

41. See, for example, the discussion of sovereignty by acquisition in *Leviathan*, chapter 20, p. 252. See also the discussion of parental authority over children, dependent on the fact that the children submit themselves (*Leviathan*, chapter 20, p. 253, and chapter 17, p. 228), even though they so submit themselves because they could be destroyed if they refuse. See also *De Cive* 9.3, pp. 212-213.

42. Paul. J. Johnson, "Hobbes and the Wolf-man," in C. Walton and P. J. Johnson (eds.), *Hobbes's `Science of Natural Justice´* (Dordrecht: Martinus Nijhoff, 1987), pp. 148-149.

43. Johnson, "Hobbes and the Wolf-man," p. 149.

44. *E. W.*, vol. 1, p. 6.

5

Natural Law and Its Effectiveness

It is the continuing security of reciprocity provided by sovereignty (or, as Hobbes revealingly points out,[1] provided by prior performance on the part of the other) that is necessary for obligation, not that my fulfillment of the obligation be in my interest.[2] In a condition of mere nature I am not bound to act first despite my covenant to do so if I fear noncompliance by the other, but in civil society, where the sovereign guarantees reciprocity, I am bound to act first if the contract so requires.[3] Where reciprocity is guaranteed, by prior performance or by the availability of coercion, I am bound by my contract. Even fear of noncompliance on the part of the other is not always enough to justify the claim not to be obligated: "Except there appear some new cause of fear, either from somewhat done, or some other token of the will not to perform from the other part, it cannot be judged to be a just fear; for the cause which was not sufficient to keep him from making compact, must not suffice to authorize the breach of it, being made."[4] And again, Hobbes insists on the distinction between what generates the obligation and the threat of coercion that might be required to enforce it:

> *Contracts oblige us. To be obliged,* and *to be tied being obliged,* seems to some men to be one and the same thing; and that therefore here seems to be some distinction in words, but none indeed. More clearly therefore, I say thus: that a man is obliged by his contracts, that is, that he ought to perform for his promise sake; but that the law ties him being obliged, that is to say, it compels him to make good his promise for fear of the punishment appointed by the law.[5]

Contracts by themselves are sufficient to impose an obligation. Noncompliance on the part of the other will free me from my obligation;

reasonable fear of noncompliance will, if I am sensible, lead me not to make a contract with somebody, and if the reasonable fear of noncompliance arises after the contract has been made, then it will free me from obligation. The function of the sovereign's sword, from my point of view, is not that it makes *me* comply and thus imposes obligation on me; it is that it makes *the other party* comply if that is necessary and thus removes any fear I might have of noncompliance. The sovereign's sword acts in the same way as prior performance by the other party, as is made clear by Hobbes's putting the two things in parallel. The threat of coercion on *the other* allows the obligation to be generated *in me*. The significance of the threat of coercion on me, if threats of coercion should be necessary to make me comply, is that they give the other party a guarantee of my compliance so that he, with security of reciprocity, is also under an obligation.

Hobbes does say that the aim of any contract is the good of the contractor, because mutual transference of right is a voluntary act and the object of any voluntary act is the good of the agent.[6] One is certainly unlikely to make a contract *simply* with the aim of hurting oneself: We would expect a psychiatric explanation of such a case rather than simply asking for the agent's reasons. But what makes me happy in some cases might be the furthering of the interests of my family and friends, and that might be the good that I seek for myself. Hobbes does not preclude my finding my good in furthering the good of others even if, on the most cynical interpretation, I do so only to get myself a good reputation or something of the sort. I might see myself as being part of the family or the group of friends, so that, to an appropriate extent, I identify my interests with theirs. But what that reference to interests explains is why I make the contract in the first place, not what conditions must apply if the contract is to be binding. The issue that concerns me here is the conditions under which contracts that people make are binding.

On Hobbes's account, contracts by themselves are sufficient to impose an obligation. I can make contracts with people I have no reason to trust (I would, of course, be silly to do so if I had any alternative), but I am bound by those contracts even though I could reasonably expect to lose by them; lack of trust frees me from the obligation only if it is grounded in events after the making of the contract.[7] I can make contracts that turn out not to be in my interests: Having formed a business partnership with you, I find that the business fails and I am left with debts, for example. On Hobbes's account, that contract is binding and I have to pay my debts. So much is clear from the account he gives of duty and injustice. A right can be laid aside by renouncing it or transferring it, he says,

By TRANSFERRING; when he intendeth the benefit thereof to some certain person, or persons. And when a man hath in either manner abandoned, or granted away his Right; then is he said to be OBLIGED, or BOUND, not to hinder those, to whom such Right is granted, or abandoned, from the benefit of it: and that he *Ought*, and it is his DUTY, not to make voyd that voluntary act of his own: and that such hindrance is INJUSTICE, and INJURY, as being *Sine Jure*; the Right being before renounced, or transferred. So the *Injury*, or *Injustice*, in the controversies of the world, is somewhat like to that, which in the disputations of Scholers is called *Absurdity*. For as it is there called an Absurdity, to contradict what one maintained in the Beginning: so in the world, it is called Injustice, and Injury, voluntarily to undo that, which from the beginning he had voluntarily done.[8]

That I *made* the contract is the crucial point for Hobbes, not whether it is paying off for me or whether I can be forced to comply; I should comply for the sake of my promise.[9] Even if I set about making only contracts that I believe will benefit me personally, I cannot guarantee success; my mistake or miscalculation when I am making the contract does not, it is clear from what Hobbes says about duty and obligation, free me from its bindingness when I discover my mistake and that the contract will not benefit me. I can enter contracts that might, at some stage, require that I put my life at risk: I could take a job as a bodyguard, or join the army, or live in a country that has military conscription.[10] On Hobbes's account, those contracts are binding. What matters is *that I made the contract*, not how it pays off or whom it pays off.

All of this is clear in Hobbes's views about the bindingness of contracts, and it is not an account that sits well with the idea that Hobbes claimed that people could act only in furtherance of their own interests. The self-interest psychology attributed to him by Hampton is not, in fact, Hobbes's. That sort of psychology would require, if obligations are to be effective, that contracts could bind only when they were in the interest of the obligated party, and Hobbes clearly does not believe that contracts are binding only on that condition.

David Johnston quotes all but the last two sentences of this passage from Hobbes:

Every man by natural passion, calleth that good which pleaseth him for the present, or so far forth as he can foresee; and in like manner that which displeaseth him evil. And therefore he that foreseeth the whole way to his preservation (which is the end that every one by nature aimeth at) must call it good, and the contrary evil. And this is that good and evil, which not every man in passion calleth so, but all men by reason. And therefore the fulfilling of all these laws is good in reason; and the breaking of them evil. And so also the habit, or disposition, or intention to fulfil them good; and the neglect of them evil.[11]

Johnston goes on to say that on Hobbes's account, "Every man is egoistic by nature and aims at his own preservation, but many men mistake the means to this end."[12]

A desire to go on living when there is no particular reason to welcome death falls far short of anything we would usually recognize as egoism. That I am prepared to protect myself against unprovoked attack or that I check the soundness of the ladder before climbing it does not show that I am in any ordinary sense egoistic; it does not even mean, when there is particular reason for risking my life for the good of others or for the Royalist cause, that I shall refuse to do so. And notice, too, that, in the last sentence of the passage quoted, Hobbes is keeping before the reader the idea that the laws of nature, properly understood, "are not properly Lawes, but qualities that dispose men to peace, and to obedience."[13] That is to say, Hobbes is not concerned simply with calculating behavior — with the person who keeps his covenants made only because he will benefit from doing so or who, on receipt of benefit from another of mere grace, endeavors to see that the giver has no reasonable cause to repent of his goodwill only because he has decided that he needs a social structure and that a social structure works better if people behave that way. As motivation in any particular case, that is different from and less effective than a sense of justice or a feeling of gratitude. Hobbes is concerned with people who actually have social inclinations: with people who have the disposition to respond gratefully to those who display goodwill toward them or to do what they promised to do simply because they promised to do it.

Goodwill makes for a better world, and a better world is a better place for me to live in, but goodwill consists of my being concerned about the interests of others and not simply about my own interest in having a better world to live in. Possession of the Hobbesian virtues will, indeed, pay off for those people who have them, but they are, nevertheless, for the most part other-directed motivations and not egoistic motivations. It is because people have these social dispositions that they are able to live in civil society.[14] Much of the apparent egoism in Hobbes consists of his pointing out that the virtues he describes, though they are really non-egoistic, do pay off, with confusion introduced by the fact that his method of argument misled him at times. I shall take up this point again in chapter 7.

Hobbes had, as many have pointed out,[15] a means-end account of reason. The crucial question is: What sorts of ends do people have? And the answer is that, unlike the rational calculators of economic theory, people have quite diverse sorts of ends. Those with the Hobbesian virtues, the "qualities that dispose men to peace, and to obedience," will have various ends, and not all of those ends will be selfish or directed toward the purely private interests of the agent. If I feel grateful and exhibit gratitude when it is appropriate to do so, then that may so affect my circumstances as to make my own life better by encouraging other people to behave well toward me when they recognize my motivation and goodwill toward them. But if I act that way only in order to achieve those effects, only to further my own interests, I am being calculating; it is not gratitude that I am exhibiting, and people who recognize my motivation will react differently. A grateful person has a different sort of end, aiming at the good of the one to whom he is grateful. People have various ends, including social ends as well as selfish ends.[16] As I shall go on to explain later,[17] Hobbes's method of argument sometimes misled him in his analyses of the virtues when he set about explaining what it is about those qualities of character that makes them virtues, or how the virtues do, in fact, pay off, but it is quite clear that what does pay off (at least insofar as people recognize the motivation — we can all misconstrue it at times) is gratitude, not calculation. Some commentators have been similarly misled, and therefore they misread Hobbes as a psychological egoist. Recognizing cold calculation as somebody's motivation, we would react in a quite different way. Hobbes was aware of this, and it was genuine virtues rather than cold calculation that he was trying to analyze.

Another way of making that point, which is not entirely misleading, is to deny that Hobbes had a purely means-end idea of reason. The laws of nature are part of reason, and the laws of nature determine certain sorts of goals for us; they do not deal only with means, but also with the choice of ends.[18] People with those qualities of character will choose certain sorts of ends and will therefore accept certain sorts of facts as reasons for acting: "I should do this because I so covenanted," or "I should do this for him because he did me a good turn."

That people differ in their judgments is enough to make it necessary for them to have a conventional decision-procedure when common action is necessary. The (limited) inclination of people to pursue their own interests and insist on having their own ways makes it necessary, in practice, to have coercive powers. The (limited) social dispositions of people, the virtues that are set out by Hobbes in the laws of nature, make it possible for people to live together in communities with conventional decision-procedures and enforcement powers. As Bernard Gert has pointed out,[19] limited benevolence is not enough to do the job; it makes the solution possible, but because it is limited and because it is met by (limited) self-interest, it is not enough by itself. Hence Hobbes concentrates on the self-interest that causes the problem and on what is necessary to deal with that.

Why can the people in the radical form of their natural condition not have the laws of nature in any effective way?[20] The answer is that the laws of nature cannot be effective in the radical form of our natural condition because, though not all of morality is conventional, it all presupposes a background of convention.

Hobbes says that the laws of nature are binding *in foro interno* in the state of nature, but binding *in foro externo* only in civil society.[21] That is to say, they are binding in conscience or in the intention in man's natural condition, but binding in the act only in civil society. This might sound somewhat strange, but it is crucial to Hobbes's moral and political philosophy. He does not mean that in our natural condition we must try to be just, kind, and so on but need not succeed, whereas in civil society we must succeed. Nor does he mean that in our natural condition we must think good thoughts while screwing all and sundry to the wall. There is no strange doctrine about the relationship between intention and action involved. We need to consider the different ways in which the same qualities of character would operate in the quite different contexts of civil society and the radical form of our natural condition to understand Hobbes's point here.

What justice requires of me depends, among other things, on how other people behave — it is a notion of reciprocity. Hobbes catches this point in his claim that the laws of nature do not oblige one person if they are not followed by the other people with whom that person must deal, as when he says:

> These laws of nature, the sum whereof consisteth in forbidding us to be our own judges, and our own carvers, and in commanding us to accommodate one another; in case they should be observed by some, and not by others, would make the observers but a prey to them that should neglect them. . . . Reason therefore . . . doth dictate this law in general, *That those particular laws be so far observed, as they subject us not to any incommodity, that in our own judgment may arise, by the neglect thereof in those towards whom we observe them.*[22]

And he catches it again with his formal definition of injustice as the breach of covenant and justice as the absence of injustice:[23] I behave justly provided that I breach no covenant, and that condition is met if

I have made no covenant to breach. In our natural condition, where I shall make no covenants if I have enough sense not to trust others, any action that I might perform will, therefore, be just. Justice, that is to say, depends on a two-way arrangement between people. And if I have any reasonable suspicion that the other person will not carry out his part of the bargain (a suspicion that will not be reasonable in civil society, where we have over us a common power sufficient to enforce compliance), then the covenant is void[24] so that I do not breach it if I do not perform my part. This, too, means that no act I perform will be unjust if performed in a natural condition riddled with suspicion. On Hobbes's account, justice will not, in fact, require anything of anybody in our natural condition.

And Hobbes seems to be right about that. If I contract to pay you for mowing my lawn, and if you then fail to mow my lawn, I am under no obligation to pay you. It is not simply that it is not then in my interest to pay you; I am under no obligation to pay you. Normally, in the relatively civilized life we lead, I am, no doubt, under an obligation not to beat you about the head with a fence paling, but if you attack me with a knife, clearly intending to kill me, that obligation lapses; that is, I am no longer under any such obligation. In both cases, what you do affects the justice of what I do, turning what would otherwise have been unjust behavior from me into just behavior. Perhaps I would not be displaying injustice in allowing you to kill me, but I would certainly not be displaying injustice in fighting back to defend myself; hitting you with a fence paling, which would otherwise have been unjust, would then be allowed by justice. Justice requires no particular action of me in those circumstances; it allows any act at all. Virtues that provide no guidance in choosing between acts are completely ineffective.

It might be best to stress a point here in order to avoid a misinterpretation of what I have just said. It is specifically *justice* that allows any act at all in those circumstances: If I beat you over the head with a fence paling, then *you* can have no reasonable complaint. It does not follow that there can be no complaint, that my behavior can give others no reason to distrust me, or that what I do displays no fault at all. If you have given up your rights, then I do you no injustice, but my actions might still show vindictiveness, spite, cruelty, and any number of other faults. They will do something of this sort if I hit you with the fence paling more often or more vigorously than is necessary to repel your attack and dissuade you from future attack. And, I shall suggest later, if I deliberately provoked your attack without infringing on any of your rights, and did so in order to give me an excuse to take to you with a lump of wood, then I display a fault that is very closely related indeed to injustice.

In man's natural condition, with everybody carrying on like a yahoo, threatening my life at every opportunity, and so on, justice will not preclude any act. When everybody else carries on like that, I have no obligations; nobody else is in a position to complain no matter what I do. If I do not have any obligations, then I cannot fail to fulfill my obligations; whatever I do, I shall be behaving justly. Hobbes makes the point with some force:

> Among these laws some things there are, the omission whereof, provided it be done for peace or self-preservation, seems rather to be the fulfilling, than breach of the natural law. For he that doth all things against those that do all things, and plunders plunderers, doth equity. But on the other side, to do that which in peace is a handsome action, and becoming an honest man, is dejectedness and poorness of spirit, and a betrayal of one's self, in the time of war.[25]

If I have any sense, then I shall protect myself against all the yahoos around the place. Indeed, I shall be likely to act preemptively rather than to wait until I have been weakened by the attack of others. And that, of course, means that I shall appear to them as a threat: The goodwill that is clear to me with my internal viewpoint on myself will not be at all clear to them from my action. This goodwill cannot show itself in action except as a stupid turning over of myself to my enemies. And so the problem becomes worse, even if the others are just as goodwilled as I am. Hobbes makes clear that the laws of nature require nothing in the way of action in our natural condition when he describes the way in which they oblige us there, that is, describes what it is for them to oblige us *in foro interno*:

> For the law of nature did oblige in the state of nature; where first, because nature hath given all things to all men, nothing did properly belong to another, and therefore it was not possible to invade another's right; next, where all things were common, and therefore all carnal copulations lawful; thirdly, where was the state of war, and therefore lawful to kill; fourthly, where all things were determined by every man's own judgment, and therefore paternal respect also; lastly, where there were no public judgments, and therefore no use of bearing witness, either true or false.[26]

Justice is a virtue, but in man's natural condition it is at best an *ineffective* virtue because it does not specify any action as one that must be performed or as one that may not be performed. This is the point that Hobbes is making: Justice is a virtue, but unless there is reciprocity and security of reciprocity, it is not a virtue that can be cashed out in any acts because any act at all will be just. As a quality of character it is a Good Thing — but in an empty way because it cannot control or guide behavior. And this creates another problem in making contracts or any other arrangements with people in the radical form of the natural condition of mankind: Because the virtues are ineffective in that way, we cannot tell anything of people's characters from their behavior. Hence we cannot know which people are goodwilled or trustworthy and which are not.

Kindness is different: It is not that one cannot fail to be kind in man's natural condition, but that one cannot be kind. One can, of course, perform those acts that would be kind in a more civilized life, but that will not show one to be kind; it will show one to be a mug. (Mug, I think, is a much undervalued moral category: Somebody who is not simply a dupe, but whose good nature leads him into foolishness with or without encouragement from others.) An example might serve to make the point. A Jew who, trying to be a kind and decent person, saved Hitler from drowning in 1942 while knowing that Hitler would not consequently change his ways but would simply send more Jews, including his rescuer, to the gas chambers would lack the discrimination necessary to the genuine virtue of kindness; he would simply be a mug.[27] In man's natural condition, in the war of each against all, anybody who performs those acts that would be kind in civil society is simply and pointlessly delivering himself to his enemies. He achieves no good thereby. He may have tried to be kind, but all he has succeeded in being is a mug. By delivering himself to his enemies, he makes the victory of nastiness more likely. Genuine kindness is a virtue, but it is impossible in man's natural condition and therefore cannot guide behavior there. It can guide behavior only in a more civil society. So Hobbes's point works for virtues other than justice.[28] As the previous quotation makes clear, he thinks that it works for all of the laws of nature.

Fairly clearly, Hobbes's point works also for gratitude, the fourth law of nature. "That a man which receiveth Benefit from another of meer Grace, Endeavour that he which giveth it, have no reasonable cause to repent him of his good will"[29] is, no doubt, an excellent thing in civil society. But somebody who exercises that inclination in the radical form of our natural condition leaves himself prey to his enemies: A display of apparent goodwill could then be used, and one should expect that it would be used in those circumstances, to lower the enemy's guard and thus make him vulnerable to fatal attack. Behaving in a grateful manner in the circumstances of the radical form of our natural condition is simply leaving oneself vulnerable to attack where attack is to be expected. It amounts to no more than silly, imprudent behavior, and that is not what gratitude is. Nor is it likely to persuade people to change their ways so that we can leave the radical form of our natural condition: If the ploy of apparent goodwill is tried on one person and it works, then the fate of the person against whom it works is unlikely to encourage others to go down the same path. The laws of nature are ineffective in the radical form of our natural condition.

The same thing does not apply to vices in our natural condition.[30] Perhaps force and fraud are the two main virtues in war,[31] but that is a matter of why they are used. If I employ them, not because I must do so in order to protect myself, but simply because I enjoy inflicting hurt on other people, then I have the vice of cruelty.[32] I exhibit that vice in my behavior, even though, in the strange and unpleasant circumstances of the natural condition and the behavior that it warrants, an onlooker might find it hard to be sure of that fact. I have the vice, or at least its material elements, even if an onlooker could not tell. But understanding what makes it a vice involves considering the significance it has with respect to civil society: What makes that quality of character a vice is that it is a quality that, if widespread, would make it difficult to leave our natural condition and move into civil society.[33] Within civil society, it makes peaceful life together more difficult. But this possibility of the vice does not rescue the virtue: Mere avoidance of cruelty is not enough to constitute kindness.

We can understand cruelty as a vice in the radical form of our natural condition only by looking forward to civil society and seeing that the vice precludes our getting there. Without looking forward in that way, we can have the same point made in what might seem a contradictory manner. To take over a distinction from Julius Kovesi's *Moral Notions*,[34] the material elements of virtues and vices might be present in people in the radical form of their natural condition, but the formal elements are not available. All the bits and pieces are there, but not what gives them the significance implied in the concept. In time of war, force and fraud are the two greatest virtues, because the context in which we operate them is not our normal peaceful context and the change of context changes the consequences and importance in our lives of those qualities of character. A delight in causing pain, which makes it hard to get along with people and is a vice in civil society, has no social consequences where there is no society. It might be a good quality for me to have if it makes people wary of approaching me and thus makes it easier for me to defend myself, or it might be a bad quality for me to have if it provokes others to place my removal from the scene higher on their list of priorities than it would otherwise have been, but in the radical form of our natural condition it cannot have the social significance that vices have.

In the radical form of our natural condition, no action is ruled out. If, after you have worked hard to grow corn (which you would not own in the natural condition[35]), I take what I want and deliberately burn the rest simply so that you will have none, then that might be wanton injury on my part or it might be preemptive self-defense, weakening your position and thereby making mine stronger in relation to you. If I kill babies, that might be simply a matter of my catching future enemies while they are weak enough for me to handle them with ease. If I burn babies to death, that might be simply a display of ferocity as a warning to my enemies that they should get on with their war with each other and not trifle with me. In so harsh a world, any of these activities might in my judgment be necessary to my preservation, and certainly we could not tell in any case whether somebody was displaying the vice of cruelty as we can, in civil society, quite frequently tell from somebody's behavior whether he is cruel. The idea of cruelty could not effectively guide our actions because, though it precludes certain motivation, actions that would be explicable in civil society only on the assumption that they were motivated in the proscribed way might, in our natural condition, be explicable as cases of preemptive self-defense. So the idea of cruelty cannot, in the radical form of our natural condition, have the significance that it has in civil society. Nor can we tell from their actions whether others in that condition are goodwilled or ill willed. In less radical forms of our natural condition, more likely to be actual forms, where small social units have been formed and the relationships of the natural condition are between social units such as families, the virtues and vices can be displayed at least within the group and can therefore affect the natural-condition relationships between the social units by making alliances more or less eligible. In those conditions, observation could tell us something of the characters of those with whom we consider allying ourselves.

Consider the significance of Hobbes's first law of nature, which requires us to seek peace where it can be found. This law does seem to come out as meaning something rather like the claim that we must think good thoughts while screwing people to the wall in our natural condition. We must prefer peaceful means of resolving our disputes, even if those peaceful means are unavailable to us; we must regard the unpleasantness of our behavior as something not enjoyable, but regrettably necessary in self-defense. But, as I have pointed out, Hobbes's claims about obligation *in foro interno* and obligation *in foro*

externo also mean more than that. The point about the first law of
nature is that people do not naturally live in their natural condition; it
is natural for people, real people with the laws of nature, to find
peaceful (conventional) ways of resolving their disputes.

So in man's natural condition, the natural passions have full scope.
It is in this sense that the laws of nature are contrary to our natural
passions (and Hobbes points out that "reason is no less of the nature of
man than passion"[36]), those passions that cause trouble in our natural
condition by leading to partiality, pride, and revenge, and Hobbes makes
clear that it is to those *natural* passions that the laws of nature are
opposed;[37] they are not simply opposed to all of our passions. But we
do not live in that version of the natural condition, and one reason that
we do not is that we have, as well as those natural passions, the civilized
passions[38] or virtues set out in the laws of nature. It is these qualities
of character that make it possible for us to live together.

We can explain why they are good qualities of character to have, as
Hobbes does in explaining why they are principles that rational people
should take up, but that story of adopting them as principles is one that
fits only into a reading of Hobbes as rough history, describing as a
chronological tale how man emerged from an actual natural condition by
means of an actual contract. And anyway, as we are all well aware,
explaining ever so carefully to unfeeling people why kindness is a virtue,
a good quality of character to have, and a quality that can give one a
better life does not change them into people who care about others, even
if they do intellectually assent. The sort of agreement required about the
laws of nature is not merely a matter of intellectual assent; it is a matter
of possession of the virtues. It need not, thank heavens, be possession
of the virtues in perfection, but possession by enough people of a degree
of the virtues sufficient to make possible life together in a community.

Men are drawn to agreement on the laws of nature,[39] but, as
Hobbes says,

> All Laws, written and unwritten, have need of Interpretation. The
> unwritten Law of Nature, though it be easy to such, as without
> partiality, and passion, make use of their naturall reason, and therefore
> leaves the violaters thereof without excuse; yet considering there be
> very few, perhaps none, that in some cases are not blinded by self love,
> or some other passion, it is now become of all Laws the most obscure;
> and has consequently the greatest need of able Interpreters. The
> written Laws, if they be short, are easily mis-interpreted, from the divers
> significations of a word, or two: if long, they be more obscure from the
> diverse significations of many words: in so much as no written Law,
> delivered in few, or many words, can be well understood, without a

perfect understanding of the finall causes, for which the Law was made;
the knowledge of which finall causes is in the Legislator. To him
therefore there can not be any knot in the Law, insoluble; either by
finding out the ends, to undoe it by; or else by making what ends he
will (as *Alexander* did with his sword in the Gordian knot,) by the
Legislative power; which no other interpreter can doe.[40]

The need for interpretation of the written law reflects back on the law
of nature, because the written law is a working out and determination
of the law of nature, and it suggests that the problem there is more than
merely one of partiality. Problems of interpretation of the written law
are problems of interpretation of the law of nature, so, of course, the
same problems can arise in interpreting the laws of nature.[41] Men, no
doubt, should keep their covenants made, but, especially if odd
circumstances arise, they can differ about exactly what the covenant was:
Words can have the same differences of signification in the natural
condition as they can have in our courts of law. Perhaps I did agree to
dig your back garden for you if you helped me to paint my house, and
perhaps you have helped me to paint my house, but does that agreement
commit me to bomb disposal if it turns out, after the agreement was
made, that your house is built on an old weapons-testing range and
there are live bombs under the ground in your back garden? I know
that I should keep my covenants made, but in such a case I would
certainly want to argue about just what the covenant we had made was.
Knowing the natural law, and agreeing on the natural law, are one
thing; agreeing on how it applies in each particular case is another thing
altogether. To take a well-known appeal case: Is a flying boat a ship or
an airplane for purposes of insurance? If you live in the middle of the
country, a thousand miles from the sea and a long way from any body
of water much bigger than your bathtub, and if I contract to supply you
with an airplane, have I met the contract if I provide you with a flying
boat? Once again, the contract must be fulfilled, but there is room for
argument about what is implied in the contract and, therefore, about
what is required in order to fulfill the contract.

It is this room for disagreement that makes the sovereign necessary
as an arbitrator. His interpretation is definitive,[42] as it must be if it is
to resolve dispute, so he is also a legislator: His declaration of the law
must be taken, in practical terms, as a making of the law. (Thus does
Hobbes deny that the old debate about whether the sovereign made law
or merely declared a preexisting law made by God has any practical
point at all.[43]) We should consider just how necessary it is to have an
interpreter of the natural law.

The main problem in social life, in Hobbes's arguments, is differences in judgments. As long as each is his own judge, as in the radical form of our natural condition,[44] there will not be peace; with disagreements unresolved, there cannot be common or corporate action. There are points here that we might want to question: just how much people do or will disagree, whether they can muddle their ways through particular disagreements even if they have no guarantee that resolutions will be reached, whether they could last an hour peacefully,[45] how much each will insist on having his own way, and how much each will be prepared to compromise with others. These are really questions about the empirical assumptions that Hobbes makes, and they are important questions, but I want to come back to them through an examination of parts of Hobbes's theories, and particularly through further consideration of what he says about the laws of nature.

I have already shown that we need not have *nasty* people in their natural condition for their natural condition to be as Hobbes describes it. For one thing, the niceness of nice people could not display itself in action. For another, people who care about what is right, and not merely about their own selfish wants, will probably be just as prepared to fight for their views, and will defend themselves and others against what they see as wrongdoing.[46] No natural and universal inclination toward vicious behavior is required for Hobbes to get his story going. The circumstances of man's natural condition are sufficient to generate the behavior that we usually think of as nasty and uncivilized.

Justice involves the idea of reciprocity. The justice of your demanding $20 from me depends on the circumstances: If I had borrowed the money from you with a promise to repay at this time, then it would be unjust of me not to give you the money. But justice involves more than simply reciprocity: It also involves convention, a point nicely caught by Hobbes when he defines justice in terms of covenant.[47] The very idea of a loan depends heavily on convention. Only by reference to conventions can we distinguish loans from gifts, for example, and the whole idea of money depends on conventions that give pieces of metal and paper, or other things, their function in our lives. But that aspect of the conventionality is just as much present if the money is given as a gift as it is if the money is lent. But justice does, indeed, work like a contract: What is required of me as a result of a contract depends on the content of the particular contract, and what is required of me by justice in other cases depends on the content of particular conventions. (The conventions might be simply those that let us make special arrangements when we want to, such as the conventions that make contracting possible.) Certainly it is not the case that justice requires in any crude way that we return the same as we got: I lecture to students for the university, but I shall be most unhappy if, on payday, the university's bursar lectures me on philosophy instead of sending me a check. And the bank, unfortunately, wants more than $20 back when I borrow $20.

Conventions, even of large sorts such as a government, can create relevant relationships between us so that one can claim something of another as a right. The behavior of the other is still relevant, as determined by the convention: I must still lecture to the students, and I must still take out the loan if the relevant consequences are to follow in either case.

If you wantonly attack me, you give up your right that I not fight you. You give up that right, on Hobbes's account, because you fail to perform in your part of the contract when you attack me. Actual nonperformance is the best of all possible reasons to suspect non-performance, and the contract is thus void.[48] I may stop you from attacking me and do whatever is necessary in my own defense, but if I go beyond that and proceed to attack you then I shall be in breach of the first law of nature which requires that I seek peace where it can be found.[49]

In our natural condition, where we have no social arrangements or conventions, and where others, for whatever reason, behave abominably, justice will require nothing of me at all. A perfectly just person, in such circumstances, would rightly feel no qualms about hitting others with fence palings, because that would be merely self-defense, even if preemptive self-defense in some cases. As Hobbes puts it,

> But because most men, by reason of their perverse desire of present profit, are very unapt to observe these laws, although acknowledged by them; if perhaps some, more humble than the rest, should exercise that equity and usefulness which reason dictates, those not practising the same, surely they would not follow reason in so doing; nor would they thereby procure themselves peace, but a more certain quick destruction, and the keepers of the law become a mere prey to the breakers of it. It is not therefore to be imagined, that by nature, that is, by reason, men are obliged to the exercise of all these laws in that state of men wherein they are not practised by others.[50]

It is not simply that justice does not pay in these circumstances and that I should therefore not bother about being just; justice simply does not require any particular behavior of me. In the civil society in which we live, we can, no doubt, list things that justice requires of us. That list might be accepted as a list of what-justice-is-in-this-society, but it is not simply what justice is. Justice is what explains why those things can properly be required of me in this society, and it does so by reference to the circumstances in which we live in this society. The circumstances in our natural condition, as described by Hobbes, are vastly different, so there is no reason to believe that justice will require the same things of us there as it does here any more than there is reason to believe that in our civil society justice will require no more of parents by way of bringing up children than it does of other people. In fact, justice will require absolutely nothing of me in our natural condition. When others are simply concerned with their own well-being, have no concern for me, try to kill me whenever the opportunity arises, and so on, I owe them nothing. I may choose to sacrifice my life (if life is so nasty and brutish, it is no bad thing that it is also short), but I cannot be *required* to do so. I may properly defend myself, and I may properly defend myself by preemptive action if that seems to me to be the correct course to take.

Justice is still a virtue. One reason that it is a virtue is that it makes it possible for us to live in conditions other than our natural condition. I should try to be just, and, more than that, I should *be* just; in our natural condition, though, that does not require that I do anything in particular. The virtue, the quality of character, does not emerge as any particular action and therefore cannot be tested by behavior. It binds *in foro interno*, that is to say, justice is still a virtue and one should be just, but it does not bind *in foro externo*, that is to say, justice does not require any particular act of us to the exclusion of any other. Even if what I have said so far about activities in our natural condition is accepted, one might think that the point applied only to the occasional nice person left in unfortunate circumstances and could not apply if all the people in the natural condition were nice. The natural condition will be like that, it might be thought, only if most of the people there are nasty. But that is not so. Apart from the impossibility of telling from somebody's behavior whether they were nice or nasty, the righteous would stand up for their views, and we should consider the many occasions there would be for dispute. Property will serve as one example. In the natural condition there is no property, no *meum* and *tuum*.[51] Anybody will take, with complete propriety, anything. Accusations of injustice could be leveled at somebody only if he took something that *he* thought was not his; every man being his own judge and accused only by his own conscience,[52] nobody's else's views on the matter are relevant. And we need not imagine anybody given to such unpleasantness as taking things that, in his own opinion, were not his. We simply have no way of determining what is whose in the natural condition, whereas we have the appropriate conventions in civil society.

An example might make the point about the difficulties of interpreting actions in the absence of shared conventions. Suppose that, at the appropriate time, I turn up, point at Manhattan Island, and offer some beads to an Indian who accepts them and nods his head. Have I then (1) bought Manhattan Island; (2) leased Manhattan Island for a year; (3) bought a lifetime interest in Manhattan Island; (4) bought myself the right to go onto the island provided that I do not inconvenience anybody else; (5) given some beads to a bemused fellow who has politely agreed with what he took to be my commendation of the scenery; or (6) none of the above? In the absence of shared conventions that would limit the possibilities dramatically, no arrangement would have been entered into at all. Different civil societies have quite different property systems; we simply do not know what the property system in the natural condition is — because there is none — and that means that there is no way of determining what is whose.

Nor is it as though there were arguments that obviously settled the matter, though we sometimes speak as though there were. Sometimes we assume that there are such arguments simply because there are arguments that operate that way in *our* own civil society, but even then the arguments are much more complex than we usually give them credit for. "This land is mine," you say when I approach you in the natural condition. "My family has lived on and worked this land since 1501, so it is mine by right of first possession." I, unused to farming but used to supervising children playing on the seesaw in the park, reply with a sincere and what seems to me an obvious response: "Then the right thing for you to do is to get off, say `Thank you,´ and give somebody else a turn." In different contexts we accept each of those arguments, but in that circumstance they come into conflict. Neither of them is satisfactory as a "natural" argument to establish property rights in the natural condition. That problem is present in the natural condition, and the only way we can get around it, Hobbes says quite correctly, is to establish what our conventions are; not just yours or mine, but ours. The conventions must be shared if they are to enable us to settle our disputes. In Hobbesian terms, we need a sovereign.

Similar points apply with the other virtues, or laws of nature. Gratitude is, no doubt, a virtue; one should not make another repent of a good deed. However much I am inclined to gratitude, though, and however unwilling I am to make anybody repent of a good deed, it will not show through in my behavior in circumstances in which nobody does good deeds to anybody and everybody is constantly trying to kill me. I shall have nothing to be grateful for. The fourth law of nature, too, is binding *in foro interno* but does not require any particular action of me.

Hobbes's laws of nature generally have these escape clauses. I am required to endeavor peace only *insofar as I have hope of attaining it;*[53] to be willing to lay down my rights *when others are so too;*[54] to keep my covenants made,[55] but not, by that law of nature, to make any; to show gratitude to those who help me,[56] but not to start things off by helping them otherwise; to accommodate myself to others, but only on the consideration that I cast out of society as cumbersome thereto anybody else who does not behave in that way;[57] and so on. Being in the radical form of our natural condition brings all the escape clauses into play; the laws of nature require nothing of us when they are ineffective with other people. Hobbes's point that in our natural condition, the laws of nature bind *in foro interno* but not *in foro externo* expresses in general terms the ineffectiveness of the laws of nature in the radical form of our natural condition.

Jean Hampton, after noting Hobbes's remark that the laws of nature are immutable and eternal moral truths, asks, "But if this is so, then why don't people in the state of nature follow them, such that the state of nature becomes a state of relative peace?"[58] As should be clear, this is a question that does not need to be answered. People in the state of nature *do* follow the laws of nature; no action, in the conditions that constitute the radical form of our natural condition, could break the laws of nature. The laws of nature cannot be effective there because they require nothing of anybody in those circumstances: They require only that I seek peace insofar as others will do so too, which is not very far at all in the radical form of our natural condition, or that I not make people repent of good deeds they do me, which requires nothing of me when nobody does me any good deeds. The laws of nature cannot be effective without civil law.[59] Whole people (that is, people who fit Hobbes's full account of human nature, including the qualities of character that are the laws of nature) are social beings found in civil society, beings to whom it is natural not to live in the Hobbesian natural condition. The virtues cannot be effective without a background of community life and the conventional decision-procedures involved therein. There is no need to call on the passions to explain why the laws of nature are not obeyed in the natural condition, because there is nothing to explain.

The point might be made generally by using the idea of kindness as an example. Kindness requires judgment in a variety of ways: One must judge the recipient properly (one helps the victim, not the mugger); one must judge whether it is one's business (unless the circumstances are extraordinary, I may not interfere with my neighbors' bringing up of their child even if the child really does not want to learn Latin); and so on. That one helped somebody else is not enough to show that one was kind. Handing my attacker a knife so that he can get me out of the way and slaughter my family is not kind, it is stupid.

Kindness, put briefly, is not simply undiscriminating care for others, but a discriminating care, and it is a virtue because of the contribution that this quality of character makes to social life. That background of social life is lacking in our natural condition, so the quality of character of kindness cannot come into play. Helping anybody there is like handing a knife to my attacker: I merely help my enemy to kill me.

That point applies even in cases in which it might appear not to. If I find somebody with both arms and both legs broken, he surely cannot be a threat to me. If I put his arms and legs in splints and care for him, it is not as though he would be likely to beat me to death with the splints, even if only because he would shortsightedly be leaving himself without a benefactor and as prey to all the others. But if I return him to health and strength, he will become a threat to me again. I was taking a stupid risk in approaching him in the first place because, given the way we live in our natural condition, he may have been going in for a little sly preemptive self-defense against me and feigning injury to get my guard down. If he was not doing so, other people who saw my action would soon recognize the chance to exploit my weakness in that way. At best, I would have been severely disadvantaging myself by burdening myself with prisoners in a vicious war. (This difficulty and danger in approaching other people is one thing that makes it hard to see how people could ever have emerged from their natural condition had it ever existed all over the world.)

If I am in the natural condition and have done nothing especially (for that condition) obnoxious, there is no reason at all why I should give up my life for others who carry on like yahoos. Even genuinely kind people will not help others; kindness will be another quality of character that in those circumstances will not be exhibited in behavior. Part of Hobbes's point about our natural condition is to show what sorts of conditions are necessary if virtues are to be effective.

The virtues, then, have no chance to be effective in man's natural condition. Even people who possess all the virtues to perfection will, in those circumstances, be forced to behave in a way that seems abominably uncivilized, and they will have no way of showing in their behavior that they do possess the virtues. All of Hobbes's laws of nature have this sort of let-out, which means that they will have no effect in that condition.

Obedience to the laws of nature is unavoidable in man's natural condition and therefore makes no difference to that condition. Neither obedience to the laws of nature nor agreement on the laws of nature at a purely intellectual level would be sufficient to remove people from their natural condition if they were in its radical form, that is, if they were so related that each person was in his natural condition with respect to' each other person.   Agreement on the laws of nature, understood in that way, could not play a significant role in a theory of the state despite Hobbes's description of them as "convenient Articles of Peace, upon which men may be drawn to agreement."[60] Possession of the virtues, or obedience to the laws of nature, plays a different role: It explains why we do not live in that condition, even if it could not explain how we could get out of that condition if we were in it.[61] It explains how we are the sort of beings who make conventions, which are natural laws becoming effective in the form of civil law, and the sort of beings whose nature is to live in civil societies. And that suggests another way in which agreement might enter the story, because people who possess the virtues will agree on the importance of certain sorts of things.

Notes

1. *Leviathan*, chapter 15, p. 204.
2. Cf. Jean Hampton, *Hobbes and the Social Contract Tradition* (London: Cambridge University Press, 1986), p. 56.
3. *Leviathan*, chapter 14, p. 196.
4. *De Cive* 2.11n, p. 127.
5. *De Cive* 14.2n, p. 273.
6. *Leviathan*, chapter 14, p. 192. As Bernard Gert points out in "Hobbes and Psychological Egoism" (*Journal of the History of Ideas*, vol. XXVIII, 4, December 1967) as reprinted in Bernard H. Baumrin (ed.), *Hobbes's Leviathan: Interpretation and Criticism* (Belmont, CA: Wadsworth, 1969), p. 112, this means only that the object of a voluntary action is something that the agent desires. It does not mean that the agent cannot desire, for example, to benefit somebody else.
7. *Leviathan*, chapter 14, p. 196.
8. *Leviathan*, chapter 14, p. 191.
9. *De Cive* 14.2n, p. 273.
10. Cf. *Leviathan*, "A Review, and Conclusion", pp. 718-719.
11. *The Elements of Law* 1.17.14, pp. 93-94.
12. David Johnston, *The Rhetoric of Leviathan* (Princeton: Princeton University Press, 1986), p. 55.
13. *Leviathan*, chapter 26, p. 314.

14. I shall take up this point in greater detail later.

15. See, for example, Johnston, *Rhetoric*, pp. 54-55; Hampton, *Contract Tradition*, pp. 36-37; Gregory S. Kavka, *Hobbesian Moral and Political Theory* (Princeton: Princeton University Press, 1986), p. 339.

16. Bernard Gert, in the Introduction to *Man and Citizen* (Brighton: Harvester Press, 1978), p. 17, with an appropriate reference to *De Homine*, makes the point that the end of the virtues — what it is in terms of which they pay off insofar as they are virtues — is the preservation of people as social beings, not as atomistic, asocial individuals: "It is not the self-preservation of individual men that is the goal of morality, but of men as citizens of a state."

17. I shall do this in chapter 7.

18. Gert (*Man and Citizen*, pp. 13ff) suggests something like this interpretation of Hobbes. For the development of an argument of this sort about reason, see my *Co-operation and Human Values* (Brighton: Harvester Press, and New York: St. Martin's Press, 1981), especially chapter 6.

19. Gert, *Man and Citizen*, p. 9.

20. Cf. Howard Warrender, *The Political Philosophy of Hobbes: His Theory of Obligation* (Oxford: Clarendon Press, 1957), p. 103: "The dilemma of man outside civil society is constituted, in Hobbes's theory, not by the absence of a moral law, but by the total or partial frustration of that law."

21. *Leviathan*, chapter 15, p. 215. Jean Hampton's discussion of this (*Contract Tradition*, pp. 89ff) sets about solving a problem that disappears when one recognizes that Hobbes is writing about virtues and what is required to make them effective. Hobbes's concern is with what is required if the virtues are to be effective, and not primarily with whether moral terms are *meaningless* outside civil society (cf. Kavka, *Hobbesian Theory*, p. 350).

22. *The Elements of Law* 1.17.10, pp. 92-93. See also *The Elements of Law* 1.19.1, p. 100, and *De Cive* 3.27, pp. 148-149. Chapters 13-15 of *Leviathan* make clear that Hobbes's account of the laws of nature is concerned with people living together in a community and that they appear as part of his theory of civil society.

23. *Leviathan*, chapter 15, p. 202.

24. *Leviathan*, chapter 14, p. 196.

25. *De Cive* 3.27, p. 149n.

26. *De Cive* 14.9, p. 278.

27. Rescuers of disabled enemy soldiers in wartime *might* be mugs, but they need not be. The point of war is to return to a decent, peaceful world, and the rescuer's action might help in making the postwar world a more decent one. More to the immediate point, the rescued soldier would normally be held captive and not be capable of constituting any further threat.

28. For a literary work on this sort of point, see Bertolt Brecht's *The Good Person of Szechwan*, translated by John Willett (London: Eyre Methuen, 1965).

29. *Leviathan*, chapter 15, p. 209.

30. Hobbes makes clear that action from sheer nastiness is contrary to the law of nature even in our natural condition: *De Cive* 3.27, p. 149n.

31. *Leviathan*, chapter 13, p. 188.

32. Cf. Warrender, *Political Philosophy of Hobbes*, p. 62.

33. Cf. *Leviathan*, chapter 13, p. 188. The laws of nature enable us to live otherwise than in our natural condition, and I am taking the vices as simply acting in the opposite direction. This line is suggested by Hobbes's remark (*Leviathan*, chapter 15, p. 209) that somebody lacking the virtue of complaisance "for the stubbornness of his Passions . . . is to be left, or cast out of Society, as cumbersome thereunto." I have developed a similar line of argument about virtues and vices in *Co-operation and Human Values*.

34. Julius Kovesi, *Moral Notions* (London: Routledge and Kegan Paul, 1967), *passim*.

35. *Leviathan*, chapter 13, p. 188.

36. *The Elements of Law* 1.15.1, p. 75.

37. *Leviathan*, chapter 17, p. 223.

38. Because passions are the beginning of voluntary actions (*The Elements of Law* 1.5.14, p. 23), the laws of nature cannot be effective unless they partake, at least in part, of the nature of passions. And Hobbes makes clear (*Leviathan*, chapter 13, p. 188) that the way out of our natural condition (that is, the laws of nature) consists "partly in the Passions, partly in [our] Reason."

39. *Leviathan*, chapter 13, p. 188.

40. *Leviathan*, chapter 26, p. 322.

41. I shall take up this point again in the next chapter.

42. *Leviathan*, chapter 26, p. 322.

43. The sovereign plays both roles, which amount to the same thing: It is by the sovereign's authority that the law, including the law of nature, is interpreted and thus declared (*Leviathan*, chapter 26, pp. 322-333); it is the sovereign power alone that can make the law of nature binding (*Leviathan*, chapter 26, p. 314); and the sovereign alone makes civil law (*Leviathan*, chapter 42, p. 593), thus definitively declaring the law of nature. Cf. *Leviathan*, chapter 42, p. 586: "And the Makers of Civill Laws, are not onely Declarers, but also Makers of the justice, and injustice of actions."

44. *Leviathan*, chapter 14, p. 189. See also, for example, *The Elements of Law* 1.19.1, p. 100.

45. Cf. *The Elements of Law* 2.5.2, p. 139.

46. Psychological egoism is not needed to explain willingness to fight in our natural condition. Nor, *contra* Kavka (*Hobbesian Theory*, p. 98), is predominant egoism. People do not fight only because they are nasty or self-interested, but sometimes because they want to achieve truth, justice, and various national ways of life. In our natural condition, private people are the judges of good and evil (*Leviathan*, chapter 29, p. 365).

47. *Leviathan*, chapter 15, p. 202.

48. *Leviathan*, chapter 14, p. 196.

49. *Leviathan*, chapter 14, p. 190.

50. *De Cive* 3.27, pp. 148-149.

51. *Leviathan*, chapter 13, p. 188.

52. *Leviathan*, chapter 27, p. 337, and chapter 15, p. 215.

53. *Leviathan*, chapter 14, p. 190.

54. *Leviathan*, chapter 14, p. 190.

55. *Leviathan,* chapter 15, p. 201.
56. *Leviathan,* chapter 15, p. 209.
57. *Leviathan,* chapter 15, p. 209.
58. Hampton, *Contract Tradition,* p. 63.
59. *Leviathan,* chapter 26, p. 314.
60. *Leviathan,* chapter 13, p. 188.

61. So Hampton (*Contract Tradition,* p. 22) is mistaken in her remark that "for purposes of his political argument, [Hobbes] might as well be a psychological egoist . . . because other-interested desires play no role whatsoever in his justification or explanation of the formation of the state." This comes from her not recognizing that the laws of nature are qualities of character and part of Hobbes's account of human nature, which, in turn, comes from a failure to see that Hobbes has followed the method of argument set out in his account of the circle.

6

Agreement on the Laws of Nature

Agreement on the laws of nature, we saw, is not sufficient to remove people from the radical form of their natural condition because obedience to them is not sufficient to do the job; hence Hobbes's point that the laws of nature bind only *in foro interno* in our natural condition.[1] The natural law and the civil law contain each other, and the natural law needs the civil law if it is to be effective.[2] One of the roles of the sovereign is to interpret the laws of nature and make them effective.[3] This is not, on the face of it, simply a problem of needing an arbitrator to deal with disagreement, because agreement does not avoid the need for the sovereign in conditions in which the laws of nature do not bind *in foro externo*, but it is worth considering just which laws of nature need to be interpreted by the sovereign and what contribution his interpretation makes. Laws must be interpreted, and it is the earthly interpretation of the laws that governs what we do if the laws are to be effective. Even if God's laws are there, we cannot look to God to interpret them for the same reason as we cannot make a covenant with God;[4] the legislator has to fit into that slot and must interpret the laws.

Hobbes's claim that the laws of nature are easy to see, so that violators have no excuse for their violation, warrants some comment. In civil society the natural law appears as the civil law; Hobbes is quite clear that it is possible to misunderstand the civil law, even if he would not be prepared to recognize ignorance of the law as an excuse.[5] The natural law that there is no excuse for misunderstanding is the natural law in our natural condition, and the reason that violators cannot use misunderstanding of the natural law as an excuse for their misbehavior there is that all that was required of them was sincerity. Each is his own judge, and nobody else's judgment takes precedence over mine until the sovereign is set up. In those circumstances, the only way that I can violate a law of nature is by doing something that I regard as a breach of the natural law. If I regarded it as a breach of the natural law when I did it, then I can hardly plead that I would not have broken the law had I not misunderstood it in such a way as to make me think that I was not breaking it: "The Civill Law ceasing, Crimes cease; for there being no other law remaining, but that of Nature, there is no place for Accusation; every man being his own Judge, and accused onely by his own Conscience, and cleared by the Uprightnesse of his own Intention. When therefore his Intention is Right, his fact is no Sinne: if otherwise, his fact is Sinne; but not Crime."[6]

The sense in which the laws are clear to all not blinded by passion, so that nobody can plead misunderstanding of them as an excuse, therefore, is not a sense that excludes disagreements about them between people. The point about the clarity of the laws of nature in the natural condition is not that they are so clear that everybody gets them right, and it is certainly not that right reason declares itself inescapably to all.[7] The point is that each person cannot help but get them right in the judgment of the only judge who matters in his case, that is, himself. One can, not surprisingly, see a version of this in present-day relationships between sovereign states: One can see both the intrusion of self-interest and passions concerning such things as national honor into judgments of propriety, and also quite serious and honest disagreements about what are just ways of treating people, what constitutes a threat, and so on.

Adding the services of the sovereign to interpret the laws of nature seems not to help very much, especially when we bear in mind the problems, noted earlier, about our retention of inalienable rights. The first law of nature, for example, that we seek peace and follow it insofar as others will do so too,[8] is completely undermined by our retention of the right to self-defense. The sovereign will prohibit those actions that he sees as threats and will thus, no doubt, reduce the threats with which I see myself as faced, but that is a different point. Leaving the matter in his hands would make my right to self-defense derisory. Insofar as I retain the right to defend myself and am myself the judge of its application, the sovereign is precluded from helping me by interpreting this law of nature. If I am the judge of when I am threatened, then I am the judge of the extent to which others are seeking peace and, therefore, of what is required of me by this law of nature. The sovereign, by giving and enforcing his interpretation of this law, might reduce the number of threats facing me, but that is merely a help to me; as far as I am concerned, I am the primary interpreter of this law of nature. Were it not so, I should have alienated my inalienable right to self-defense.

The second law of nature, "That a man be willing, when others are so too, as farre-forth, as for Peace, and defense of himselfe he shall think it necessary, to lay down this right to all things; and be contented with so much liberty against other men, as he would allow other men against himselfe,"[9] seems quite clearly to rule out interpretation by the sovereign because of the words that Hobbes has chosen.   It is an instruction to the particular person, couched in terms of what *he* shall think necessary. The stage in the chronological story at which this law of nature appears seems to rule out its being interpreted by the sovereign, because it is a central part of the story of how the sovereign is set up, and the fact that Hobbes immediately proceeds to a discussion of the inalienable right to self-defense stresses again that what is involved in this law is a matter for the private judgment of the particular person. Leaving this law to be interpreted by the sovereign would ruin the whole story.

The oddity of handing over interpretation of the second law of nature to the sovereign might be removed by going on to the third law of nature, "That men performe their Covenants made,"[10] which is a working out in more detail of what is involved in the second; Hobbes says that it follows from the second,[11] so it is, presumably, to be read as an explication of the second. With the third law of nature we do need interpretation, or, at least, we need application to the particular case. The sovereign, as arbitrator, will be needed to interpret contracts and rule on such matters as what is a reasonable time within which to finish a house one has contracted to build, or whether a flying boat is a ship or a plane for purposes of an insurance contract. Here private judgment will not do the job, so the sovereign's role is necessary.

But this is an extended notion of interpretation. The parties to the dispute know perfectly well what the third law of nature requires: It requires that they keep their covenants made, and that means doing what they covenanted to do. Their problem is not about the interpretation of the law of nature, but about the interpretation of the particular covenant. In this extended sense, though, the sovereign is needed here as an interpreter.

To leave to the sovereign the interpretation of the fourth law of nature, about gratitude,[12] would turn this law into a version of the third law of nature and would therein distort the notion of gratitude. Some of Hobbes's later laws of nature are concerned simply with what people are to do as a matter of applying the earlier laws, but others, of which this is one, are more concerned with the usefulness of certain sorts of motivation. People who are inclined to respond to somebody else's doing something for them by returning the good turn are less likely to respond to the other's completing his side of a contract by forgetting all about the arrangement because they have got what they wanted. Such people are more readily trusted when contracts are to be made, and they are generally easier to get along with in communal life.[13] To have the sovereign determine what gratitude required and coerce somebody to the performance, though, is treating a situation in which gratitude is appropriate as one that is contractual. That would be unfair, because it means that I can force contracts on you (you want A but would rather keep B; I can get B from you simply by providing you with A even if you did not want the deal), and it loses the point of gratitude. Gratitude, as distinct from the simple payment of debts, is significant at least partly because it displays something about my attitude to the person to whom I am grateful. It is, in that way, specifically a display of private judgment and takes its significance from that fact, so it cannot be turned over to the sovereign's interpretation. Having the sovereign interpret this law of nature is no help at all.

If we are to have communal life, then it is required that people have the virtues to the requisite degree, but that is quite different from saying that all the virtues deal with requirement. Gratitude, for example, does not. As far as Hobbes is concerned, justice is the virtue that deals specifically with requirement. That is because justice goes with law, and law goes with requirement. Laws bind us as part of our covenant,[14] and breach of covenant is the sum of injustice.[15] Where there is no law, we are at liberty to decide on our actions for ourselves.[16] Where there is no law, we are subject only to our own consciences and are not required to meet any outside standard. The laws of nature impose no such objective requirement on us until legislation enforcing them is passed, and, given Hobbes's account of justice, they then become matters of justice.

Justice is concerned with requirement, but not all aspects of morality are. If I borrow money, then I am under an obligation, or a debt of justice, to repay it; I can be required to repay it, and I do a wrong (theft) to the person from whom I borrowed it if I do not repay it. I cannot, in the same way, be required to give money to a beggar on the street. The point is not simply one about legal requirement; it is a moral point. If I borrow money from somebody, then that fact puts him (specifically) in a special relationship to me (specifically) so that I do him a wrong if I fail to repay the money even if the debt is one for which I could not be taken to court. That somebody is a beggar does not put him in that relationship to me. If it did, all beggars would be in that relationship to me, and I cannot be required to give money to all beggars (including those in the poorer countries of the world) because I haven't that much money even if I gave only one cent to each beggar. Charity goes beyond requirement. If nobody gives the beggar any money, we cannot (unless there is a special story) pick out the particular person who should have done so. If I owe the beggar money, I can be picked out as the particular person who should have done so. Debt picks out a particular person as obligated in a way in which simply the fact that somebody needs help does not.

This is not, of course, the phenomenology of charity or the other virtues in a decent person. A decent person will be concerned about behaving decently, not simply doing what is required of him and not a jot more. The demands of charity, courage, and so on might well be just as insistent for such a person as the demands of justice, but what is at issue here is not simply how the matter seems to the agent. The issue is one of what *objective* requirements there are, or what can properly be *demanded* by somebody else as of right rather than supplicated for.

We talk of a debt of gratitude, but that is not the same thing as a debt proper. Suppose I owe the grocer a debt proper, or debt of justice, of $100. He can require payment. If he, seeing that I am on hard times and because he is a kindhearted fellow, forgives me the debt, then I owe him a debt of gratitude. If a debt of gratitude is the same thing as a debt proper, I have gained nothing; if I have gained nothing, why should I be grateful? Gratitude makes sense only if it is a different sort of relationship from requirement or obligation. Gratitude is appropriate if somebody provides me with something for my good that he could not have been required to provide. If the grocer simply gives me what I have paid for and can therefore require, or if he provides me with goods so that I shall pay him, then gratitude is not appropriate. If somebody does something for me in order to get me to do something for him, and if I accept what he does for me even though I know what he expects in return, then I probably have a debt of justice to him and owe him what he wanted in return, but gratitude is not appropriate: He·did what he did in order to get something for himself. If gratitude is appropriate, then there is nothing that the other person can require of me, but I shall be a nasty person if I do not help him in any way that I can when he needs help.

Another way in which the difference between the two comes out is in the different ways of working out how much return is appropriate. If I owe the grocer a debt proper of $100, I repay it when I give him $100. Giving him more would simply be odd; it would not be a matter of repaying my debt. Repayment of debt is precise in that sort of way. Debts of gratitude, though, are not precise in that sort of way: I do not repay a debt of gratitude to the grocer by later giving him exactly the

$100 he forgave me in debt if he then needs $500 and I have that amount readily available. The debt of gratitude would there be met by giving him the $500, as it might be met in other circumstances by simply giving him a cheerful smile and a bit of encouragement. Requirement goes with precision about the actions required; gratitude goes with simply trying to help in whatever way possible as a response to goodwill.

Gratitude is importantly a matter of the motivation of the agent. Actions can be required of somebody, but motivation cannot.[17] One might perform the actions of a grateful person for different reasons, such as to make it more likely that help will be forthcoming again next time, but then the actions are prudent rather than expressive of gratitude. Justice is done, even if I do not display a sense of justice or the virtue of justice, if my debts are paid no matter what the motivation. I need not even pay them myself. That sharp distinction between the virtue and the action makes possible the sort of requirement that justice involves and that Hobbes saw that it involves. The sovereign's sword can make me keep my contract, thus giving the relevant security to those among whom I live. The requirement is of the *action*, not of the motivation. The sovereign's sword can also make me refrain from insulting other people[18] and obey the other laws of nature, but only insofar as the sovereign legislates to make them part of civil law, thus part of the contract, and consequently, given Hobbes's account, matters of justice.

Gratitude, then, is not a matter of requirement as just actions are a matter of requirement, even if peaceable and comfortable life in a community requires that a reasonable number of people have a reasonable inclination to feel gratitude when gratitude is appropriate. The actions that would be appropriate to gratitude can be required only insofar as the sovereign makes them matters of justice by legislating. Gratitude is Hobbes's fourth law of nature,[19] and he clearly does mean gratitude as a matter of motivation. Gregory S. Kavka's claim[20] that Hobbes's moral theory deals only with requirement and not at all with the morality of actions that are desirable though not required is false. There is a clear Hobbesian distinction between requirements pertaining to justice and the nonrequired nature of charity. John Aubrey's anecdote[21] of Hobbes's giving sixpence to an old man in the Strand is relevant here because, in response to Jasper Mayne's rhetorical question about Hobbes's motives, we are given the famous rejoinder about other available motivations. Aubrey clearly thought that compassion was the motive, but Hobbes seemed more intent on pointing out that charity is not strictly required. And at the end of *The Elements of Law*,[22] Hobbes makes the point that charity is not required by civil law but is enjoined by divine or moral law. Insofar as the sovereign has made no definitive interpretation of those laws, they remain matters for the conscience of the agent rather than matters of objective requirement.

Exactly the same sort of point applies to the fifth law of nature, "That every man strive to accommodate himselfe to the rest."[23] The law can require various sorts of behavior from me, and it does so under the third law of nature, which requires that I keep my covenants made. Breach of the civil law is unjust, according to Hobbes, not merely stubborn or unsociable: "The difference between Injustice, and Iniquity is this; that Injustice is the Transgression of a Statute-Law, and Iniquity the Transgression of the Law of Reason."[24] Hence the sovereign, being legally unlimited, can do iniquity but not injustice.[25] The requirement that I be sociable, as distinct from the requirements that (in accordance with the third law of nature) I behave in the ways required by the laws, is not one requiring the sovereign's interpretation. It requires more than merely obedience to the law, which is what the sovereign's command would make it, even though my obedience to the law is one thing that is likely to follow from my adherence to this law of nature. Again, it is, in fact, a remark about useful motivations. Somebody sociable is easier to get along with, more likely to enter cooperative relationships with others, and so on. As a point about motivation, it depends on the fact that the relevant behavior reflects the private judgment of the agent and not merely the conformity of his behavior to law.

This general point can be raised over and over again: What the sovereign imposes on us is law, and law derives its binding force from the third law of nature. Of the other eighteen laws of nature listed by Hobbes in his first approach to the subject (he says that there are others that it would not be pertinent to list in the context of his endeavor, and he lists another in "A Review, and Conclusion"), some, those from the eleventh on with the exception of the sixteenth,[26] appear to be directed to the sovereign and will, therefore, be interpreted by him. That is because they are concerned with the sorts of laws and social arrangements that should be made: The sovereign should practice equity; he should therefore see that those things that cannot be divided are used in common, that those things that can neither be divided nor used in common are allocated by lot, and as a specific version of that he should apply the principle of primogeniture; he should see that mediators have free passage; he should allow no man to be his own judge, or to judge a case in which he has natural cause to partiality; and, if there is nothing else to distinguish the cases in a dispute about fact, he should decide on the basis of the numbers of witnesses on each side.[27]

The third law of nature, and the second insofar as the third is an explication of it, require that the sovereign interpret or apply them to resolve disputes about what the contracts require. That is to say, the sovereign must prohibit theft, murder, adultery, and other such things, but he must also define what theft, murder, and adultery are.[28]

The fourth to the tenth laws of nature, inclusive, are about motivation and do not require interpretation by the sovereign. They deal, roughly, with gratitude, complaisance, mercy, and humility:

> That a man which receiveth Benefit from another of meer Grace, Endeavour that he which giveth it, have no reasonable cause to repent him of his good will. . . . That every man strive to accommodate himselfe to the rest. . . . That upon caution of the Future time, a man ought to pardon the offences past of them that repenting, desire it. . . . That in Revenges . . . Men look not at the greatnesse of the evill past, but the greatnesse of the good to follow. . . . That no man by deed, word, countenance, or gesture, declare Hatred, or Contempt of another. . . . That every man acknowledge other for his Equall by Nature. . . . That at the entrance into conditions of Peace, no man require to reserve to himselfe any Right, which he is not content should be reserved to every one of the rest.[29]

These might reasonably be summed up as requiring gratitude, complaisance, mercy, humility, and perhaps a certain sort of temperance, along with some workings out of what those virtues require in the way of types of action. That is, they deal with the sorts of ends that people set for themselves and the sorts of motivations that they tend to have. In fact, those laws of nature do not allow interpretation by the sovereign: For the sovereign to interpret them and enforce them on us brings the relevant behavior under the third law, not under any from the fourth to the tenth. And the sovereign's interpretation is not much help with the first and second laws of nature — those laws of nature must already be in operation for the sovereign to hold any sway.

So introducing the sovereign as interpreter of the laws of nature is not a great deal of joy to us. Nevertheless, there is another way in which agreement with respect to the laws of nature might feature in the argument. The laws of nature are the second part of Hobbes's account of human nature and are his account of the virtues.[30] People who share the virtues will agree in their judgments of the importance of certain sorts of things. If we can remove the errors in Hobbes's account of the virtues, errors into which he was led by his model of explanation, then perhaps we can escape the problem about the relationship between private and public judgment in Hobbes's moral theory, and perhaps we can avoid some of the more worrying parts of his theory of sovereignty.

What makes government *necessary* on Hobbes's account is, as we have seen, that people (in civil society as much as in their natural condition) differ in their judgments and in their wants and therefore need a second-order decision-procedure if they are to have common action and peaceful life in a community rather than a war of each against all. As we have also seen, people need not be nasty, self-interested beings for those problems to arise, but, quite plainly as a matter of common experience, at least most people have at least some self-interest, and that exacerbates the problem. On the other hand, were people entirely self-interested, government and life in a community would be impossible. What makes government and peaceful life together *possible* is that people are not entirely self-interested but also have other, more sociable, inclinations: They have those qualities of character that Hobbes sets out in the laws of nature. What makes peaceful life together possible is that enough people have, to the requisite degree, an inclination to keep their covenants made, to fit in with other people, to respond pleasantly when others help them, and so on: They have the laws of nature, which is to say, "Morall Vertues, as Justice, Equity, and all habits of the mind that conduce to Peace, and Charity."[31] "The Lawes of Nature, which consist in Equity, Justice, Gratitude, and other morall Vertues on these depending, in the condition of meer Nature . . . are not properly Lawes, but qualities that dispose men to peace, and to obedience."[32] Because these qualities of character are part of human nature, government and life in community are possible.

Hobbes's account of the laws of nature, as he makes perfectly clear, is his moral philosophy: "The way, or means of Peace, which . . . are, *Justice, Gratitude, Modesty, Equity, Mercy,* and the rest of the Laws of Nature, are good; that is to say, *Morall Vertues;* and their contrarie *Vices,* Evill. Now the science of Vertue and Vice, is Morall Philosophie; and therfore the true Doctrine of the Lawes of Nature, is the true Morall Philosophie."[33] And his moral philosophy is a philosophy of virtues and vices, of qualities of character rather than of rules, as is made clear in the passages quoted at the end of the preceding paragraph and when he goes on to complain that moral philosophers had hitherto misunderstood morality, writing as though it were the quantity of a gift, not the cause, that made the gift liberal.[34] It is further clear when he distinguishes justice in men, that being a matter of the conformity of their manners to reason, from justice in actions, and says that "the Injustice of Manners, is the disposition, or aptitude to do Injurie; and is Injustice before it proceed to Act; and without supposing any individuall person injured."[35] It is also clear when he says: "That which gives to humane Actions the relish of Justice, is a certain Noblenesse or Gallantnesse of courage, (rarely found,) by which a man scorns to be beholding for the contentment of his life, to fraud, or breach of promise. This Justice of the Manners, is that which is meant, where Justice is called a Vertue; and Injustice a Vice."[36] Hobbes was struck by and insistent on his departure from Aristotelianism, but we need not be surprised if some traces of Aristotle remain in Hobbes's moral philosophy.

It might seem to be surprising that Hobbes should be read as a virtues theorist, and it is easy to see how he might be read otherwise. Indeed, I shall try to show that at least some of the excesses of his doctrine of sovereignty come from his having misconstrued himself in a crucial respect, treating his model of explanation as though it were more than a model, and therein making mistaken assumptions about the nature of the virtues. Seeing how that model works with his moral theory and how easily it is misconstrued helps in understanding how Hobbes reached the position he did reach.

If Hobbes is using, as I have argued that he is, the method of explanation exemplified in the discussion of the circle,[37] then the story of people being drawn to agreement on laws of nature should not be taken literally. Indeed, there could be no sense in taking that story literally if the stories of the contract and the radical form of the natural condition of mankind are not taken literally: People can be out of their natural condition as a result of deliberation on the question of which set of rules pays off only if they were not in civil society when they deliberated. I have already argued that just as we have never left our natural condition in some of its forms, so we were never in it in the relevant radical form. And I have argued also that the contract must be taken as merely a model, as suggested by the discussion of the circle. If my arguments on those points have been correct, then reading Hobbes's moral theory as one of people's making economically rational choices among possible sets of rules is mistaken. In the case of Hobbes's moral theory, the model is mistaken, and that mistake, especially when allied with Hobbes's positivistic insistence on guarantees of outcomes,[38] makes it impossible for him to remove the tension between private and public judgment. Hence Hobbes builds up the authority of the sovereign in an attempt to overcome that tension.

Hobbes makes perfectly clear in overt statements that his moral theory is one of virtues and vices: "*Justice, Gratitude, Modesty, Equity, Mercy,* and the rest of the Laws of Nature, are . . . Morall Vertues; and their contrarie *Vices;*[39] . . . Morall Vertues, as Justice, Equity, and all habits of the mind that conduce to Peace, and Charity;[40] . . . the Lawes of Nature, which consist in Equity, Justice, Gratitude, and other morall Vertues on these depending;"[41] and so on.

And it is clear that he means what he says. He is not, when he refers to moral virtues, referring simply to behavior in accordance with the appropriate rules. Whether one offends against the laws of nature is not simply a matter of whether one's actions fail to accord with the rule; the natural law is distinguished from the civil law in that it commands the will.[42] Hence, what determines whether I have broken the laws of nature is not whether my actions are in accordance with them but whether I *believe* that my actions are in accordance with them.[43] That is, the laws of nature are concerned more with the person than with the person's overt actions. And Hobbes does mean that: The laws of nature, he says, are habits of mind.[44] They are qualities of people that make it possible for them to live a peaceful life together.[45]

His disagreement with Aristotle, then, is not a wholesale disagreement. Both of them hold virtues theories of morality; Hobbes differs from Aristotle on what it is for something to be a virtue:

> But because men cannot put off this same irrational appetite, whereby they greedily prefer the present good (to which, by strict consequence, many unforeseen evils do adhere) before the future; it happens, that though all men do agree in the commendation of the foresaid virtues, yet they disagree still concerning their nature, to wit, in what each of them doth consist. For as oft as another's good action displeaseth any man, that action hath the name given of some neighbouring vice; likewise the bad actions which please them, are ever entituled to some virtue. Whence it comes to pass that the same action is praised by these, and called virtue, and dispraised by those, and termed vice. Neither is there as yet any remedy found by philosophers in this matter. For since they could not observe the goodness of actions to consist in this, that it was in order to peace, and the evil in this, that it related to discord, they built a moral philosophy wholly estranged from the moral law, and unconstant to itself. For they would have the nature of virtues seated in a certain kind of mediocrity between two extremes, and the vices in the extremes themselves, which is apparently false.[46]

Plain men disagree in their moral judgments, and they are able to continue to do so with no remedy available as long as morality has not been made a science.[47] And it has not been made a science because people got the formal element wrong or provided no formal element at all.[48] As far as Hobbes is concerned, the formal element — the guiding principle in determining which qualities of character are virtues — is their contribution to peaceful coexistence. *That* is what Aristotle got wrong: A virtues theory of morality is still what we need, but a properly scientific virtues theory such as that of Hobbes, not the mistaken and unscientific theory of Aristotle. What it is that Hobbes picks on in his attack on Aristotle is itself sufficient to tell us what sort of theory Hobbes is setting up as an alternative.

And a virtues theory is what we should expect if we read Hobbes as employing the model of explanation set out in the discussion of the circle. What is a method of making one of these qualities of character that would guarantee that this is what we would turn out with, even if it is not the method by which the thing in fact came into being? In the case of civil society, the answer is one about people calculating and contracting to make a state. In the case of the laws of nature, it is one of people working out what line they must follow in order to achieve peace, which is the formal element of the virtues. What is being explained is the significance of various qualities of character. As will emerge, the explanation is not a good one: At least some of the virtues could *not* be produced by such calculation. Hobbes makes the mistake of treating the formal element of the virtues as though it were one of the material elements.

Once we see that Hobbes was a virtues theorist, it is much easier to make sense of claims he makes, such as that the laws of nature in man's natural condition bind *in foro interno* but not *in foro externo*.[49] The laws bind in the intention but not in the act, perhaps, but just what that amounts to is far from clear until one sees that Hobbes is a virtues theorist and is pointing out that virtues can be effective and can guide action only in conditions of reasonable security. One can see how the laws of nature can play the important role they do play in Hobbes's political theory despite the fact that people did not live in the radical form of their natural condition and did not emerge from it into civil society by contracting.

And this interpretation of Hobbes fits the actual laws that he lists, covering justice, gratitude, loyalty, humility, mercy, and so on, and working out in some of them what sort of behavior the various virtues will require in certain circumstances or in the general circumstances of civil society. Somebody would not show much of the virtue of justice if he avoided breaking faith only by never making covenants, entering conventional relations involving obligation, or making faith in any other way, even though he would then have satisfied Hobbes's third law of nature that men should keep their covenants made.[50] Such a person would not have failed to keep any covenants, but more is required for the virtue of justice: It is necessary also that one follow the first law of nature by seeking peace where it can be found,[51] that is, that one be prepared to enter conventional relationships involving obligation with others who are prepared to enter such relationships.[52] Hobbes, indeed, sets that out as the basic law of nature from which all the others follow, or as the fundamental virtue, and we should read it as part of all the others. As particular expressions of the way the virtue of justice works out, we then get the claims that mediators must be allowed safe conduct,[53] that we be prepared to submit disputes to an arbitrator,[54] that nobody be judge in his own case,[55] and so on.

The laws of nature that appear early in the list set out the virtues, and the later ones set out implications of those virtues for policy. And we know how to draw out those implications because Hobbes has made clear what the formal element of the laws of nature is: The laws of nature are what we must have in order to have a life of relative peace and security rather than the war and ceaseless strife of the radical form of man's natural condition. The laws of nature are articles of peace.[56] They are qualities fitting man for peace.[57] Hence, the reason that we must be prepared to submit our disputes to an arbitrator is that we shall, otherwise, be as far from peace as ever.[58] It is the recognition of this formal element, a principle for generating a list of the virtues or laws of nature rather than leaving the listing as a matter of whatever strikes the particular person as appropriate, that constitutes, for Hobbes, the creation of a science of morality.

Hobbes's moral theory is not simply a virtues theory, and his moral theory is inextricably intertwined with his political theory. Had Hobbes heard of the doctrine of the autonomy of ethics, he would have rejected it. Hobbes's virtues theory requires a rights theory to make it work: As we have already seen, the virtues are ineffective without a suitable background of security that, Hobbes has argued,[59] requires the idea of rights and obligations. Were the virtues not present in a sufficient degree in a great enough number of people, it would be impossible to set up the system of rights. That can be created only if people are prepared to seek peace and, in that, to keep their covenants made, submit their disputes to arbitration, and so on. But if the possession of those virtues is not expressed in the setting up of a system of rights and obligations through a conventional second-order decision-procedure, specifically a sovereign on Hobbes's claim, then the virtues will not be able to flourish. It is natural, on Hobbes's account, for people to form conventions of the sort that is necessary.

Natural and civil law are also necessarily close together because the law of nature, in order to become effective and to become a law, is declared in the civil law: "Theft, murder, adultery, and all injuries, are forbid by the laws of nature; but what is to be called *theft*, what *murder*, what *adultery*, what *injury* in a citizen, this is not to be determined by

the natural, but by the civil law."[60] Natural law requires that we keep
our covenants made, but the detail of what we do depends on the
content of the covenant. And whether I made a covenant or a
nonbinding statement of what I might do tomorrow is itself something
that will be determined by the civil law. Property and ownership will be
determined by the civil law. And in all of this, most obviously in the
case of property, the civil law is giving us rights with respect to what
other people must do or refrain from doing and duties with respect to
what we must do or refrain from doing. So Hobbes's moral theory ties
together rights theory and virtues theory with a closeness that seems
nowadays commonly to be regarded as impossible.

The laws of nature are set out by Hobbes initially as those rules on
which people must agree if they are to leave the radically individualist
natural condition. Because that radically individualist natural condition
never did exist and never could have existed, the laws of nature must
actually be taken as something else: as those qualities of character that
enable us to live as we do and *not* in the radically individualist natural
condition. Because we are, by and large, like this, we do not live like
that, and *only* because we are like this can we not live like that.[61] The
story about people agreeing to follow the laws of nature as a matter of
policy emerges because of Hobbes's use of the compositive method, the
application to moral philosophy of the type of explanation set out in his
account of the circle. Reading what he says about the laws of nature in
the light of that passage about the circle and what he says there about
appropriate forms of explanation makes clear that his references to
virtues and vices are not accidental or careless but are precise references
to the sort of moral philosophy that he is setting out.

His account of what makes a rule a law of nature, or what makes a
quality of character a virtue, is very strongly in terms of what is required
for people to live a peaceful life on this earth. Virtues do have a point
in terms of which they are understood to be virtues: Hardness is a
virtue in a diamond because of the uses to which diamonds are put, for
example, or in terms of the point of our picking out diamonds from
other stones. In the same way, we must have some idea of a point in
terms of which moral virtues are understood to be virtues. On Hobbes's
account, that point is very much an earthly one rather than a heavenly
one. It might at least appear, therefore, that he was begging questions
against some of his opponents in the seventeenth century, who were not
prepared to accept that the point of human life was merely earthly. The
point of life, they might have thought, was to glorify God, or to make
one's way to heaven, or they might have thought that life had any
number of other theological points beyond the merely mundane.

George Lawson, for example, took up this point: "To think that the sole or principal Cause of the constitution of a civil State is the consent of men, or that it aims at no further end than peace and plenty, is too mean a conceit of so noble an effect."[62] He then developed the point further:

> For there is a twofold end of regular civil Government; The first is Peace; The second is Godliness and Honesty, to which Peace is subordinate. . . . Government is for Peace, and Peace for Godliness, and the performance of our duty towards God, and Honesty: That we may live soberly and justly towards men. . . . These earthly States are erected, and subordinated to an higher end than peace and plenty here on earth: they should be so ordered as to prepare men for eternity: otherwise *Regna* are but *latrocinia*, a den of thieves and a combination of devils.[63]

And Lawson went on to give a definition of a commonwealth: "It is a community of men orderly subjected to a supreme power civil, that they may live peaceably in all godliness and honesty."[64] Lawson is quite clear that the end of civil government and communal human life is not merely peace, but that it is much more complex and includes at least godliness. Such a difference about the ends in view is likely to lead to disagreement about what qualities are virtues, so this point needs to be taken up if the argument about virtues is to be a tight one.

Hobbes does take up this point, whether or not he does so satisfactorily. The idea of a virtue requires some point if it is to make sense: A virtue is a power, and a power is a power to do something. We look for some qualities in an automobile and for others in a fishing rod: What the item is *for* will determine what is a virtue in it. One way in which people can differ about what is a virtue, therefore, is by differing about the end in view. Hobbes is quite clear that the end in view with the laws of nature is earthly, human good: "They come to be praised, as the meanes of peaceable, sociable, and comfortable living."[65] He does recognize, though, that others might disagree with him on the matter:

> There be some that proceed further; and will not have the Law of Nature, to be those Rules which conduce to the preservation of mans life on earth; but to the attaining of an eternall felicity after death; to which they think the breach of Covenant may conduce; and consequently be just and reasonable; (such are they that think it a work of merit to kill, or depose, or rebell against, the Soveraigne Power constituted over them by their own consent.) But because there is no naturall knowledge of mans estate after death; much less of the reward

that is then to be given to breach of Faith; but onely a beliefe grounded upon other mens saying, that they know it supernaturally, or that they know those, that knew them, that knew others, that knew it supernaturally; Breach of Faith cannot be called a Precept of Reason, or Nature.[66]

There are several arguments that Hobbes might be calling on here, though none of them seems to be really satisfactory. One of them is that all laws need interpretation.[67] Hobbes uses this argument primarily to show that the laws of nature require the civil law, that is, that they require interpretation by the sovereign, if they are to be effective. Knowledge of God's purposes would be required if God's purposes were to guide our actions or to determine our judgments of what is a virtue and what a vice. We have no such "natural" knowledge, and, in fact, people differ about God's purposes and requirements about all sorts of things, so reference to God's purposes will not be effective as a *social* control of action. People will be acting on different rules, not on the same rules, so common action will disintegrate. The problem could be escaped if a definitive interpretation of God's purposes and law were to be recognized, but such a definitive interpreter would be the sovereign. The practical implications of the idea that heavenly considerations determined the laws of nature would then be equivalent to Hobbes's view: In either case, right and wrong is determined by the sovereign's say-so, and what determines whether he keeps together a community over which to be sovereign is very much a matter of earthly considerations. Lawson suggests that his own views are like that: "Therefore in all States of the world, they who have possession of the Sword do rule, let the Title be what it will; neither can it be otherwise. And no Prince can rule, when God hath taken away his Sword."[68] The suggestion here is, clearly, that possession of the sword is the appropriate sign of God's blessing on a ruler, though the flavor is quite different from Hobbes's insofar as it suggests that anybody can try the ruler to see if God would prefer a change. Successful revolutionaries, or successful organizers of coups d'état, would be God's agents of change.

This suggestion that the two things would come to the same in practical terms is not a sufficient reply for Hobbes, and only partly because of the role left for revolutionaries in Lawson's theory. Part of the point comes out if the sovereign holds the requisite religious beliefs: He might then prohibit or require all sorts of things and, provided that they included those things necessary for communal life, would keep his job. Having the sovereign determine what is to be done does not mean that what is to be done will be determined by considerations of what is necessary or helpful to earthly life with other people. More important, even though the sovereign determines what is to be done, he does not determine what is a virtue and what is not: That job, according to Hobbes, is done by Hobbes's arguments about the laws of nature. (Hobbes says that his claims about the moral virtues and their necessity for procuring and maintaining peace, though not presently law, are evident truth.[69]) The argument of the preceding paragraph does not really meet the claim that the point at which virtues are aimed is a heavenly point rather than an earthly point; it certainly does not refute that claim.

The point about our lack of "natural" knowledge of God's purposes might be that the points about earthly good are the only ones on which agreement can be guaranteed, but that claim certainly will not do: People do differ about earthly good when they argue about the values of different ways of living. More important, the point about our lack of "natural" knowledge of God's purposes does not meet the claim of the person who agrees about what is for our earthly good but goes on to say that it is our heavenly good, not our earthly good, that matters, and that it is therefore our heavenly good that determines which qualities of character are human virtues. I might be able to agree with you about what makes a fishing rod a good fishing rod, but that agreement will not help if what I want is an automobile for traveling across difficult terrain. My different purpose means that I am looking for something with quite different virtues from those in the fishing rod.

And if what constituted our earthly good were all that we could agree on, that would be merely a matter of fact. People *might* be able to agree on religious matters, too. Perhaps it seems unlikely that everybody in the world could agree on all religious matters and in the interpretation of what they take to be God's law, but we can surely imagine the possibility of communities, especially comparatively small religious communities, where there was such agreement. It might be, if the differences were very great, that such a community could not live as a part, or at least as an ordinary part, of a wider community that had a different idea of the point of the virtues, for want of sufficient agreement where common action was necessary, but that does not show the impossibility of such a community itself.

Hobbes says that covenants with God are impossible without special revelation[70] and that one can make a covenant with the author by mediation of the actor only if the authority is shown.[71] Putting these two conditions together with the denial that we can have "natural" knowledge of God's purposes might look as though it gave us an argument to show that only considerations of earthly good can fill the role of determining virtues. But revelation to another does not wear its authority on its face (hence Hobbes's acerbic reference to "those that knew them, that knew others, that knew it supernaturally"[72]), so we have no way of telling what was true revelation from what was mere seeming. Similarly, we cannot know what really shows that God has granted authority to a private citizen to speak for him. But this will not do the job for Hobbes, either; it does not meet the point. Whether we can make covenants with God, either directly or by means of an intermediary, affects whether we can be unjust to God and whether God can be unjust to us, but it does not meet the point of whether what matters, what determines which qualities of character are virtues and which are vices, is earthly good or heavenly good. Most of the laws of nature do not require that one have covenanted with the other person specifically on the matter at hand; they might require a background of cooperation and reciprocity, but the only virtue that has its action *determined* by covenant is justice.

One might develop further arguments by asking why we should consider God's wishes if they are at variance with our view of our own good, though the argument seems not to go far: Heaven, presumably, would be part of our good, though not part of our earthly good. Hobbes certainly does not follow the line of querying the propriety of obedience to God. His idea seems to be that given that we have no certain knowledge of God's purposes or of the existence of heaven or hell or of their nature if they do exist, the sensible thing is to work in terms of our earthly good. This is not a position likely to move those who think that they do have certain knowledge of such things, either through their own revelation or through their recognition of the authority of some people to speak for God.

So Hobbes seems not to have made good his point about why virtues should be determined by considerations of earthly good rather than heavenly good. On the other hand, I am not sure that he really needs to. He might, perhaps, quite satisfactorily (at least in our own less religious age) sit on the claim that his laws of nature set out qualities of character that are virtues in the context of our earthly life with other people, and that such virtues are important in the circumstances in which we live, that is, the circumstances of earthly life with other people. Certainly, qualities of character that are virtues in terms of some other point cannot make it *more* likely that we shall have peaceful human coexistence, and they might make it less likely.

If we take morality to be a sort of limitation on human behavior growing out of human interaction, then Hobbes will have given an account of moral virtues. Other people might give an account of religious virtues. Or one could simply let the term "moral" go, because there is really nothing magic about the word itself, and say that Hobbes has given an account of human social virtues. That would be a sufficiently impressive achievement. And whatever their theological beliefs might be, people can live together peacefully on this earth only if they are, by and large, as Hobbes claimed in his account of the laws of nature that they must be.[73] Even if earthly social life does have the point of preparing us for eternal life in heaven and should develop in us the qualities appropriate to eternal life in heaven, it will have much time to do so only if people also have the earthly virtues set out by Hobbes in the laws of nature. If life is solitary, poor, nasty, brutish, and short, then none of us will develop many qualities at all. What makes social life possible is necessary to the achievement of any point that social life might have.

A community might have more than one point, and different communities might have different points. One community might have as one of its points the glorification of itself; another might have as one of its points the glorification of God. Whatever disparate points different continuing communities might have, each must have at least the point of making it possible for its members to live peacefully together. Hobbes has, therefore, given an account of qualities of character that are virtues for people in any community, even if different communities might recognize other qualities of character as virtues as well.[74]

Hobbes says things about the laws of nature other than that they are qualities fitting men for peace. He says that they are laws of God, or, more accurately, that they are laws when considered as God's commands.[75] That is because law is the command of him who has authority to command,[76] and God has that authority.[77] This does not tie them especially to God; the laws of nature are also laws, properly understood, when they are commanded by the sovereign: "The Lawes of Nature . . . are not properly Lawes, but qualities that dispose men to peace, and to obedience. When a Common-wealth is once settled, then are they actually Lawes, and not before; as being then the commands of the Common-wealth; and therefore also Civill Lawes."[78] The only difference between God and the sovereign in this respect is in the source of the authority to command: God's authority rests on his might,[79] whereas the sovereign's authority rests on consent.[80] And the sovereign takes some secular precedence, because it is by his authority that the scriptures are obeyed as the word of God.[81]

This legislation is an important part of making the laws of nature effective, as we have already seen: People can, and do, differ about what justice requires in the given circumstances, or about what actions

courage could lead one to perform.[82] Those disagreements sometimes
need to be resolved if we are to live peacefully together, and the
sovereign must define for us what murder, theft, and adultery are.[83]
This is a point about what is required if the virtues are to be effective;
it goes no way toward showing that Hobbes's moral theory is a theory
of externally imposed rules rather than a theory of virtues. What status
they have in that way depends on the backing that they are given: They
are divine laws insofar as the rational backing for the choice of action is
God's command, and they are virtues insofar as they provide the
backing for the action by being qualities that make people suitable for
peaceful life together.

Secular law is important for Hobbes's moral theory in several ways.
It resolves disputes and defines murder and other wrongdoing for us,
but it also provides guarantees of reciprocity for us by filling in the gaps
in people's characters. Hobbes had a low opinion of people in general;
he was not unaware that people, by and large, do not possess the virtues
to perfection, and he knew how successful wrongdoing could provoke
even the virtuous.[84] Those who give in readily to temptation, who
look more to the short term than to the long term and see that particular
wrongful acts can be profitable, need to be given a reason not to perform
those acts. It is quite obvious that particular people on particular
occasions can get away undetected with particular wrongful acts;
nevertheless, as a general policy this will not work, or cannot be a
reasonable policy, because it makes one dependent on the mistakes of
others for one's place in social life,[85] and such dependence is not
reasonable. But some people, blinded by their passions or reasoning
falsely, are likely to offend against the laws of nature, and they must be
stopped if they are not to provoke the others who will content
themselves with equality. That men content themselves with equality is,
Hobbes says, the foundation of the natural law,[86] but those who are
otherwise prepared to content themselves with equality and thus follow
the natural law can be provoked to untoward behavior if the others are
allowed to get away with their wrongdoing.[87] Legislating to stop them
is part of setting up the conditions that allow the virtues to be effective.

Hobbes makes clear that it is not a matter of calculating in every
particular case what is in my interest. Not every virtuous act will pay off
for the agent. What pays off is the virtue, a habit (a term taking over all
the obscurity it has in translations of Aristotle, and partly explained here
by reference to the idea of a disposition) that means that I do not
calculate in that manner in every particular case:

The fulfilling of all these laws is good in reason; and the breaking of them evil. And so also the habit, or disposition, or intention to fulfil them good; and the neglect of them evil. And from hence cometh that distinction of *malum poenae,* and *malum culpae;* for *malum poenae* is any pain or molestation of mind whatsoever; but *malum culpae* is that action which is contrary to reason and the law of nature; as also the habit of doing according to these and other laws of nature that tend to our preservation is that called VIRTUE; and the habit of doing the contrary, VICE. As for example, justice is that habit by which we stand to covenants, injustice the contrary vice; equity that habit by which we allow equality of nature, arrogance the contrary vice; gratitude the habit whereby we requite the benefit and trust of others, ingratitude the contrary vice; temperance the habit by which we abstain from all things that tend to our destruction, intemperance the contrary vice; prudence, the same with virtue in general.[88]

It is the disposition that is at issue, not simply the particular act. Those who concentrate on the particular act each time are likely to go wrong.

Possession of the virtues does pay off for us. It pays off for us, as Hobbes has shown, by making it possible for us to live peaceful lives together instead of being in the radical form of our natural condition. Hence Hobbes says that the laws of nature are also principles of prudence: Prudence, he says, is the same with virtue in general. Standing back from the hurly-burly and looking at Hobbes's account of the virtues, we can see that the virtues pay even if particular virtuous actions sometimes do not. But to stress that paying off in the wrong way, treating it as part of the calculation that precedes the performance of a virtuous act and not simply in terms of the quite different issue of what it is that determines which qualities of character are virtues, leads to a misconstruction of the virtues.[89] Hobbes made that misconstruction because of the way he applied to the virtues the model of explanation that he set out in his account of the circle.[90] He took as his model for the virtues self-interested people calculating the policies that would best serve their long-term interests. He misled himself in doing that; the model will not do and does not fit what Hobbes says when he writes straightforwardly about the laws of nature as virtues. Calculation and reasoning do not play quite that role in the virtues. If Hobbes had not made that mistake, I shall go on to show, he need not have committed himself to the more excessive elements in his theory of sovereignty and especially to the idea that public judgment must have unfettered rule over private judgment.

Notes

1. *Leviathan*, chapter 15, p. 215.
2. *Leviathan*, chapter 26, p. 314, for both claims.
3. *Leviathan*, chapter 26, p. 314.
4. *Leviathan*, chapter 14, p. 197, and chapter 18, p. 230; *De Cive* 2.12, p. 128; *The Elements of Law* 1.15.11, p. 79.
5. *Leviathan*, chapter 26, p. 321, places on citizens the onus of finding out the law concerning their proposed actions if they have any doubt about the legality of what they are considering doing; chapter 27, p. 338, says that ignorance of the law excuses them only if the law was not sufficiently declared. Hobbes stresses elsewhere (chapter 26, p. 317; chapter 27, p. 345) that the law must be made known if it is to be obligatory and that a law's not being sufficiently made known is therefore an excuse for disobedience in the case of a civil law. The requirement that the law be promulgated does not apply to the law of nature (*Leviathan*, chapter 26, p. 319).
6. *Leviathan*, chapter 27, p. 337. See also *The Elements of Law* 1.17.13, p. 93.
7. *Leviathan*, chapter 5, pp. 111-112.
8. *Leviathan*, chapter 14, p. 190.
9. *Leviathan*, chapter 14, p. 190.
10. *Leviathan*, chapter 15, p. 201.
11. *Leviathan*, chapter 15, p. 201: "From that law of Nature, by which we are obliged to transferre to another, such Rights, as being retained, hinder the peace of Mankind, there followeth a Third."
12. *Leviathan*, chapter 15, p. 209: "That a man which receiveth Benefit from another of meer Grace, Endeavour that he which giveth it, have no reasonable cause to repent him of his good will."
13. Howard Warrender, in *The Political Philosophy of Hobbes: His Theory of Obligation* (Oxford: Clarendon Press, 1957), pp. 51-52, points out that this law of nature catches those who take protection from the sovereign but have not covenanted. As gratitude, it does not require their obedience as covenant-based justice would, but certainly people of this sort will be less likely to seek the advantages offered by a community and reject all responsibility on the ground that they have not consented.
14. See, for example, *De Cive* 14.2, pp. 273-274.
15. *Leviathan*, chapter 15, p. 202.
16. See, for example, *Leviathan*, chapter 21, pp. 264 and 271.
17. Cf. *The Elements of Law* 2.6.3, p. 146: "No human law is intended to oblige the conscience of a man, but the actions only."
18. Cf. Hobbes's eighth law of nature, which is against contumely: *Leviathan*, chapter 15, pp. 210-211.
19. *Leviathan*, chapter 15, p. 209.

20. Gregory S. Kavka, *Hobbesian Moral and Political Theory* (Princeton: Princeton University Press, 1986), pp. 437-438. David Gauthier, in *The Logic of Leviathan* (Oxford: Oxford University Press, 1969), pp. 56-57, recognizes that gratitude is not a matter of obligation in Hobbes's theory.

21. Oliver Lawson Dick, ed., *Aubrey's Brief Lives* (Harmondsworth: Pelican, 1949), p. 317.

22. *The Elements of Law* 2.10.5, p. 187.

23. *Leviathan*, chapter 15, p. 209.

24. *A Dialogue*, p. 70.

25. *Leviathan*, chapter 18, p. 232.

26. The sixteenth law of nature requires that people be prepared to submit their disputes to arbitration: *Leviathan*, chapter 15, p. 213.

27. *Leviathan*, chapter 15, pp. 212-214.

28. *De Cive* 6.16, p. 185.

29. *Leviathan*, chapter 15, pp. 209-211.

30. Warrender, in *The Political Philosophy of Hobbes*, p. 99, says, "If it is denied that God plays an essential role in Hobbes's doctrine, the laws of nature in the State of Nature cannot be taken to be more than prudential maxims for those who desire their own preservation." I am suggesting another possibility. Gauthier, in *The Logic of Leviathan*, notes on p. 69 a passage in which Hobbes says that the laws of nature, properly understood, are qualities fitting man for peace, but his formal account of the laws of nature (p. 36) overlooks that claim.

31. *Leviathan*, chapter 26, p. 330.

32. *Leviathan*, chapter 26, p. 314.

33. *Leviathan*, chapter 15, p. 216.

34. *Leviathan*, chapter 15, p. 216.

35. *Leviathan*, chapter 15, p. 207.

36. *Leviathan*, chapter 15, p. 207.

37. *E. W.*, vol. 1, p. 6.

38. Hobbes's argument often seems to depend on the idea that Murphy's Law is true and that what can go wrong will go wrong. Hence he builds guarantees into his political theory. The function of a sovereign sometimes seems to be not simply to resolve the disputes that come up, but to make sure that no dispute could possibly come up that could not be resolved. If there should be some area in which disputes did not arise, because of widespread agreement or for some other reason, then the fact that the sovereign's power was limited with respect to that area seems to have no consequences for the effectiveness of the sovereignty; the requirement that his or her power be unlimited seems to depend logically on the idea that the sovereign must be capable of dealing with all possible disputes, and not simply with all actual disputes. In fact, it seems clear that people can often muddle through for quite a while. The liveliest election I can remember in Australia was the federal election of 1975, which was especially interesting because it centered around the discovery of obscurities in the Constitution and surrounding conventions. Despite those obscurities, Australia had managed to muddle through seventy-five years of federation, and it managed to muddle through that dispute, too.

39. *Leviathan*, chapter 15, p. 216.

40. *Leviathan*, chapter 26, p. 330.

41. *Leviathan*, chapter 26, p. 314.

42. *De Cive* 14.14, p. 281.

43. *The Elements of Law* 1.12.13, p. 93, and *Leviathan*, chapter 27, p. 337.

44. *Leviathan*, chapter 26, p. 330.

45. *Leviathan*, chapter 26, p. 314.

46. *De Cive* 3.32, p. 151.

47. Cf. *De Cive* 2.1, pp. 121-122. See also *The Elements of Law* 1.15.1, pp. 74-75.

48. On formal and material elements of concepts, see Julius Kovesi, *Moral Notions* (London: Routledge and Kegan Paul, 1967), *passim*.

49. See, for example, *Leviathan*, chapter 15, p. 215.

50. *Leviathan*, chapter 15, p. 201.

51. See *Leviathan*, chapter 14, p. 190.

52. Cf. the discussion of the raw form of injustice in my *Liberty, Community, and Justice* (Totowa: Rowman and Littlefield, 1987), *passim*.

53. *Leviathan*, chapter 15, p. 213.

54. *Leviathan*, chapter 15, p. 213.

55. *Leviathan*, chapter 15, p. 213.

56. *Leviathan*, chapter 13, p. 188.

57. *Leviathan*, chapter 26, p. 314.

58. *Leviathan*, chapter 15, p. 213.

59. Starting with the right reason argument, *Leviathan*, chapter 5, pp. 111-112.

60. *De Cive* 6.16, p. 185. See also *De Cive* 14.10, p. 278.

61. So one function of Hobbes's account of the natural condition of mankind might be taken as providing a *reductio* argument to show that what the laws of nature set out are, indeed, virtues in people.

62. George Lawson, *An Examination of the Political Part of Mr. Hobbs his Leviathan* (London: Francis Tyton, 1657), p. 1.

63. Lawson, *Examination*, pp. 11-12.

64. Lawson, *Examination*, p. 5.

65. *Leviathan*, chapter 15, p. 216.

66. *Leviathan*, chapter 15, pp. 205-206.

67. *Leviathan*, chapter 26, p. 322.

68. Lawson, *Examination*, p. 9.

69. *Leviathan*, chapter 26, p. 323.

70. *Leviathan*, chapter 14, p. 197.

71. *Leviathan*, chapter 16, p. 219.

72. *Leviathan*, chapter 15, p. 206.

73. Here one can see Hobbes's account of man's natural condition playing a role in a form of *reductio* argument to show that the qualities set out in the laws of nature must be virtues for social life.

74. The possibility that there might be this distinction between sorts of virtues seems to be overlooked in Alasdair MacIntyre, *After Virtue* (Notre Dame, IN: University of Notre Dame Press, 1981), *passim*.

75. *Leviathan*, chapter 15, p. 217, and elsewhere.

76. *De Cive* 3.33, p. 152; *The Elements of Law* 1.17.12, p. 93.

77. *Leviathan*, chapter 15, p. 217.

78. *Leviathan*, chapter 26, p. 314.

79. *Leviathan*, chapter 31, p. 397.

80. *Leviathan*, chapter 40, p. 502.

81. *Leviathan*, chapter 33, p. 426.

82. *Leviathan*, chapter 26, p. 314.

83. *De Cive* 6.16, p. 185.

84. See, for example, *The Elements of Law* 1.14.5, p. 71.

85. Cf. Hobbes's discussion of the Fool in *Leviathan*, chapter 15, pp. 203-205.

86. *The Elements of Law* 1.18.6, p. 96.

87. *The Elements of Law* 1.14.5, p. 71.

88. *The Elements of Law* 1.17.14, p. 94.

89. In an important way, I am agreeing with Gauthier, *The Logic of Leviathan*, p. 28: "There are two opposed lines of argument which have been pursued by Hobbes's scholars, and which are equally mistaken. The first is to claim, correctly, that Hobbes's *conclusions* have a prudential basis, and to infer, incorrectly, that Hobbes's conclusions are prudential. The second is to claim, correctly, that Hobbes's concepts are not prudential, and to infer, incorrectly, that Hobbes's conclusions do not have a prudential basis."

90. *E. W.*, vol. 1, p. 6.

7

The Virtues and the Roles of Reason

The tension between public and private judgment remains a problem throughout Hobbes's moral and political theory. His main argument is for the necessity of giving primacy to public judgment if there is to be communal life, but the necessity of recognizing a natural right to self-preservation as something carried over from the natural condition of mankind works away insidiously at that argument, undermining the theory of sovereignty that Hobbes has tried to show is necessary. The solution to this problem is that, given Hobbes's virtues theory of morality and not the misconstruction that he made of it because of the application of his model of explanation, public judgment need not play quite the role that he assigns to it.

If we are to live together peacefully, we must be able to agree on an arbitrator or on some sort of decision-procedure to resolve our disputes. According to Hobbes, this always means deciding on people to do the job: The idea that we can have rule by law, as opposed to rule by men, he says, is an absurdity taken over from Aristotle's politics.[1] Enforcement is needed, and so is interpretation and application of the law;[2] the arbitrator must give a decision, or somebody must have the job of ruling on whether the coin came down heads or came down tails. The procedure by itself is not enough; there must be an authoritative declaration of what its decision was. We cannot dispense with people when it comes to resolving disputes, because they are necessary to operate the procedures and to interpret their outcomes. And, Hobbes says, it must always be the same person or body of people, subject to no legal limitations.

As a matter of fact, we can usually manage to agree between ourselves whether a coin came down heads or came down tails. As a result, given enough honesty and decency, we can use this agreement to get by with the rule of law and not feel the need of any sovereign to operate the decision-procedure for us. At least, we can do the job for ourselves without setting up a legally unlimited ruler who decides his sphere of authority, has taxing powers and the right to raise an army, and cannot be replaced when the next dispute comes up. We might disagree about how to take it if the coin lands on an uneven surface and comes to rest leaning on something instead of lying flat, but even if the coin, by chance, lands on its edge and stays there, we can usually sort out what to do. In such a case we should probably agree to toss again.

Every now and again there might (and there does, even in international relations) appear on the scene a thug who agrees to toss a coin and sticks righteously to the procedure if it goes his way, but who, when it does not go his way, will, with a dangerous smile, look at a coin lying perfectly flat and clearly showing tails and announce firmly that it shows heads. If one has sufficient force, one can get away with ignoring the procedure in at least some cases. Less powerful dishonest people, as soon as they see that the coin has gone against them, might snatch up the coin with a cry of "Bad luck!" and give a false report of which side was showing before the other person has a chance to see it. We all know that such cases occur, but they are sufficiently unusual to be upsetting when they occur in our everyday lives. We expect better of people; enough of them have enough of the virtues described by Hobbes for us to get by otherwise in most cases and to feel let down when we cannot. We have enough security for the virtues to be effective, and enough people have them to a sufficient degree. Were that not the case, we should be in the radical form of our natural condition.

Nor is that simply a point about our everyday, matter-of-fact expectations. We should expect exactly the same of the people Hobbes described. Somebody who is inclined to abide by the first law of nature will not willfully misinterpret the toss of the coin, though he might if he thought that the other person had deliberately tossed a coin that had a tail on either side or in some other way tried to get away with an unfair procedure. People who are inclined to seek peace and follow it insofar as others will do so too will not be inclined to cheat about the outcome of the tossing of the coin unless they have reason to believe that the other person has cheated in the choice of the coin. To put the point very bluntly, the people for whom Hobbes thinks that government is possible will not be quite as much in need of government as he suggests. Private judgments will often manage to do the job; they need not always be subject to public judgment.

Jean Hampton[3] develops an argument that, though I believe its dependence on claims about self-interest to be mistaken, applies interestingly here. Hobbes makes clear that the arbitrator or sovereign need not be a monarch, but any "committee" form of sovereignty leaves a problem: There must be rules to determine what constitutes a decision of the committee (What is a quorum? Is an absolute majority required? Is a two-thirds majority required?). And those rules, like all other rules on Hobbes's account, stand in need of definitive interpretation and application. Giving the job of interpretation and application to a committee leaves us with the original problem again. *Either* an absolute monarch is needed *or* the committee can get by without undue problems about interpretation and application simply because its members manage to agree on all important cases.

If the latter is possible, then there must be an alternative to the Hobbesian sovereign, and, if Hobbes thought that his sovereign need not be a monarch, it must be an alternative that he could have countenanced. A decision-procedure will be necessary for the committee, but the issue is whether the decision-procedure needs to be a Hobbesian sovereign. In recognizing the possibility of a sovereign other than an absolute monarch, Hobbes clearly recognized the possibility that people could, in fact, get by, at least in small, face-to-face groups in which each was known to each of the others. How big such groups can be, what steps must be taken to maintain peace when they become too big, and whether such groups would be large enough to have security against external attack are questions of fact rather than questions of logic. Hobbes, even if he did not realize it, did contemplate the alternative:

> A *Commonwealth* is said to be *Instituted,* when a *Multitude* of men do Agree, and *Covenant, every one, with every one,* that to whatsoever *Man,* or *Assembly of Men,* shall be given by the major part, the *Right* to *Present* the Person of them all, (that is to say, to be their *Representative;*) every one, as well he that *Voted for it,* as he that *Voted against it,* shall *Authorise* all the Actions and Judgements of that Man, or Assembly of men, in the same manner, as if they were his own, to the end, to live peaceably amongst themselves, and be protected against other men.[4]

This account of sovereignty by institution bears clear signs of the two-contract doctrine. There are two stages to the contract: The first requires a unanimous vote to go along with the second part of the procedure, which is a majority vote determining which person or people will actually play the part of the sovereign. (It is not, of course, that everything would stop if one of those present voted against at the first stage of proceedings; that person would simply be out of the game thereafter.) Hobbes realized, therefore, that it was not logically impossible for a group of people without a sovereign to come to decisions. The first stage does not count against Hobbes's claims about the sovereign because there is no decision-procedure operating: Unanimity is required, and it is achieved by having those who do not agree go away. No community with much disagreement could operate for long with that as its decision-procedure. But there is still no sovereign when the people go through the second part of the proceedings, and they manage to do that. Hobbes's own model requires the making of decisions and the operating of a decision-procedure (majority vote) without a sovereign.

Hobbes argued that private judgment must be subordinate to public judgment in the form of the sovereign, but he did not succeed in removing private judgment from his theory when it kept on turning up in places into which it would not fit. One reason for this is that his model of explanation misled him when he came to accounting for the virtues. What I want to show now is that removing the misconstruction into which Hobbes misled himself can solve the problem. A Hobbesian sovereign might or might not be necessary as a matter of fact in some communities or in others, but it is not logically necessary to all communities. Morality may be, in some ways, unavoidably conventional, but the community itself, and not only the sovereign, can provide that conventional element. General possession of the virtues is necessary, Hobbes argued, if sovereignty is to be possible, but general possession of the virtues also means that sovereignty is not logically necessary and that private judgment can, without disaster, continue to play a healthy part in our lives. Community takes precedence over sovereignty; about that much, George Lawson was right. This might appear to suggest that John Locke was nearer to being right than Hobbes was: It suggests that communal life without government is at least logically possible and that citizens retain a proper private judgment about the government. But Locke put the emphasis about private judgment in the wrong place and did not balance it with the *appropriate* emphasis on toleration: He had citizens using their private judgment to judge the performance of the government, that is, to judge the particular decisions that it produced, rather than concentrating on the *fairness* of the decision-procedure.

The laws of nature, on Hobbes's account, are necessary if people are to live in civil society rather than in the radical form of man's natural condition. If people were not inclined to follow the laws of nature, there could be no life in communities. If people are inclined to follow the laws of nature, on the other hand, then we can reasonably expect that there will not be the number of disruptive disagreements that Hobbes suggests and can expect that where serious disagreements do arise, people will be more capable of sorting things out for themselves or muddling through in some way. Rather than having *a* sovereign, they might have different sorts of procedures for different sorts of cases, or, rather than having standing procedures at all, they might do the job in a piecemeal way and simply agree among themselves on an appropriate procedure when a problem arises.

For those who are inclined to follow the laws of nature, there are many possible ways of resolving disputes. There is no guarantee that those procedures will always work without degenerating into violence, but, even though revolution might be demonstrably improper, there can be no *guarantee* that there will be no revolution against even a Hobbesian sovereign. The right reason argument shows only that communal life requires that there be a binding decision-procedure for each dispute about a matter requiring common action. Anything more than that is simply an empirical matter of what works: It will be a matter of what particular passions these particular people have, just how selfish they are, just how willing to accommodate themselves to others, and so on. There is no reason to believe that different groups of people, with different histories, different economic systems, different family systems, and so on, will not differ in those respects.

Hobbes's moral theory is a theory of virtues and vices. He uses those terms, and, like those of his contemporaries (such as Eachard) who used those terms in describing his moral theory, he understood them in a context of Aristotelian theory; that is, he understood them to be qualities of character. Lawson picked up the point, though he did not see its significance and therefore did not develop it: "Equity, justice gratitude, and other moral vertues, are not Laws of nature, but either habitual or actual conformities unto the Laws of Nature."[5] Hobbes, indeed, had changed the idea of a law of nature from what that term meant for most writers of the period, which is what gave rise to Lawson's complaint; mere rules would not do the job without motivation, without people's being the sorts of creatures who were inclined to behave in the appropriate ways. The role of virtues in Hobbes's theory is the same as the role of laws of nature in the theories of more historically and less philosophically inclined writers of the period, so he has, here as elsewhere, taken over the term and used it for his own purposes. His quarrel with other writers on virtues and vices is that they had not seen what it is that makes a virtue a virtue.[6] And Hobbes stresses the role of the virtues, as opposed to a merely legalistic signing of a contract, in making life in communities possible when he refers to "this Treatise, concerning the Morall Vertues, and of their necessity, for the procuring, and maintaining peace."[7]

Hobbes does not commit the crude error of arguing that people ought to be like this because they are like this; his premise is not simply that people *are* like this, but that they *must* be like this if they are to live in communities, which, as his argument about the radical natural condition shows, is the only way for people to live.   In the radical natural condition, humankind could not last more than one generation, so it is a presupposition of continuing human life that these qualities of character are virtues.   The argument is not a means-end argument. Hobbes is not arguing that continuing human life is a good thing, so what is necessary for human life to continue must be a good thing. He is arguing that it is a necessary truth in continuing human life that these qualities of character are virtues.   He has stayed with the idea of the apodictic, as is required by his attempt to argue in a way modeled on geometry.   (Hobbes says that the claim that monarchy is the most commodious form of government is the "one thing alone I confess in this whole book not to be demonstrated, but only probably stated."[8])

Hobbes's general account of the virtues (those qualities of character that are necessary if people are to live peaceably and comfortably together) seems to me satisfactory, but the model taken over from the account of the circle is inadequate.   The virtues are not qualities of character that, no matter how they were in fact gained, could have been gained by people calculating in that sort of way.   To see them that way means misconstruing some of the ways in which reason enters into morality. The model Hobbes took to explain the virtues does misconstrue the role of reason in that way.

The question "Why should I be moral?" has seemed to many people to be an unanswerable one because of the role that reasons have in morality.   To be moral, it is sometimes said, is not simply to do the right thing, but to do the right thing for the right reasons.   One can see the point of this: Refraining from thumping the kids only because the neighbors are watching does not show one to be patient or tolerant or understanding.   In asking why one should be moral, therefore, one seems to be asking for reasons for accepting reasons, and that appears to leave a problem: If my reason for doing X is Y, and if the only reason I am prepared to accept Y as a reason for doing X is Z, then, it seems, my real or basic reason for doing X is Z. If Y was the right reason, the reason that would have made my act a moral act, then I have moved away from that reason; by giving myself a reason for being moral, I have precluded my being moral.   The reasons seem to be transparent: We seem to see right through the surface reason to the real one.   And Hobbes, misled by his model of people calculating about policy, writes as though that is how things work with the virtues. Because of that, he feels that he has to cover with his theory of sovereignty problems that are properly handled with an adequate theory of virtues. An adequate account of virtues explains how many disputes can be settled without recourse to a Hobbesian sovereign. And it is clear that, on Hobbes's view, a sovereign could not be set up without the virtues or natural law.

It matters that we be able to argue out what is a virtue and what is not. There are genuine arguments about such matters: about whether chastity is really a virtue, whether prudence is properly distinguishable from selfishness, whether generosity is really no more than foolishness encouraged in some by others, and so on. The problem mentioned in the previous paragraph arises here, too. If one thinks that the reasons why a particular quality of character is a good thing are the reasons on which somebody is acting in exhibiting that quality of character, one will misidentify the virtues. This is the mistake into which Hobbes's model of argument misled him. The quality of character of kindness, for example, might be a good thing because it is socially useful in that it promotes trust and makes social intercourse easier. If one takes that to mean that being kind is intentionally acting so as to make social intercourse easier (or so as to produce any other advantage put forward as showing that kindness is a good quality of character), then one is inclined to point out that this is not why kind people act, and one is inclined to think that no such argument about which qualities of character are virtues can be carried on.

These problems arise because of a misunderstanding of the different ways in which reason enters into morality and into moral philosophy. I shall try to disentangle part of the confusion.

When the circumstances are such that a kind act is possible, there is still a number of ways in which one can fail to be kind. The most obvious, and the least interesting, ways are by being cruel or callous; I shall bypass those and suggest seven other ways of failing to be kind. I do not suggest that the list is exhaustive, but it should be sufficient for my point, which is to bring out some of the relationships between kindness and reasoning.

The first way of failing to be kind is by pretending to be kind. Faced with a situation in which it is possible to be kind, but unmoved by the plight of the other person, I seize the chance to win myself a reputation as a kind and warm-hearted person. "What would a kind person do here?" I ask myself, and then I go ahead and do that, making sure that my action is not hidden from public view. I have acted as a kind person would have done, and the other person's suffering is eased, but I have not been kind: The aim of my action was some good to myself, and I aimed at the good of another only incidentally, as a means to achieving my own good. I was, ultimately, self-seeking, and along the way I have been deceitful in my pretence of concern for the other.

This is not to deny that I can, in a case of genuine kindness, be aware while I help another person that some good will accrue to me as a result of my action. And it is not to say that if, given a choice between two ways of helping somebody, I choose the way that will also help me, then it follows that I was not really kind. What is at issue is whether I am moved to action by the plight of the other or am merely pretending to be so. If I am actually moved by the plight of the other, I am acting within the realm of kindness; if I am merely pretending, I am being calculating. If I am so moved by the plight of the other that I plunge into action without all the necessary thought and get things wrong, so that I do not succeed in helping, then at least I was kindhearted or well intentioned. If, as a result of my passionless calculation, I get everything right and, for everybody to see, help as much as it would be possible to do, I am still a calculating person (and a useful one) rather than kind.

The second way is, in some respects, like the first: It is a case of taking out insurance. Again I am faced with a situation in which it is possible for me to be kind, and again I am unmoved by the plight of the other. This time, though, I am moved by the possibility that I may find myself in a similar plight and needing help at some time in the future. I seek no false reputation as a kind person; I seek only to make myself a creditor who will have debts to call in when he is in need. Pointing out that one good turn deserves another and that I may call on him for help at some time, I relieve the poor fellow's distress. Again I have done what a kind person would have done, and again I have failed to be kind. Depending on the nature and severity of the other fellow's distress, I may even have been callous in not being moved by it and in treating it simply as an opportunity to protect myself. I have not been deceitful, though: I did not even think in terms of what a kind person would do, but in terms of what would be a useful arrangement. And this need not be wholly bad: In being mindful of such possible reciprocation, and perhaps going further because of that than one would have gone out of simple goodwill, one might show the quite proper virtue of prudence. That one failed to be kind does not mean that one failed to have any virtue at all. That one calculated does not mean that one must have failed to display a virtue.

The third way of failing to be kind is by being muddleheaded, or confusedly kind; it is a way we often describe in a forgiving manner by saying that the person meant well. It is different from the first two ways in that the agent does aim at the patient's good for its own sake, but gets things wrong. Moved by the suffering of somebody who has just struggled in from the desert suffering from dehydration, I give him a whole bucket of water to drink. Seeing that somebody is suffering from hypothermia, I put her by a roaring fire and give her rum to drink. Seeing that my aged and infirm neighbor is suffering from a leaky roof, and ignoring my lack of the relevant knowledge and skills, I get up there to repair his roof and do such a job that the roof collapses on him the next night. In each case I showed myself to be kindhearted; in each case I meant well; but in each case the outcome of my efforts was foreseeably disastrous. I am certainly not callous or cruel, though I may be stupid. On the other hand, if I am generally given to such actions rather than merely being mistaken in this particular case, to describe me as kind without a very long story to qualify the description almost out of existence would be, at best, very misleading. That is why we say, rather, that such people are confusedly kind or mean well.

The fourth way of failing to be kind is by being a busybody. Faced with a situation in which the kind, or at least considerate, thing to do might be to discipline one's desires and leave somebody alone, I interfere. Seeing the infant I love to cuddle trying to crawl across the room, I pick him up and carry him there. Seeing my son, for whom I want a life with less worry than my own, trying to do his math homework, I tell him all the answers. In each case, I intervene in such a way as to inhibit somebody else's development. Seeing that my neighbor's son is deliberately left alone to do his own math homework, that my neighbor refuses all requests for the answers, and that the boy would rather go and chase girls, I provide the answers. In that case, I interfere in something that is simply not my business. In each of the three cases I have been moved by some sort of goodwill or desire for the benefit of the other, but my goodwill is vitiated by lack of discipline and extremely poor judgment of what is my business and what is really for the good of the other. Another example of the way in which goodwill can ally itself with poor judgment so as to come out as stupidity rather than kindness can be found when appropriate discrimination is not made, as when one's desire to help expresses itself just as readily in coming to the aid of a mugger meeting with spirited resistance from an old-age pensioner as it does in coming to the aid of his victim.

A fifth way of failing to be kind when the opportunity arises is by trying to make oneself do the right thing. A Boy Scout might help an old lady across the street, not self-seekingly in order to win a badge and not because he is moved by her difficulty in getting to the other side, but because he wants to be a good Boy Scout and he knows that this is what Boy Scouts are supposed to do. Such a person is conscientious: He acts in order to meet certain standards that he recognizes. If the standards are of the appropriate sort, they will require that he do what a kind person would do out of immediate concern for the other. An act performed for that reason does not display kindness, but, again, it does not follow that it shows no virtue: Conscientiousness has its good points.

Similar situations can arise without requirements quite so formal as those made of a Boy Scout. I might, for example, notice in myself, and worry about, a certain callousness, a failure to be moved by the sufferings of others as much as I think I should be. Recognizing this as a lack, and wanting to be a decent person, I carefully set about turning myself into a kind person, my plan being to do so by developing in myself the habit of kind behavior. Faced with a choice between actions, I work out what a kind person would do and, despite my lack of any immediate inclination, make myself do it. Until and unless my plan succeeds, I shall not be kind. At least in the early stages of the project, my aims are not appropriate. My primary concern is not the easing of somebody else's suffering, but the meeting of certain standards that I have set for myself. Were I being kind, the focus of my attention would be the person I helped, but, in fact, the focus of my attention is myself: I want to improve myself. Again, it does not follow that no virtue is involved, because this is not just any old case of self-improvement. It is not the same as if I had set about learning to speak Japanese or how to play the violin. Each of those might be a case of self-improvement, but the plan here is to improve me in a quite public and social way, to make me a better person for others to live with. There is, in my project, a moral concern for others, but not by way of an immediate reaction to their specific suffering; it is more a reasoned-out concern for what ought to be done, something of a fairly impersonal sort, than an empathetic sharing of the distress of others and desire to relieve it.

A sixth way of failing to be kind is by being squeamish. If I never discipline my infant son because I cannot bear to see him frustrated and do not think of the years ahead when he might suffer from not having developed appropriate habits of discipline, or if I cannot put back in place somebody's dislocated shoulder because I cannot bear to cause anybody that much pain, then I have some sort of concern for the feelings of others. But it is a misguided sort of concern that is not kindness and is not a virtue.

The last of the ways I shall list of failing to be kind is by being patronizing or arrogant: Helping another because, by doing so, one shows one's superiority. Again, the focus of one's attention is oneself; relieving somebody else's distress is merely a means to one's own end.

I have not argued that these seven cases are cases of failing to be kind, because I take it that there will be agreement about that claim.

Given our normal operations with the concept of kindness, it seems obvious that they are such cases as soon as they are described. What I want to do is ask what lessons we can draw from them about the nature of kindness.

One thing that seems fairly clear is that the motivation in a case of kindness is an immediate desire to help another who is in distress. The desire is not mediated by an intention to serve one's own purposes; relieving the distress of the other is the end of the action and not merely a means. This means that the motivation in a case of kindness is not that of making oneself a better person and not that of meeting some standard one thinks one should meet. The focus in an act of kindness is the distress of the person being helped, not the agent and how good he is. Kindness is not a duty, and to treat it as one is to turn it into something else like the Boy Scout's conscientiousness. Kindness goes beyond mere duty. Reason can play a number of different roles when one is kind, but it does not play the role of working out what kindness requires under that description. It is a good thing that one perform the appropriate actions even if one does not do so out of kindness; other virtues can be exhibited in the action; but those other virtues are not kindness, and they are important partly *because* some people lack the virtue of kindness or do not have it to a very high degree.

Kindness is a nonreflexive virtue: If one aims to be kind, in those terms, then one necessarily fails. To aim to be kind, in those terms, is to aim to meet a standard; that might be conscientious or exhibit some other virtue, but it is not kind. In being kind, one does not consider what the kind thing to do would be under that description; one considers how to relieve distress or promote welfare.

Kindness is, in that respect, different from justice, which is a reflexive virtue. If one exhibits the virtue of justice, then one *has* considered what justice requires, in those terms. If justice requires that I do *B*, I might do *B* simply because I am in the mood for such action and without giving any thought to justice. I might do *B* because, and only because, doing so serves my interests or those of somebody I favor. In such cases I perform the action a just person would perform, but I do not exhibit the virtue of justice. If I borrow money, then justice requires that I repay it. If I forget the debt but see my creditor in need and immediately respond by giving him a gift (as I consider it) of the amount of money that I owe him, then I may have shown myself to be kindhearted, and I may accidentally have carried out my duty, but I have not shown myself to be a just person. If I am to exhibit the virtue of justice, then I must be trying to meet a standard because that standard is set by justice; I must reflect on justice and what it requires. In that way, justice is a calculating or ratiocinative virtue. Kindness, on the other hand, is importantly a matter of what one's natural inclinations are rather than of one's calculations of what is due from one. Reason can play different roles with different virtues. Prudence, for example, can be reflexive or nonreflexive, and it can be calculating or noncalculating.

It is clear, though, from the list of ways of failing to be kind, that kindness is not simply a matter of feeling and reflex action, like jumping when one feels pain. Reason, judgment, and knowledge have their parts to play. I am irresponsible, not kind, if I offer to help by rewiring all of my neighbor's electrical circuits when I lack the required knowledge. Judgment must be exercised in such cases. Unless I can work out how to solve various problems or to bring about certain states of affairs, my attempts to be helpful will fail. And consideration of other virtues will sometimes be necessary: With no consideration of justice, my desire to help will leave me just as likely to help the mugger who meets resistance as to help his victim.

What might seem odd about all this is the idea that there could be a virtue like kindness. It is, I have suggested, a matter of one's natural inclinations, and, even though one might be able to keep one's natural inclinations under control, one cannot help what they are. How can my moral virtue or vice be something that I cannot help? There is a common inclination to think that one can properly be morally judged only for what one can help; this seems to be required by the conditions for responsibility. If I cannot help whether I am kind or not, how can I be held responsible for that? And if I cannot be held responsible for it, how can it be a moral virtue?

Perhaps kindness is not a moral virtue; it is not at all obvious that this is a point worth worrying about. Physical strength is not a moral virtue, but it does not follow that we should be indifferent to its development: Any parent who kept his children from exercise so that they would grow up to be physically weak would, other things being equal, be falling down on the job. And kindness is clearly a human and social virtue however we want to use the word "moral."

On top of that, the *acts* expressive of kindness are free acts; that is why they can display something of one's character. Perhaps it is not a matter of my choice whether or not I am naturally inclined to help people who are in need, but it is a matter of my choice whether I do help people who are in need: Immediate natural inclination is not the only provocation to action. What I shall be held responsible for, or blamed for, is what I do or fail to do, not what I am. That I lack the virtue of kindness is not, by itself, something to blame me for. Somebody who lacks kindness but is conscientious might perform all the actions that a kind person would perform, and such a person might, in some respects, be the more admirable in that he had to struggle to overcome his natural inclinations in order to behave decently. He is certainly not blameworthy in that case for performing the acts that a kind person would have performed. (Somebody else might be blameworthy for so doing if what he did could properly be redescribed as deceiving people.) That somebody has a failing he cannot help is, by itself, no reason for punishing him.

So the problem about the conditions for responsibility does not really arise. One is responsible for one's action or inaction — for one's display of the lack of a virtue — not simply for the lack of a virtue. Nevertheless, lack of kindness is a failing. That one is not responsible for this quality of one's character is irrelevant to the point. Even if it is through no fault of my own that I have lost all my limbs, my incapacity may properly be considered in deciding whether to choose me on a football team. Native stupidity is equally a failing, and equally one for which its possessor is not responsible. That somebody is not responsible for his stupidity does not mean that it cannot properly be considered in deciding how to act toward a person, because it is a failing that can be, and is likely to be, displayed. If a grader failed an examination paper because it displayed stupidity, he would not be discriminating improperly. Except that there are more qualities of character that can compensate for lack of kindness in doing the jobs that kindness does than there are that will compensate for lack of intelligence in doing the jobs that intelligence does, lack of kindness is like stupidity in that respect. Lack of kindness is a failing in people because it makes social life harder for social beings, both the person who lacks the kindness and those around him. Conscientiousness may come into the gap left by the lack of kindness, but that takes more effort and means that life will be less easy. Life in a community simply is easier for people who naturally enjoy helping and making allowances for each other.[9]

People are social beings. We recognize ourselves, not as pure Cartesian mental substances, but as parents, philosophers, carpenters, and so on, all terms that have their meanings in a social framework. If we were not social beings, capable of living peacefully in communities and inclined to do so, then, given that there are enough of us for us to be constantly coming into contact with each other, we should be in a Hobbesian natural condition. If we are willing to get along together, then we shall form peaceful conventional means of resolving disputes arising from clashes of interests or differences of judgment; if we are not, any such differences will be provocation to fighting, and that fact would itself be further provocation to preemptive defensive action. What enables us to avoid this is that people, or enough people, *are* social beings with the qualities of character appropriate to social life. Those qualities of character will be virtues in social beings in much the same way as clear type is a virtue in a typewriter. What is a virtue is not simply something that each of us can decide for himself, but it is set by the necessity of people's having social ends: Different people might set different ends for themselves, but that the human race has lasted more than one generation presupposes that people, by and large, are social beings with social ends. What makes it possible for the human race to survive in this way must be a matter of qualities of character and natural inclinations to behave in certain ways rather than of people's formulating and agreeing to abide by certain rules that would enable them to achieve their ends: If there were no such natural inclinations, people would wipe themselves out before they could formulate rules. They would be unable to get together peacefully, and if they were not trustworthy and willing to get along together, they could not be trusted to keep the agreement even if they had made one. A lack of trust would again make preemptive action no less than reasonable.

Working out whether or not some quality of character is a virtue is clearly an activity of reason, which I take not to exclude empirical research. If kindness is a virtue, it is so because it eases social relationships and facilitates and encourages cooperative relationships of the sort that constitute community. If kindness is a virtue, therefore, it will, in the long run, help the kind person as well as others because of the sort of community life that it creates. That people will act simply out of concern for each other, even if only on a limited scale, might make social relationships a lot easier than would each person's willingness to act so as to ease social relationships because he thought it might provide some long- or short-term benefit for himself. That people aim for each other's good — rather than for what makes it a good thing that they aim for each other's good — can make them easier to get along with. That is why such a quality of character would be sufficiently important in human life for us to have formed a concept marking it off.

At least apparently, kindness facilitates cooperation and communal life in a number of ways. It is easier to begin a cooperative endeavor with goodwilled people; those who have some care for others and are not completely self-absorbed will be more inclined to enter cooperative relationships. There is less need to worry about whether kind people will be constantly looking for loopholes in the rules by means of which to do one down. That a kind person would not be inclined to take advantage of such opportunities brings out a relationship between kindness and the trustworthiness that is basic to cooperation and communal life. A cooperative endeavor is likely to be more productive if each of its members knows that he can take worthwhile risks in the security of the knowledge that the kindness of others will not leave him to bear all the costs alone if things go wrong. Kindness is likely to pay off for all, including the kind, and for that reason it is an important quality of character and one worth inculcating whenever possible.

All of this leads to an apparent inconsistency. Kindness facilitates social relations and pays off for all, including the person who is kind. That is why kindness is a good thing, so it is, presumably, why one should be kind. But if one does perform acts because they facilitate social relations and pay off, one is only pretending to be kind. This comes out in the ways in which people respond to help from others. A genuine attempt to help out of concern for the other, even if it is materially unsuccessful, as when Mary tries to help Fred by cooking the dinner but produces a singularly tasteless meal, can be a help: The concern of the other can itself cheer somebody who felt that things were getting them down. The awareness that one is not alone is one of the benefits of kindness. If, on the other hand, Mary cooked a magnificent meal but did it only so that Fred would feel bound to prepare dinner the next night or because she thought it would somehow improve social life in general, and did it with no particular concern for Fred, his reaction would probably be quite different.

A similar point can be raised with respect to justice. If justice is a virtue, it is so because it facilitates social relations and pays off. In fact, it seems clear that a sense of justice is necessary for cooperation: One cannot cooperate with somebody who cannot be trusted at all, and one cannot trust somebody who keeps to his agreements only when they require that he do what it would have suited him to do anyway. More accurately, one cannot trust such a person unless enough of us do not have that problem but do have a sense of justice so that we can combine and make sure that it will pay the other fellow to keep his word. And if justice keeps us from the Hobbesian natural condition, then clearly it pays off for each and every one of us.

Somebody who performs an act that is required by justice might do so for a number of different reasons: because he fears that he will be penalized if he does not; because he seeks a reputation as a just person; because what justice requires in this case is also, in fact, in his interests; because it is required by justice; and so on. The person who actually exhibits the virtue of justice performs the act because it is just. Otherwise she might be pretending to be just or simply performing an act the justice of which is merely coincidental, but she would not really be exhibiting justice even if an outside observer could not tell. Acting from a sense of justice and acting from self-interest are different — a point often brought out by reference to Gyges' ring — though the fact that we have to live our lives among other people means that the two will often lead to the same action.

But we do need to have some explanation of why justice is a good thing or of why we should be just. As has been pointed out, the explanation is that, in a particular way, it pays. What pays is genuine justice, that is, acting because justice requires the act and not simply because the act is in one's interest. It is plainly not true that every act required of me by justice is also the act most in my interests, but having the virtue of justice is in my interest because it makes possible life in a community with others and keeps us from the Hobbesian natural condition. If self-interest is my *only* motive for keeping the contract, then it will often lead me to break the contract. This point has often been made in terms of the Prisoners' Dilemma, and, in a life as short as that in the Hobbesian natural condition, the dilemma is nonreiterable.[10]

So justice pays each of us by making life in community possible. That is why justice is a good thing, and it is, presumably, why we ought to be just. And again we seem to have the inconsistency. I ought to do X because it is just; I ought to be just because it pays; therefore the real reason I ought to do X is that it pays; but doing something because it pays is not really being just. And we cannot short-circuit this problem by refusing to go beyond the claim that I ought to do X because it is just: Doing X because it is Y with no care for whether Y is a good thing exhibits no virtue whatsoever. It is merely slavish rule-following or something of the sort.

The problem with kindness is not quite the same, because the kind person does not argue that he ought to do X because it is kind; kindness is nonreflexive, so he argues that he ought to do X because it will help another. A very similar problem seems to arise, though, as long as the explanation of why it is a good thing to act so as to help another is that the quality of character expressed in kind acts is one the possession of which pays.

The problem is the apparent transparency of the reasons — the way we seem to see through the facade of reasons that are put up and to find revealed to us that people who act kindly or justly are either hypocrites or fools. If justice is a good thing only because it pays, and if I go around performing acts because they are just without consideration of whether justice pays, then, it seems, I am a fool in two ways: I am ignoring my own interests when I have no particular reason to do so, making myself a mere tool of others, and, in my futile attempts to be a decent person, I am blindly following some sort of conventional morality without considering whether what my action expressed really is a virtue or not. If, on the other hand, I put myself forward as a just person but will accept the justice of an action as a reason for performing it only when or because justice will pay me, then I am a hypocrite; I am concerned only with furthering my own interests, and not at all with justice itself.

If we think that justice is important because it pays, and if we also think that being just is different from simply acting out of self-interest, then the virtues seem to collapse into incoherence. When moral concepts are misconstrued in this sort of way, unpleasant consequences follow: For example, if the point of the concept of murder, or what makes some sorts of homicide sufficiently important for us to have developed this concept marking them off, is that life in a community is impossible without some limitation on wanton killing, then any killing that does not make life in a community impossible is permissible. Another example is the idea that kindness is a fraud: Helping others where there can be no expectation of return is mere foolishness because only the fact that kindness has social utility makes it a good thing. Such arguments improperly telescope an account of what the concept is and, a different though related matter, an account of why the concept is important and therefore takes that form.

It is easy to see how this idea of the transparency of the reasons gets a grip on our thinking here. If I know that X is required by justice but I will not move until I am persuaded that being just will pay me, then I am being self-interested and not just. Or I might be simply confused, improperly mixing my moral philosophy and false ideas of the role of reason, on the one hand, with my practical morality, on the other, by insisting that the particular act meet the conditions that make the concept important. The problem seems to disappear, though, if we shift from an entirely first-person case to a third-person case.

The problem of transparency appears to arise when I accept X as a reason for accepting Y as a reason. It does not seem to arise when, without mentioning X to him, I so bring up somebody else that he will accept Y as a reason. There is no temptation to say that he is a hypocrite, or that *his* real reasons for acting are the ones *I* had for what I did.

So suppose that, like a lot of people, I have limited care for others. In particular, I care a lot about my son and want him to live a life in which his own interests are satisfied as much as possible. I do not care a great deal about others except insofar as they will affect whether my son can satisfy his interests. Having thought about the way possession of the virtue pays, I might set about bringing my son up to be just. That is to say, I might bring him up to perform acts required by justice simply because they are just and without consideration of whether they will pay. Assuming that I knew how to do so, I might bring him up to have the virtue of justice. (Similarly, I might bring him up to care for the interests, as well as the rights, of others.)

If I am so selective in my concerns, then I might have to do a good deal of pretending in order to bring him up to be just and kind, but I might succeed. If I did, there could be no temptation to say that my son was really self-interested simply because *my* reasons for developing that quality of character in him concerned only his interests. He has no reason for accepting reasons of justice, though he might have worked out what reasons there are for believing justice to be a virtue. It is a good thing that my son be just, but I cannot give him reasons for being just: Just is something that he is, not something that he does. I can give him reasons for performing just actions; if he is a just person, it will suffice that I give him those reasons that show the action to be just.

The problem of the transparency of reasons is merely apparent; it arises from a confusion. Moral philosophy has a practical point, but the role of reason when a kind person or a just person works out what to do is not the same as the role of reason when a moral philosopher (though perhaps the same person as the practical moralist) sets about working out whether kindness and justice are virtues.

The practical moralist will be concerned about what to do, but, if serious, he will also need to be a moral philosopher who works out which qualities of character are social virtues and which are merely weaknesses. Any sharp distinction drawn between practical moralists and moral philosophers is drawn only for reasons of convenience in certain circumstances. Recognition that justice and kindness are virtues, that they pay in the appropriate way, does not remove the virtue from the agent. For one thing, the appropriate form of payment is not direct payment to the agent by the act. What we recognize in seeing that virtues pay is that it is important in community life that people commonly have these qualities of character; the payment is in the possibility of community life, which is not, by and large, one of the direct aims that we have. It is not really a matter of giving people reasons for being just or kind, but of showing why certain general facts about people are important and a good thing because of the roles they play in community life. What the serious moral agent asks himself in the more philosophical parts of the endeavor is not "Should I be kind?" but "I am like this (inclined to care about people, or unmoved by other people's problems); is it a virtue or a vice? Should I give it free rein or curb it?" And as we saw in the discussion of the first way of failing to be kind, if in a particular case of responding warmheartedly to somebody's problems or fulfilling your obligations because justice requires that you do so, you can see that you will gain some quite direct benefit too, that does not change the morality of your act from what it would have been otherwise. The threat of personal gain would not stop kind people from helping others or just people from paying debts, even though that threat is also not necessary to move them to action.

The relationship between reason and virtues is complex. What is required if there is to be peaceful life in a community is agreement in the outcome of our practical reasoning. Despite what Hobbes says, agreement is required not so much *on* the laws of nature[11] as *in* the laws of nature. Given the nature of virtues, as opposed to the odd story of policy-formation that Hobbes tells when he follows the model of the circle in accounting for virtues (not when he is arguing straightforwardly that they are qualities of character necessary for life in communities), that is the only sort of effective agreement that we could have with respect to them. What is especially required is agreement in the first[12] and fifth[13] laws of nature — that we seek peace where we can find it and that we strive to accommodate ourselves to others — because these lead to toleration and to our being able to find means of resolving our disputes. Agreeing in those is recognizing that we are social beings, not the selves of liberal individualism; the selves of liberal individualism are the selves of people in the radical form of their natural condition.

How can there be practical reasoning, an argument the conclusion of which is an action rather than a proposition? In one sense the answer is easy: Two people can have an argument, for instance, with the argument ending in a fight. Or a young man in the springtime might contemplate all the solid virtues of Martha and then go chasing the flashy Margaret instead. Contemplation of relevant facts, or the presentation of relevant facts in a dispute, can be followed by action, and the facts might well have been contemplated because of their relationship to the prospective action. The real problem, though, is how the reasoning can be good or bad in relation to the action.

Everything seems to be straightforward when the conclusion to be drawn from an argument is itself a proposition, but it does look as though there is a problem arising when the conclusion is an action. An action cannot contradict a proposition. An action might falsify a proposition, or fail to accord with it, but the contradictory of a proposition is another proposition. If an action cannot contradict a proposition or set of propositions, then it cannot be entailed by a proposition or set of propositions. So the reasoning, if it is good, cannot be good as a piece of deductive reasoning.

Nor could it be good as a piece of inductive reasoning: The premises would make the action more probable only with additional information (which the agent does not contemplate, though it might affect him) about how reasonable the premises were, what axes the action might allow to be ground, how reasonable the agent was, how given to self-deception, and so on. Information not forming part of the premises would be necessary to the probability argument, and suggestions that whether the premises make the action probable depends on how reasonable they and the agent are bring out a circularity in the idea that the argument could be inductive.

As a general point, actions are performed or not performed, but they are not true or false, and the notion of truth seems central to explaining what it is for a conclusion to follow from premises. (This is actually misleading: Actions, aim, and friends can all be true or false, though not in the sense required to explain the notion of "following from"; the problem is that the notion of "following from" would probably have to be called on to explain the relevant notion of truth.)

Such is the grip of the idea of theoretical reason that it seems a very simple move to conclude from this that the conclusion of a practical syllogism must be a proposition rather than an action. The conclusion must be a proposition such as that this act would be kind, or that I ought to do this. Moral argument is then misconstrued as having the form of a theoretical argument leading to a propositional conclusion of that sort: "Stealing is wrong; taking away Margaret's good name would be stealing; therefore I ought not to take away Margaret's good name." It is this sort of agreement that would be agreement *on* the laws of nature.

But there is an oddity about such a move in an explanation of practical argument: It seems very odd that somebody who was unmoved by the fact that Mother was very tired after putting in hours of work every day for the good of the family, that she had been treated in a rather cavalier fashion and felt unappreciated, that she really does enjoy having breakfast in bed (so much so that she can still remember when it last happened twenty-five years ago), and so on, should suddenly be moved by the information that giving Mother breakfast in bed would be kind. If he didn't care about all those other facts, why should he care about kindness? Indeed, one might want to ask *how* he could care about kindness if he did not care about all those other facts. How can the fact that an act would be kind give somebody a reason for acting if the fact that Mom would really like breakfast in bed does not?

Of course, as many a person who continues to smoke can attest, it is possible to give somebody reasons for acting without moving him to act. Nevertheless, it does seem, at least intuitively, that there is a relationship between reasons and motivation: At least a reasonable person *ought* to be moved by good reasons. And if a reasonable person *ought* to be moved by good reasons, then it seems that good reasons, and hence reasons, *can* move somebody to act. But how could reasons move somebody to act? If reason alone could do that, business computers would take over the world. Hence there arises the mistaken idea that practical reason is theoretical reason with the addition of wants, emotions, attitudes, or whatever. That there is a restaurant on the corner is not, by itself, a reason for anything. Add to it the fact that I am hungry and have the necessary money, and I have a reason for crossing the road. My desire for food, when added to the fact, produces a reason for acting, and facts, it seems, could become reasons for acting only in that sort of way. If we give somebody all the facts we like, but he does not have the relevant wants, we shall not succeed in giving him a reason for acting.

Let us return to an earlier stage: the idea that the conclusion of a practical argument must be a proposition. That idea is false. Seeing why it is false will also lead us into the problem of how facts can be reasons for a particular person to act even in the face of that particular person's particular wants.

The reasons that lead a kind person to act, and that show what he did to be kind, do not refer to kindness or to what he ought to do. That he be straightforwardly and untaintedly kind requires that he *not* feel it necessary to draw the propositional conclusion. The kind person responds to the facts that Mom is tired and would much enjoy breakfast in bed. The one who responds *not at all* to those facts, but only to the information that it would be kind to his mother to give her breakfast in bed, may be a dutiful son (and there are worse things to be), but he is not kind.

There are, as we have seen, many ways of failing to exhibit kindness when the opportunity for kindness presents itself, and not all of those ways of failing to be kind require that one display a vice. If Mom, in the bad old days, decided to use the money that she saved out of the housekeeping to employ a live-in maid, then it is no act of kindness on the maid's part to give Mom breakfast in bed: Rather, the maid is simply doing her job. And that is no vice on the maid's part, though that is so partly because her job means that she has no opportunity to be kind simply by providing breakfast in bed. If Dad, despite his tiredness after eight hours of gainfulMom a machine employment followed by half the housework and a night spent looking after a baby with colic, decides that Mom deserves the best to start off a day in which she will have to look after the baby, and therefore gives her breakfast in bed, that would be kind even though he would have done, under one description, the same thing as the maid would have done in the previous story. If Dad, despite his tiredness after eight hours of gainful employment followed by a night on the town with the boys, decides that breakfast in bed for Mom might put her in a good mood and distract her from the fact that he didn't get home until 6:00 A.M., then his giving her breakfast in bed might show cunning, cowardice, prudence, or whatever, but it does not show kindness. If the maid, however, despite eight hours of gainful employment followed by a night on the town, seeing that Mom has had a hard night with the baby, makes sure that, though it is an effort, breakfast in bed is served with a smile, *that* might be kind.

It is not simply a matter of what act was performed, but of the motivation for the act and the attitude displayed by it. Kindness goes beyond duty, but not necessarily by doing more of the same and giving somebody two breakfasts in bed instead of one. Kindness is a matter of motivation and attitude that cannot be required of one as action can, and it can consist of performing no more actions than are required by duty, but performing them with a certain attitude. The idea of going the second mile is, in many ways, a poor model for this sort of thing, even though the relevant aspect of what is involved here is not something that can be required but is more like supererogation. The maid, in the first case, was simply doing her job, and that is what she was concentrating on. Dad, when hung over, was aiming at his own well-being. The maid, in the second case, did no more than her job, but she did her job differently. And Dad, in the first case, acted for different reasons.

A Boy Scout who helps old-age pensioners across the road because that is what Boy Scouts are supposed to do, and for no other reason, is like the maid serving breakfast in bed because that is her job. His concentration is on himself and whether he meets the exacting standards of good Boy Scouting; he sees old-age pensioners as opportunities to do his thing. That need not be a bad thing: Given that the Boy Scout rules restrict the field of those to be helped to those who want to be helped, and given that it might be dangerous for those old-age pensioners who have failing eyesight to cross the road alone, it might be a good thing to have punctilious and dutiful Boy Scouts. But that a Boy Scout is punctilious and dutiful means that he is punctilious and dutiful; it does not mean that he is kind. One reason why it might be a good thing that the Boy Scout be punctilious and dutiful is that those qualities of character might fill in for and do part of the job of kindness when kindness is lacking. Indeed, they might fit in for any other virtue, and, for anybody who had not all the virtues to perfection, that would make them very important qualities of character indeed.

The Boy Scout, like the maid, might also be kind: That he is aware of what is expected of a Boy Scout does not mean that he is unaware of, or unmoved by, the problems of old-age pensioners or people who cannot see very well. Nor does it mean that he is unaware of the fact that it is considerations of kindness that lie behind the requirement made by Boy Scouts; he might be well aware of that and approve of the rule because he is a kind fellow.

Somebody else, without joining the Boy Scouts, might set himself standards of decency and take them very seriously. He might even find it worthwhile to make for himself a rule with the same content as the rule requiring that Boy Scouts help old-age pensioners across the road. And he might see the same point to that rule as the kind Boy Scout saw. But the point of his making a rule of that sort would have to be that he would not, in the normal run of things, help old-age pensioners across the road, or would be too willing not to do so if he felt tired, or knew that the old-age pensioner voted for the Republican party or wrote in library books, or generally if he found excuses far too readily. Seeing this shortcoming, and seeing it *as* a shortcoming, he could make himself a rule to rectify it. The shortcoming is a lack in his kindness. It is not a complete absence of kindness, or he would not be bothered about it, but it is a lack in his kindness. So, thinking that kindness is important, he makes a rule for himself requiring that he do kind acts such as helping old-age pensioners across the street. Were he completely lacking in kindness, he would not make the rule; but were he being kind in the particular acts, he would not need the rule. And he is not performing a kind act when he makes the rule, because there is nobody to whom he is then being kind.

The case of this fellow is not the same as that of another who made the same rule simply in order to keep on the right side of an aged and rich aunt who offered the chance of a large inheritance, or of somebody else who adopted the rule simply in an attempt to keep himself from the fires of hell. In those two cases, there is no reason for saying that the person is kind. Nor is it like the case of somebody who usually does respond to the suffering of others in particular cases, without the need of a rule, but has discovered that there are hard cases that slip by his notice. Some people, perhaps, are unaffected by bereavement, but others are so greatly affected that they go into a sort of shock and show no signs of suffering; in such a case one might fail to be kind simply because the suffering was not apparent. So one might form the rule that one will help and support the bereaved until it becomes obvious that they are not really suffering or that one's ministrations are making things worse because they want to be left alone. The point of forming this rule is that one *does* care about the particular case, not that one is bothered by the fact that one does not. These people are not like the person we are considering.

This person that we are considering shows his concern for others by making the rule, and that concern therefore comes out in the particular act because the act would not have been performed had he not made that rule for himself. The concern shown for others in the particular act, though, is not an immediate concern; it is like giving money to organized charities but being unmoved by suffering that he comes across except for finding that it makes him uncomfortable. (And, in some cases, such discomfort might not reflect concern at the plight of another as much as worry about one's own future or feelings of guilt to be explained simply in terms of one's upbringing.) That he has adopted a rule aimed at kindness shows something about him because he, unlike the Boy Scout, made the rule for himself, but what it shows about him is complex. This person has some kindness, and without that he would not have performed the act, but the kindness is displayed in the fact that he has adopted the rule that led him to perform the act. What he displays in the particular act is more like the Boy Scout's punctiliousness and dutifulness. It is something like general decency, making up for the deficiency in his kindness. That he has to go through the *theoretical* reasoning to conclude that the act would be kind, having been insufficiently moved by recognition of the plight of the other, and act on his theoretical conclusion are what show the *deficiency* in his kindness. That there is a deficiency in his kindness does not mean that he is nasty or behaves reprehensibly, because he is calling on other virtues to make up for that deficiency, and he might even be more admirable than a kinder person in that it cost him more effort and resolve to behave that way.

One thing that all of this suggests is that genuine, untainted kindness does involve the use of a practical syllogism in which the conclusion is not the proposition that this act would be kind, drawn as in theoretical reasoning, but an action: Mom has had a hard time and is feeling poor, therefore I get her a cup of tea. It is not that Mom has had a hard time and is feeling poor, therefore it is true that I *ought* to get her a cup of tea. The genuinely kind person, as Aristotle points out, wants to help and takes pleasure in providing the service; the person who is tempted not to perform the act is the one who needs to be told, or to tell himself, that he *ought* to do it. The theoretical conclusion does not matter if one has the relevant virtue to a great enough degree.

It is agreement in practical reasoning that matters for Hobbes's argument. Agreement in such practical reasoning, the possession of a virtue, is primarily an inclination to accept or seek certain sorts of ends in one's actions, and thus to be moved by certain sorts of facts. Agreement merely at the level of theoretical reasoning will not do the job, especially because the need to use theoretical reasoning in these cases indicates the inclination not to act. But agreement in practical reasoning will go a long way toward making peaceful life in communities possible. Agreement in theoretical reasoning will help to fill in gaps.

Another thing that this consideration of theoretical reasoning suggests is an important, though secondary, role for moral judgments, or for the conclusions of theoretical reasoning about practical matters. The role is secondary because it is simply making up for imperfections in people (or doing so to some extent): A perfectly kind person would not need to use moral judgments in this way to make up for the deficiency in his kindness. And it is important, obviously, because people are imperfect. We may be, to some extent, kind, courageous, just, and so on, but we are also liable to temptation, bad moods, and fits of laziness that impair our practice of those virtues.

Courage is usually thought of as the overcoming of fear, and it matters that people be able to do that, given that people are as they obviously are. The strongest case of the virtue, though, would be in somebody who did not even feel fear when the risk was worthwhile, and who therefore was not distracted from the task ahead; this would be the true virtue of courage, the quality of character most worth having of all those in this area. It would be the version of courage parallel to kindness as we actually understand kindness. But that is not how the word "courage" is commonly used. The shift recognizes human frailty: We do not commonly have true courage, but it matters that the job of that virtue be done, so we need something to keep us to the task even if we do not delight in it. It is not simply a matter of overcoming fear to no end, looking around to see what pointless risks are there to be taken and then taking them; one asks oneself "What would a (truly) courageous person do here?" and then does what that person would have done.

One can see, then, how true courage must be the prior virtue of the two, because use of the other virtue requires calculation in terms of true courage, but one can also see why the more common idea of courage, actually a species of dutifulness, is so important. To the extent that I am afraid, I do not want to perform the task, but, I tell myself, I *ought* to perform the task, so (at least on a good day) I do perform it. And if the task was worthwhile, then it matters that it was done. It matters that I did what would have been done by somebody with true courage if and only if true courage is a virtue (and that is why true courage is prior to common courage), but, in a world that has gone to the dogs, it matters that we have the back-up virtue. Just how much it matters that we have it is suggested by the fact that the virtue-word is now commonly used to refer to the back-up virtue. But to treat a genuinely kind or courageous act as though the agent's reasoning must have included the conclusion that the act would be kind or courageous is to imply imperfection where it is absent.

These moral judgments that play the important, though secondary, role are moral judgments on our own prospective actions. Moral judgments on the actions of others can have a similar, though less direct importance: When we ponder the activities of Governor Phillip and Major Ross, of Oliver Cromwell or John Brown, we are contemplating fairly dramatic versions of matters not too far from our own experience and seeing versions of problems that we come across in our own lives. As a result, one hopes, we respond better to those problems when they do arise in our own lives; we have gained some idea of where fortitude can get us and what traps can be fallen into. Apart from that, moral judgments on others serve mainly to distance us from a situation and to fill in conversational gaps at tea parties.

Of the primary virtues, as opposed to the make-up virtues, justice is special in that it does require the making of a judgment. Prudence, of the other primary virtues, allows the making of a reflexive judgment that prudence requires certain action as perfect kindness precludes the reflexive judgment that kindness requires the action, but justice *requires* such a reflexive judgment. Justice requires that one reach a theoretical conclusion. Justice is concerned with one's rights and duties, so, unsurprisingly, it is like what I have called dutifulness. If little Tommy has to be threatened and bludgeoned into making Mom a cup of tea, then, even though he has done the act that a kind person would have done, he has not done a kindness or been kind. If I am threatened and bludgeoned into paying my debts, then I *have* paid my debts, even though unwillingly; justice has been done, though not with good grace. But I have not exhibited the virtue of justice. Even if I do willingly what justice requires be done, it does not follow that I have exhibited the virtue of justice. Perhaps I owe little Tommy ten dollars, but I forgot that I owed him ten dollars because I do not take my debts seriously. When I saw his disappointment at not being able to buy Mom a machine that would brew her tea each morning, I gave him ten dollars willingly so that he could buy the machine and not be disappointed. My giving him the money might be a matter of kindness (or at least of good intentions), or a matter of trying to curry favor, or any other of a number of things. It is a matter of justice only if I perform the act because justice requires it; exhibition of the virtue of justice requires that I do the theoretical reasoning and reach, as a conclusion, the moral judgment that justice requires that I give little Tommy ten dollars. In this way, justice is different from the other primary virtues.

There is another way in which moral judgment *might* matter: If one is to be kind or courageous, it matters that one help the victim and not the mugger. That is to say, exhibition of any of the virtues depends on our distinguishing in certain ways. In particular, it depends on our distinguishing in terms of justice, seeing who has what rights in any given situation. That is a matter of setting limits. The other virtues can be exhibited properly only within the limits of justice, and not in being unjust. That does not mean that being kind entails that one judges that kindness requires the act. It means that genuine kindness requires that one recognize that the act is not unjust, and the judgment that an act is not unjust is not, by itself, any reason at all *for* acting. Were there injustice, that would be a reason for not acting: As Hobbes has shown, peaceful life in communities requires that we recognize rights and obligations, so the other virtues, especially those dealing with making life comfortable, have their values only within those limits. Given the absence of such reasons about injustice, the reasons for acting in a genuine and straightforward case of kindness act as a practical syllogism with no theoretical conclusion reached or required.

The story about people's reasoning out a set of laws will not do as an account of the virtues. It is not simply that the virtues *were* not produced that way: They *could not have been* produced that way. Hobbes was wrong about that. Reasoning, and the making of judgments in theoretical reasoning, play complex roles in virtues, but they do not play the role that they are given in Hobbes's model of explanation. That role is one of calculating policy in terms of one's interests. Hobbes's model is inadequate for the virtues: That procedure is not one that *could* produce the virtues, let alone one that *guarantees* that they be produced. What it leaves us with is something suggesting that there will be many more disputes, and disputes harder to resolve, than in fact there are between people who possess the virtues to a reasonable degree. For such people, the Hobbesian sovereign is not a logical necessity.

It helps each of us that others have the virtues, and it helps us in living with others that we have them. Two people get along better if each has the virtues. Self-interested calculation might lead people to follow such policies as pretending to have certain virtues, acting as though they had the virtues so that they could get along better with other people (though that exercise of self-interest depends on other people's actually having the virtues; it could not be the story for everybody), but it could not lead people actually to have the virtues. The virtues pay in that they enable us to live in communities rather than to die in the radical form of our natural condition, but that cannot be a reason for us to adopt them. They are qualities of people, not policies.

Hobbes saw an important point about the virtues, and his general account of them as qualities of character necessary to peaceful and comfortable life for anybody seems to me entirely adequate. Problems indeed remain about the point toward which the virtues are directed if somebody wants to suggest a different aim for them, but Hobbes has undeniably picked out *social* virtues, a class of qualities of character that are of great importance in human life. But the methodological account he gives, drawing on the model of the circle, is false. (The same sorts of argument that show that Hobbes was mistaken there show that Rule Utilitarianism, or any account in terms of the calculation of policies, cannot give an adequate account of the virtues.) That does not matter: Because Hobbes is not committed to any actual social contract, he is not committed to any story about people's developing the virtues in that way. That is merely an unnecessary addition to his theory. He is right about the virtues' being qualities of character, and he is right about what makes them important qualities of character.

Because the virtues enable us to live in communities rather than to die in the radical form of our natural condition, it is a good thing for each of us that most people have the virtues to the requisite degree. That people have the virtues in that way is not a matter of calculation on their part; people simply *are* so inclined. It might be explained genetically; it might be explained in terms of their being brought up that way because they are brought up with, and have to live with, other people; but, whatever the reason, most people are so inclined to a reasonable degree.

Because people are sociable, inclined to an appropriate degree to seek nonviolent ways of resolving disputes with others who will similarly seek nonviolent means, inclined similarly to keep their words and to be well disposed to those who help them, and so on, it is possible for people to sort out disagreements. Hence, if we do agree to resolve a dispute by tossing a coin, we do not usually need to nominate an independent party to rule on whether the coin came down heads or came down tails; we can agree between ourselves which it did. People who disagree about accounts[14] can usually sort out the matter in-house without setting up an unlimited and eternal sovereign. Hence there is not always a need for a Hobbesian sovereign to interpret the law and apply it to us. (People who, simply as a matter of self-interested calculation, had adopted a policy of acting as though they had the virtues would be more likely to cheat. Their aim is simply to get for themselves the best that they can, in whatever way possible. Acting as though they had the virtues will often be the best way, but sometimes cheating will be.) People who have the qualities of character described by Hobbes in the laws of nature will not be in quite the parlous condition that he describes.

What it is, on Hobbes's account, that makes it possible for us to have government also means that it is not *necessary* for us to have a Hobbesian sovereign. Most of us, most of the time, can sort out our disputes. Public judgment can be set up with a binding decision-procedure only in terms of private judgments of the justice of that procedure; that we can do that shows that people are prepared to consider decision-procedures and their outcomes in exercising their private judgments. We can often recognize the injustice of simply forcing our own views of justice on others. (The fact that not everybody can recognize that is one of the main practical reasons that we do sometimes need enforcement procedures.) We can exercise our private judgments on decision-procedures not only once, but many times. There is no reason of logic (though there may be matter-of-fact reasons, especially in larger communities) why we cannot simply sort out a decision-procedure for each individual dispute.

We must have conventional decision-procedures if we are to resolve our disputes in the face of continuing disagreement after discussion of the merits of a case, but whether we need a Hobbesian sovereign is a quite different matter. As a matter of fact, we manage to operate with many different decision-procedures; we have decision-procedures in our families quite apart from those that constitute the state, decision-procedures in other social groups, and so on. The state provides us with one source of decisions resolving disputes; tradition is quite a separate source. There is no problem at all when the two do not come into conflict, and, when they do come into conflict (as they seem to have done in a few recent legal cases around the world in which children were allowed to "divorce" their parents, apparently setting the state against the traditional organization of the family), we often manage to muddle through. Hobbes is right about the necessity for conventional decision-procedures. He is, therefore, right about the necessity of a community's operating in terms of rights and obligations. He is right about the necessity of our being prepared to set aside merely private judgment if we are to live together. But he is also right about the virtues and their roles in our lives, so he is wrong about the need for a Hobbesian sovereign.

How strong people's natural inclinations to follow the laws of nature are (people possess the virtues to different degrees) and how strong their other passions are will determine how strong and how absolute the enforcement powers or the government must be. That is an empirical matter that cannot be settled by *a priori* argument. History suggests that we can get by with something a good deal less than a Hobbesian sovereign, or at least that we can often get by for long periods of time with something a good deal less than that. People can live peacefully for long periods of time without guarantees of continued peace, and the peace can be genuine peace, not merely the inactive enmity of our natural condition as Hobbes describes it.

Hobbes was right about what makes government (at least in a fairly broad sense of the term "government") necessary, and he was right about what makes government possible, but because he was right about what makes government possible he was wrong about what forms of government are likely to be necessary. People's private judgments, given that the people possess the virtues to a reasonable degree, will be such that the people will not insist on having their own way all the time. They will be prepared to compromise, or to toss a coin, or to use some other decision-procedure as the occasion demands. People with the virtues will, as they do, agree on a good many more moral matters than they disagree on, so that problem will not be as frequent as Hobbes suggests it is likely to be. But Hobbes is surely right in stressing that the people who disagree with me, or with you, can be both honest and intelligent, and any of us must be prepared at times to live with decisions that are binding on us even though we believe them to be wrong. That is toleration, and lack of toleration is likely to be the main thing requiring enforcement of decisions on people who have the virtues.

It is not a logical truth that a community requires a Hobbesian sovereign. If it is a truth at all, it is an empirical truth depending on the particular people who find it necessary that they live together. The idea of a community is logically prior to the idea of government and does not depend on the idea of government. Lawson was right about that:

> For a community is the immediate subject of a Common-wealth, and must be associate before they can be capable of a form of Government. . . . Thus a free people may invest one man or more either with original power, or trust him and them only with the administration. And they may put conditions upon them, either to give them an unlimited or

limited power, as the wisest men amongst them shall think fit. And there is great reason so to do: For, 1. They are free. 2. He with whom they purpose to contract, hath no right to command them, no power over them before he be made Soveraign: He is but a private person, and they are mad men if they will subject themselves upon unreasonable conditions: They are very unwise, who will make a Butcher their Shepherd, or set a Woolf over their Flocks. And surely its no point of wisdom in any free-people, to trust any one man, or assembly of men, with an absolute unlimited power.[15]

Hobbes goes some way toward recognizing this point in the two-contract view that is still discernible in *Leviathan*.

Notes

1. *Leviathan*, chapter 46, pp. 699-700.

2. *Leviathan*, chapter 26, p. 322.

3. Jean Hampton, *Hobbes and the Social Contract Tradition* (London: Cambridge University Press, 1986), pp. 105-106.

4. *Leviathan*, chapter 18, p. 228.

5. George Lawson, *An Examination of the Political Part of Mr. Hobbs his Leviathan* (London: Francis Tyton, 1657), p. 98.

6. *Leviathan*, chapter 15, p. 216.

7. *Leviathan*, chapter 26, p. 323.

8. *De Cive*, "Preface to the Reader," p. 104.

9. Some of what appears in this paragraph has been taken further in my "Pride, Prejudice and Shyness," *Philosophy*, vol. 65 no. 252, April 1990.

10. Hobbes's discussion of the Fool (*Leviathan*, chapter 15, pp. 203-205), setting aside all the argument about the details of what he says, is clearly an argument that possession of the virtue of justice pays.

11. *Leviathan*, chapter 13, p. 188.

12. *Leviathan*, chapter 14, p. 190.

13. *Leviathan*, chapter 15, p. 209.

14. Cf. *Leviathan*, chapter 5, pp. 111-112.

15. Lawson, *Examination*, pp. 21-22.

8

Conclusion

Hobbes cannot adequately account for a natural right to self-defense within his system. It is the natural right to self-defense, along with things that must accompany that right, that lies at the base of the radical form of our natural condition: In that condition one has the natural right to defend oneself, and, crucially, one is one's own judge with respect to the exercise of that right. One may, therefore, with propriety, act preemptively to defend oneself. The only sin in that condition (no crime exists there) is to act in a way that *the agent* thinks is in contravention of the laws of nature,[1] so there is no action that can be objectively ruled out as prohibited. What is prohibited depends solely on the views of the agent, over which the rest of us have no authority. Hence the natural right to defend oneself becomes, practically, a right to all things, and, if all men have a right to all things, conflict follows.

If one retains a natural right to self-defense in civil society, then all the problems remain. (One will, of course, expect to have a right to defend oneself in civil society; what is at issue is whether it could be a *natural right*.) One has actually given up nothing, so one is still in the natural condition. One cannot, in any significant sense, retain the right to self-defense if one has given up one's right to be one's own judge with respect to its exercise, as Hobbes clearly recognized. One retained one's right to self-defense when threatened by the sovereign (even if one was threatened by the sovereign as a punitive response to one's own reprehensible behavior), and one was not expected to leave to the sovereign the judgment of what one could do in defending oneself against the sovereign. That one is one's own judge of what is necessary to one's preservation in the natural condition is what turns the right to defend oneself into a right to all things; if one must still be one's own judge of what is necessary to one's preservation in civil society, then the

195

right to defend oneself will become, in practice, a right to all things. No move will have been made, and nothing will have been given up. One might feel threatened by the sovereign's lack of military preparedness, or one might feel threatened by his military preparedness because one fears that it will provoke other states; it might even be that some citizens feel threatened in the first way while others feel threatened in the second way. It is not unknown for citizens of the one state to disagree in that sort of way, some wanting disarmament and others a military buildup. Some might feel that their lives, or the comfort of their lives, are threatened by the sovereign's economic policies, and others might feel that the comfort of their lives is threatened by any policies that will alleviate what the first group sees as a threat. Again, there are such disagreements. It is worth noting that mayhem does not necessarily follow.

Hobbes needs the natural right to self-defense in his argument, and he needs to retain it in civil society because that is what gives the point to civil society in his account. Civil society must have some point, because institutions are to be understood in terms of their points. One could differ from Hobbes on what that point is, as, for example, Lawson did when he claimed that there was a religious point to social life, but that is the point that Hobbes saw civil society as having. In that way, the right to defend oneself is crucial to his whole argument. It is not just something that he could drop from his theory without changing anything else. So Hobbes's theory seems to have the problem that we can live in a way other than our natural condition only if we alienate an inalienable right — a right that his theory requires to be inalienable.

The right to defend oneself, taken along with the necessity of one's being one's own judge of what is necessary to one's preservation, becomes in practical terms a right to all things. It is necessary that each be his own judge because right reason does not wear a sign that makes it obvious to all, so we cannot resolve disputes by reference to right reason. Each will take for right reason his own reason, and that is a matter of logic, not a matter of arrogance or some other human failing: I believe what I believe, and that is to believe that what I believe is true. For me to believe that something is false is for me not to believe it. If my reason tells me one thing and then right reason tells me another, what happens is that I change my mind. I can recognize that I am fallible, but in particular cases I can no more distinguish between what right reason tells me and what my reason tells me than I can distinguish between what is true and what I believe to be true. We can discuss things, and one of us might change his mind as a result of the discussion, but if we still differ after exhaustive discussion, we cannot resolve the dispute by reference to right reason. To resolve the dispute we must go to an arbitrator or some sort of conventional decision-procedure. Then you can give me a different sort of reason for submitting to your views, a reason concerned with authority, which is different from a reason of the sort each of us presented in trying to persuade the other that he had the truth, or I can give you a different sort of reason for submitting to mine. Before that, there is no reason one of us can give the other for submitting that the other cannot, with equal sincerity and conviction, give to the one. Provided we have agreed on the significance of the coin's coming down heads, the new sort of reason does pick out one of us over the other in a quite publicly ascertainable sort of way.

The right to defend oneself becomes, in practical terms, a right to all things. What would cause conflict, though, would be attempts to *exercise* the right to all things. If each of us has a right to all things, but you spend your life growing roses on one side of the continent and I devote my life to fishing on the other side, no problem will arise. There will be no difficulty unless our attempts to exercise our rights come into conflict, or until one of us decides that our attempts to exercise our rights will come into conflict and decides to act preemptively.

How frequently do we expect other people to have really bizarre views about what is necessary to their preservation? How frequently do our exercises of our rights come into conflict without our being able to resolve the conflict ourselves? These are questions of fact, not of logic, but the answer in each case is clear: Not never, but not always, either. I may lock my door at night, but I do not sleep with a gun under the bed, a Doberman patrolling the yard, and so on, and I do not refuse to go forth in the day without a bodyguard. (If life *were* that bad, how could I trust the bodyguard?) I certainly feel no need to keep the door locked against my family and friends. I am quite sure that none of the people with whom I talk each day, people well known to me, will suddenly attack me with a hatchet. (Someday one of them might: My anecdotes might have been even more boring than usual, or the other person might have gone mad. But that would be very surprising. All it shows is that I am fallible and that odd things can happen. The ground *might* open up and swallow me sometime when I am embarrassed, but the expectation that it will not is very reasonably based.)

There are nasty people around, but people could not live in communities unless enough of them had sufficient inclination to follow Hobbes's laws of nature, that is, unless enough of them had the virtues to a sufficient degree, so I know that there are nice people out there, too. One learns to distinguish. Some people in some situations are threatening, but we live quite large parts of our lives without that sort of threat because people, by and large, have senses of decency and act accordingly. How frequently and how greatly one is threatened are (important) empirical matters; they cannot be dealt with by an *a priori* argument such as that presented by Hobbes. How it is proper or necessary to respond depends on those empirical matters of the frequency of the threats and how great they are.

If each of us retains the right to defend himself and is his own judge with respect to that right, then nothing has been given up no matter what the pieces of paper to which we might have added our signatures. We still have everything that we had in our natural condition. What people have in civil society that they lack in their natural condition is security of reciprocity, which allows their virtues to become effective, or allows the laws of nature to bind *in foro externo*. The issue of fact, which depends on other matters of fact such as questions about how selfish people are, how frequently they disagree, how insistent they are likely to be about having their own ways, and so on, is whether they can have security of reciprocity without having a Hobbesian sovereign.

It might be impossible to have a *guarantee* that the empire will last peacefully for a thousand years without a Hobbesian sovereign, but the issue is whether people could live together peacefully (even without a guarantee) without a Hobbesian sovereign. And the answer, fairly clearly, is that, at least with some people, we can have security of reciprocity without the Hobbesian sovereign. The virtues or natural laws that are necessary if a sovereign is to be set up will often enable people to do the sovereign's job for themselves. We know people, we get to know how trustworthy they are, what sorts of temptation they are likely to succumb to, and so on. Some people we cannot trust in certain circumstances, other people we can. Where problems do arise, a Hobbesian sovereign is not always necessary to their solution: Upsurges of public opinion are sometimes sufficient to provoke correct behavior from backsliders, or we can get around problems in other ways. And even if a Hobbesian sovereign guarantees that there will be one and only one resolution to each dispute, there can be no guarantee that everybody will always accept that resolution and that the empire will continue in peace for a thousand years.

This problem about self-defense mirrors a general problem about judgment. It is a specific case of a problem about the role of private judgment in Hobbes's theory and in social life. This is the central problem with which I have been dealing, and it is set up by Hobbes in the right reason argument that appears in chapter 5 of *Leviathan*:

And as in Arithmetique, unpractised men must, and Professors themselves may often erre, and cast up false; so also in any other subject of Reasoning, the ablest, most attentive, and most practised men, may deceive themselves, and inferre false Conclusions; Not but that Reason it selfe is always Right Reason, as well as Arithmetique is a certain and infallible Art: But no one mans Reason, nor the Reason of any one number of men, makes the certaintie; no more than an account is therefore well cast up, because a great many men have unanimously approved it. And therfore, as when there is a controversy in an account, the parties must by their own accord, set up for right Reason, the Reason of some Arbitrator, or Judge, to whose sentence they will both stand, or their controversie must either come to blowes, or be undecided, for want of a right Reason constituted by Nature; so is it also in all debates of what kind soever: And when men that think themselves wiser than all others, clamor and demand right Reason for judge; yet seek no more, but that things should be determined, by no other mens reason but their own, it is intolerable in the society of men, as it is in play after trump is turned, to use for trump on every occasion, that suite whereof they have most in their hand. For they do nothing els, that will have every of their passions, as it comes to bear sway in them, to be taken for right Reason, and that in their own controversies: bewraying their want of right Reason, by the claym they lay to it.[2]

This is the first, and I think the main, argument that Hobbes presents for the necessity of a sovereign. People differ in their judgments. People can be mistaken about matters of necessary truth, such as arithmetic or geometry, so people can differ in their judgments even about matters of that sort, as well as about matters of morals and politics. Right reason will not serve to resolve the dispute; the dispute can be resolved only if the parties, of their own accord, set up a conventional decision-procedure to the sentence of which they will both stand. The dispute can be resolved only if their private judgments are subject to public judgment.

But Hobbes cannot remove private judgment from his system. He needs it for the right to self-defense, and he needs it for the judgment of whether the decision-procedure is binding, that is, the judgment of whether the decision-procedure is one to the sentence of which I am prepared to stand. I cannot expect that I shall get away with having as the decision-procedure a reference to the arbitration of somebody over whom I hold significant power when it is known that I shall use this power to have the outcome favor me. And if I am to seek peace and follow it and to try to accommodate myself to others, as is required by the laws of nature, I shall not try to do so. If I am not prepared to follow the laws of nature, there is no prospect at all of a happy outcome.

Nor shall I feel bound if the only decision-procedure to which you are prepared to submit is one that strikes me as unfair in a similar way. Hobbes clearly raises these questions (we must set up the procedure of our own accord and be prepared to stand by its decision), and they require the exercise of private judgment.

An earlier version of the same argument, proceeding right through to the reference to sovereignty, appears in *The Elements of Law:*

> In the state of nature, where every man is his own judge, and differeth from other concerning the names and appellations of things, and from those differences arise quarrels, and breach of peace; it was necessary there should be a common measure of all things that might fall in controversy; as for example: of what is to be called right, what good, what virtue, what much, what little, what *meum* and *tuum*, what a pound, what a quart &c. For in these things private judgments may differ, and beget controversy. This common measure, some say, is right reason: with whom I should consent, if there were any such thing to be found or known *in rerum natura*. But commonly they that call for right reason to decide any controversy, do mean their own. But this is certain, seeing right reason is not existent, the reason of some man, or men, must supply the place thereof; and that man, or men, is he, or they, that have the sovereign power.[3]

The solution to Hobbes's problem about private judgment, I have argued, lies in allowing private judgment and recognizing that it can often be trusted. Hobbes was a virtues theorist who misconstrued the implications of his own position because of the model that he took for the virtues: the model of rational calculators seeking agreement about policies. That model is inadequate. The solution to Hobbes's problem about private judgment, in the end, is that agreement *in* the laws of nature, possession of the virtues to the required degree, gets over the problem of disagreement *about* various things, or, at least, that it does so fairly frequently. The virtues that are necessary among people if a sovereign is to be set up make it unnecessary to set up a sovereign. And if an accurate account of the virtues is given, avoiding the inadequacies of Hobbes's model, then there will be no temptation to think, as Hobbes did, that a Hobbesian sovereign is a logical necessity if people are to live together peacefully for more than an hour. It is natural for people with those virtues — complete people — to avoid the condition of mere nature and to seek and agree on conventional methods of resolving their disputes. The condition of mere nature, as described by Hobbes, is not the condition in which real people naturally live. Real people are complete people; they do not, by and large, lack the laws of nature.

The relationship that this Hobbesian argument sets up between private and public judgment is significantly different from standard views about the relationship between conscience and the law. As arguments about that relationship are usually carried on these days, only one level of agreement is considered: The question asked is "Do I agree with the law?" — as though that were the only question that could be asked. If the law does not coincide with my views of justice, it seems to be assumed, then I am in conscience bound to oppose it, and, on some views, I am in conscience bound to disobey it.

Hobbes thought that one of the importantly erroneous doctrines taught by universities of his time (the first he mentions when he comes to list them, and he plainly thought it a fundamental error) was "that men shall Judge of what is lawfull and unlawfull, not by the Law it selfe, but by their own Consciences; that is to say, by their own private Judgements."[4] The argument settles on issues of content and ignores all questions of procedure, such as whether procedure X is fair for resolving a dispute in which people honestly disagree and where common or corporate action is needed, or whether it is one by the decision of which (before we know what that decision might be) we are prepared to stand. That is a mistake; procedure matters, and it is the only hope for common action where we cannot agree on content. Those against whom the decision went might keep on arguing in public for a change to the law and continue trying to persuade others of the truth of their position; there can be common action or communal life only if, while arguing for change, they nevertheless treat the law as binding while it is on the books. Common public standards are required for common or communal action, and that conventional determination of the standards is the only way of having them in the face of disagreement.

Even though I recognize my fallibility in general terms, I (tautologically) believe that each of my beliefs is true. Sometimes I am *really* sure that a belief is true. Nevertheless, in the face of disagreement, I must be prepared to submit to a common decision-procedure and to accept its decision. For one thing, if I am to live with other people it is impolitic for me to try to have my own way all the time. But it is not simply a matter of politics. It is not morally proper for me to press for that: It would be unjust for me simply to force my views on others even if I could get away with it. As a matter of justice, their views of justice must be given equal consideration with mine.

Communal life in the face of disagreement requires that some submit to others. If we are to have communal life, that submission is inescapable. The question to be asked is whether the procedure determining who submits to whom is a just one. One cannot properly object simply that one's views on justice are not always allowed to prevail over others' views of justice, because there is no injustice in that. That one does not always win does not mean that one is not being given a fair go along with everybody else. On the other hand, one can properly object if the procedure determining who is to submit to whom is an unjust *procedure*. There is an identifiable injustice there, quite apart from the issue of whether one's views on the substantive matter prevailed.

An important part of the story just told is the necessity of common standards and action. If common standards and action are not necessary, the story provides no justification for making one person submit to another. My fishing on the West Coast and your growing roses on the East Coast are quite independent activities, so neither provides a justification for making me grow roses or making you go fishing. If one thinks that common action is not necessary on a given matter, then a different and more complex story will be necessary to justify making one submit. Such stories might well be available. Perhaps one's refusal displays a raw form of injustice, making it impossible for other people to live together in peace. That would be an infringement of Hobbes's first law of nature rather than of his third. Perhaps people in our community disagree fairly often about whether common action is necessary and have dealt with that problem by setting up a decision-procedure to determine in any case of dispute whether common action is necessary; that decision-procedure, to which I am committed by my membership of the community, might have gone against my private judgment in this case and ruled that common action was necessary. Answers could be given in particular cases, explaining why one could be made to submit even though one did not think that common action was necessary, but the story told to explain that must be a more complex story than the other. On the face of it, if I am prepared to go my own way and do without common action, others have no right to make me submit unless they can tell a special story. That matter, prima facie, is one for my private judgment. Hobbes suggests this when he says that those in dispute must set up the arbitrator "of their own accord."[5]

Even if I readily agree that common action is necessary, matters remain for my private judgment. The question of whether the procedure is a just one is a question for my private judgment. Hobbes suggests this when he says that the arbitrator on whom those in dispute agree must be one "to whose sentence they will both stand,"[6] that is, each must agree that the procedure is binding. If objections can be only to the justice of the procedure and not at all simply to the justice of the decision, it does not follow that objections must be hard to find. The procedure might be unjust in a number of ways. Corruption on the part of the officials is one straightforward way. Another is that the procedure might unfairly favor one section of the community, either because the rulers traditionally come from one class, or because employment of lawyers requires considerable wealth, because ownership of newspapers and television stations weights debate unfairly, or for a number of other reasons. Recognition of Hobbes's point shifts the focus of the debate from the decision to the procedure by which it was made, but it does not cut off all debate.

This comes out again by implication in one of Hobbes's attacks on Aristotle:

> Aristotle, and other Heathen Philosophers define Good, and Evill, by the Appetite of men; and well enough, as long as we consider them governed every one by his own Law: For in the condition of men that have no other Law but their own Appetites, there can be no generall Rule of Good, and Evill Actions. But in a Common-wealth this measure is false: Not the Appetite of Private men, but the Law, which is the Will and Appetite of the State is the measure. And yet is this Doctrine still practised; and men judge the Goodnesse, or Wickednesse of their own, and of other mens actions, and of the actions of the Common-wealth it selfe, by their own Passions; and no man calleth Good or Evill, but that which is so in his own eyes, without any regard at all to the Publique Laws; except onely Monks, and Friers, that are bound by Vow to that simple obedience to their Superiour, to which every subject ought to think himself bound by the Law of Nature to the Civill Soveraign. And this private measure of Good, is a Doctrine, not onely Vain, but also Pernicious to the Publique State.[7]

Part of the point here is that the monks and friars whom Hobbes takes as his model are not simply following somebody or recognizing some superior whom they have picked out at random. They have exercised their private judgments in recognizing the authority of that superior (that is why they chose this man, or this order, rather than devil-worship or the leadership of a passing tramp), but subsequently they must subordinate their private judgments to the public judgment of the superior when the two come into conflict. Private judgment is necessary to that story because only in terms of that exercise of private judgment can the later subordination of private judgment be legitimized.

Hobbes was right in his claim that insistence on private judgment at *all* levels gets in the way of communal life and leads to confrontation and probably violence if the people go on trying to live together. At one level, private judgment must give way to public judgment. At another level, private judgment is still necessary; we must make private judgments of the procedures by which the decisions are made. At this level we must have coalescence of private judgments. Without such coalescence we could not have communities. Because people do differ in their private judgments, and even differ, as did Hobbes and Lawson, about the point of civil society, it is a good thing that we have different communities. If two people differ sufficiently in their private judgments of justice or anything else, it may be impossible for them to live together peacefully in a community of like-minded people (other Muslims, or devotees of economic competition, or whatever it might be); if they live in separate communities instead, the two communities might be capable of behaving toward each other in a civilized manner. There can be no guarantee that everybody can live together peacefully with everybody else, and a glance around the world today suggests that it is not simply a matter of lacking guarantees, but our having different communities, and different sorts of communities, might ease that problem somewhat. Certainly it does no good to insist pointlessly that everybody must behave as we do, ignoring the question of whether common action really is necessary.

Hobbes's moral theory, perhaps oddly, is one singularly well fitted to democracy. It is well fitted to democracy because of his insistence on the necessity of toleration. The more that people are intolerant and insist that their own views of right and wrong should prevail in the face of disagreement, the more that a community needs strong enforcement powers if it is to have common action. People who are genuinely tolerant can live with others despite disagreement and without the need for strong enforcement powers. If we are willing to endeavor peace as far as we have hope of obtaining it,[8] if each will strive to accommodate himself to the rest,[9] if every man will acknowledge the other to be his equal by nature[10] (and therefore not insist on having his own views prevail all the time), and generally, if we will follow the laws of nature (that is, if enough of us have the virtues to a sufficient degree), then we shall be able to get along with each other. We shall disagree as often as, in fact, we do, but we shall be capable of sorting the disagreements out at least most of the time.

Nor shall we need a Hobbesian sovereign to do it. One must be prepared to submit, but it does not follow that one must be prepared to submit to just *anything*. We shall, as we must, exercise our private judgments on the decision-procedures that are used in resolving our disputes. As different problems come up, we might notice faults in the procedure that we had previously overlooked and might change our minds about how just it was, though the evidence we had would need to be more than simply our disagreeing with its decisions. We might choose to have different procedures in different areas of our lives, or to have a different procedure for each dispute, leaving it to the parties in the dispute to sort out a procedure on which they agree, or we might do other things. What we do, if we have any sense, will depend, at least in part, on what works. If people are less tolerant, or if too high a proportion of one particular community is given to simply pushing their own barrows, then more centralization and accumulation of power will be necessary if the community is to remain as a community. In some cases, life might be easier and better for all if a community that had a lot of disagreement did break up into smaller communities with less disagreement. That is one possible resolution of continuing disputes where common action is not necessary. The more that people recognize the basic truth in what Hobbes says, or the more that people have the virtues set out in the laws of nature (as Hobbes correctly claims is necessary if a Hobbesian sovereign is to be set up) and treat each other in the appropriate manner, the less that we shall need a Hobbesian sovereign and the more capable that we shall be of having genuinely democratic communities.

Notes

1. *Leviathan*, chapter 27, p. 337.
2. *Leviathan*, chapter 5, pp. 111-112.
3. *The Elements of Law* 2.10.8, p. 188.
4. *Leviathan*, chapter 30, p. 383.
5. *Leviathan*, chapter 5, p. 111.
6. *Leviathan*, chapter 5, p. 111.
7. *Leviathan*, chapter 46, p. 697.
8. *Leviathan*, chapter 14, p. 190.
9. *Leviathan*, chapter 15, p. 209.
10. *Leviathan*, chapter 15, p. 211.

Selected Bibliography

Aubrey, John. *Aubrey's Brief Lives*, ed. Oliver Lawson Dick (Harmondsworth: Pelican, 1949).

Baumgold, Deborah. *Hobbes's Political Theory* (Cambridge: Cambridge University Press, 1988).

Coady, C.A.J. "The Peculiarity of Hobbes's Concept of Natural Right" in C. Walton and P. J. Johnson (eds.), *Hobbes's `Science of Natural Justice´* (Dordrecht: Martinus Nijhoff, 1987).

Eachard, John. *Mr. Hobbs's State of Nature Considered in a Dialogue Between Philautus and Timothy*, ed. Peter Ure (Liverpool: Liverpool University Press, 1958).

Easlea, Brian. *Witch-Hunting Magic and the New Philosophy* (Brighton: Harvester Press, 1980).

Ewin, R. E. *Co-operation and Human Values* (Brighton: Harvester Press and New York: St. Martin's Press, 1981).

———. *Liberty, Community, and Justice* (Totowa, NJ: Rowman and Littlefield, 1987).

Filmer, Sir Robert. "Observations on Mr. Hobbes's *Leviathan*" in Peter Laslett (ed.), *Patriarcha and Other Political Writings of Sir Robert Filmer* (Oxford: Basil Blackwell, 1949).

Gauthier, David.*The Logic of Leviathan* (Oxford: Oxford University Press, 1969).

———. *Morals by Agreement* (Oxford: Oxford University Press, 1986).

Gert, Bernard. "Hobbes and Psychological Egoism," *Journal of the History of Ideas*, vol. XXVIII, 4 (December 1967).

———. Introduction to his own edition of *Man and Citizen* (Brighton: Harvester Press, 1978).

Hampton, Jean. *Hobbes and the Social Contract Tradition* (London: Cambridge University Press, 1986).

Hart, H.L.A. *The Concept of Law* (London: Oxford University Press, 1961).

Herzog, Don. *Happy Slaves: A Critique of Consent Theory* (Chicago: University of Chicago Press, 1989).

Hohfeld, W. N. *Fundamental Legal Conceptions* (New Haven: Yale University Press, 1964).

Johnson, Paul J. "Hobbes and the Wolf-man" in C. Walton and P. J. Johnson (eds.), *Hobbes's `Science of Natural Justice´* (Dordrecht: Martinus Nijhoff, 1987).

Johnston, David. *The Rhetoric of Leviathan* (Princeton: Princeton University Press, 1986).

Kavka, Gregory S. *Hobbesian Moral and Political Theory* (Princeton: Princeton University Press, 1986).

Kovesi, Julius. *Moral Notions* (London: Routledge and Kegan Paul, 1967).

Lawson, George. *An Examination of the Political Part of Mr. Hobbs his Leviathan* (London: Francis Tyton, 1657).

MacIntyre, Alasdair. *After Virtue* (Notre Dame, IN: Notre Dame University Press, 1981).

Nozick, Robert. *Anarchy, State, and Utopia* (Oxford: Basil Blackwell, 1974).

Oakeshott, Michael. *Hobbes on Civil Association* (Oxford: Basil Blackwell, 1975).

Stoffell, Brian F. "Hobbes's *Conatus* and the Roots of Character" in C. Walton and P. J. Johnson (eds.), *Hobbes's ˜Science of Natural Justice´* (Dordrecht: Martinus Nijhoff, 1987).

Tuck, Richard. *Hobbes* (Oxford: Oxford University Press, 1989).

Warrender, Howard. *The Political Philosophy of Hobbes: His Theory of Obligation* (Oxford: Clarendon Press, 1957).

Watkins, J.W.N. *Hobbes's System of Ideas: A Study in the Political Significance of Philosophical Theories* (London: Hutchinson University Library, 1965).

Watt, E. D. *Authority* (London: Croom Helm, 1982).

Wellman, Carl. *A Theory of Rights* (Totowa: Rowman and Allanheld, 1985).

Wolff, R. P. *In Defense of Anarchism* (New York: Harper Torchbooks, 1970).

Wolin, Sheldon S. *Politics and Vision: Continuity and Innovation in Western Political Thought* (Boston: Little, Brown & Company, 1960).

Index

About the Book and Author

This book is a timely new interpretation of the moral and political philosophy of Thomas Hobbes. Staying close to Hobbes's text and working from a careful examination of the actual *substance* of the account of natural law, R. E. Ewin argues that Hobbes well understood the importance of moral behavior to civilized society. This interpretation stands as a much-needed corrective to readings of Hobbes that emphasize the rationally calculated, self-interested nature of human behavior. It poses a significant challenge to currently fashionable game theoretic reconstructions of Hobbesian logic.

It is generally agreed that Hobbes applied what he took to be a geometrical method to political theory. But, as Ewin forcefully argues, modern readers have misconstrued Hobbes's geometric method, and this has led to a series of misunderstandings of Hobbes's view of the relationship between politics and morality.

Important implications of Ewin's reading are that Hobbes never thought that "the war of each against all" was an empirical possibility for citizens; that his political theory actually presupposes moral agency; and that Hobbes's account of natural law forces us to the conclusion that Hobbes was a virtue theorist.

This major contribution to Hobbes studies will be praised and criticized, welcomed and challenged, but it cannot be ignored. All philosophers, political theorists, and historians of ideas dealing with Hobbes will need to take account of it.

R. E. Ewin was educated at Sydney and Oxford universities and has taught at Sydney University, The University of East Anglia, and Makerere College in The University of East Africa. He currently holds the position of associate professor of philosophy at The University of Western Australia. He has also been a visiting lecturer at Trent University and The University of Auckland.

His publications include *Co-operation and Human Values* (1981) and *Liberty, Community, and Justice* (1987). He is working on a book about business and professional ethics.